JACK MEYER
of Millfield

'Boss'. Portrait by Cecile Crombeke presented to Jack Meyer in 1962 by the Millfield Society to mark the school's Silver Jubilee

JACK MEYER
of Millfield

Michael Goater

ALAN SUTTON

First published in the United Kingdom in 1993
Alan Sutton Publishing Limited · Phoenix Mill · Far Thrupp
Stroud · Gloucestershire

First published in the United States of America in 1993
Alan Sutton Publishing Inc · 83 Washington Street · Dover
NH 03820

British Library Cataloguing in Publication Data

Goater, Michael
Jack Meyer of Millfield
I. Title
373. 222092

ISBN 0-7509-0405-4

Library of Congress Cataloging in Publication Data applied
for

.

Typeset in Baskerville 10/13.
Typesetting and origination by
Alan Sutton Publishing Limited.
Printed in Great Britain by
The Bath Press, Avon.

To Jenny, Ruth, Mark and Simon

Contents

List of Illustrations

Foreword

Jack Meyer was a genius. Whenever his interest was fired his intuitive flair for original, unorthodox solutions took over and produced a series of unique achievements. Millfield was the chief of them, and that great school was his life's work and remains his monument, but he left an indelible mark on county cricket, too, and will not be readily forgotten at Fenner's and Taunton. He was an outstanding all-round games player at Haileybury and won cricket and racquets Blues. He would certainly have played golf for Cambridge if he had had time and had been less adventurous in his experimentation with new methods. Not many greater theorists have graced the games field than he, and Jack was a fascinating raconteur who wove his spells over young and old alike, embroidering his stories with anecdote and fancy in about equal proportions.

His secret as a schoolmaster was that he genuinely loved young people and knew how to get the best out of them. He was much more a man of the world than any other headmaster I have known, and he was unencumbered with undue reverence for scholarship. The boys and girls at Millfield were led by a man who wanted them to know excellence in whatever field they could achieve it, and he did not much mind whether it came about in music or cricket, classics or the long jump. Jack believed that it was when a young person came to know what excellence meant that life 'took off' and ceased to be grey and humdrum. At the same time it should be said that no man did more for those with learning problems than he did, and he was one of the first teachers to recognize and overcome dyslexia.

The mandarins of the Headmasters' Conference disapproved of his deep love of sport, especially when he adopted a Robin Hood policy which allowed outstanding young sporting prospects like Gareth Edwards, J.P.R. Williams and Mary Rand to come to Millfield free, paid for by foreign potentates or native tycoons who scarcely noticed the extra burden of fees. I well remember taking what I thought was a very good first XV from Marlborough to play Millfield in the first match of the season. We lost 55–0 and were taught a lesson we never forgot, to the extent that we did not lose another match that season. Gareth Edwards scored seven tries from the base of the scrum and Jack spent all of tea time in his study apologizing to me for the drubbing his boys had handed out to mine, sensitive to the fact that in the early 1960s no other public schools would play Millfield because they were too frightened or too jealous to do so.

The study in which we sat that afternoon gave many clues to his unique character. The floor was littered with waist-high piles of back copies of *The Times* and *The Sporting Life*, and there were two large dustbins full of corn for his latest craze, ornamental Muscovy ducks which came flooding in through the French windows at feeding time. He was delighted when they waddled up to sit on his knee. There was a boyishness, almost a naïvety, about him which was strangely endearing. At intervals boys and girls knocked and came into the study to report to 'Boss', as everyone called him, on the performance of their team that afternoon. He treated them all with great courtesy and friendly ease. One could not help noticing their warm affection and deep respect for him.

Golf clubs, cricket bats, tennis rackets and indeed every imaginable item of sports gear was stacked in all corners of the room. 'A good young golfer came here last week hoping for a place. I gave him an eight iron and took him out of those windows and challenged him to get down in two (indicating a 40-yard pitch and putt hole outside the window). He did so and I'm giving him half fees. The boy had the right temperament.'

My old captain, Maurice Tremlett, played his earliest cricket for Somerset under Jack Meyer and never forgot it: 'Much the most original and exciting captain I ever played under. He was always trying something new to outwit the opposition. He once moved every fielder into the covers in the middle of an over, and bowled long hops on the leg stump to a bewildered batsman who, mesmerized by this manoeuvre, managed to get inside the line of the third delivery he received and spoon it into the forest of cover points.' No two balls were ever quite the same and each was delivered to a fascinating running commentary. He took 408 first-class wickets, among them Bradman's, and an innings of 202 not out against Lancashire in three and three quarter hours in 1936 is still spoken of by Taunton greybeards.

There was a nervous energy about Jack which showed in his expansive gestures and quick speech. The fingers were long and delicate, made for wrapping around the seam of a cricket ball. The eyes were bright and wise and often had that faraway look of the visionary who sees further than an ordinary man. And so it was in education where he will be remembered by a multitude of impecunious and talented young people, many of them future Somerset cricketers and international athletes to whom he gave a chance in life. In that sense he might have been mistaken for a socialist, and how he would have chuckled at such an imputation. But what a Secretary of State for Education he would have made; we would very soon have become unbeatable in the Test arena at the very least.

Dennis Silk

Acknowledgements

Since 1966 Jack Meyer's biography has had several potential authors, and it has been a privilege to bring the work to fruition. The writing has been aided by the generous support of Millfield School and The Millfield Society.

Rupert Martin was the first biographer, and like the present author received much support and practical advice from Jack Meyer's friend and advocate, Dr John Paxton. This book owes much to the anecdotes collected some twenty years ago by Rupert Martin and Jack Meyer's secretary, Amothe Sankey; many of these memoirs would not be available to today's researcher. Despite Jack Meyer being 'flabbergasted to see that I might become biog-worthy', work began in 1972 and Dr Paxton found a publisher. Although by that time the founder had retired from Millfield, the school was not ready for the biography and two years later, almost on the point of signing the contract, the publisher's interest evaporated.

The present work originates from a request by Wyndham Bailey to Jack Meyer, asking him to put down some memoirs of his time at the school for posterity and The Millfield Society. The idea blossomed into an autobiography, but was not altogether supported by Jack Meyer's overwhelming preference for talking, as compared to writing, about his life. Wyndham Bailey, Michael Gambier and the author came to his aid with dictaphones, and these notes form the background to the present work.

This biography owes much to Joyce Meyer, who has 'set the record straight' on many occasions, and given frank and fascinating insights to her late husband's character. Jack Meyer's sister, the late Hon. Constance Ponsonby, also provided many delightful details of his family background, childhood and school years. Gratitude also goes to Amothe Sankey, Millfield's secretary for thirty years, who could provide enough additional information to quadruple the size of this volume.

Thanks are also due to Millfield staff who remember the unpredictable excitement of working under 'Boss', as Jack Meyer was known. Through the *Millfield Chronicle*, old boys throughout the world have sent anecdotes and memoirs of their time. Contributions have also been received through the *Haileyburian*, and special thanks must be extended to Alastair

Macpherson, Bill Tyrwhitt-Drake and David Rimmer for the valuable information which they provided on Jack Meyer's formative years in cricket.

The author is also grateful to Dennis Silk for providing an excellent foreword, and *The Cricketer* magazine from where the material originated. It is an inspired piece of writing which captures Jack Meyer's extraordinary character with enviable fluency.

In conclusion, thanks are due to Jean Rock and her magic word processor: to say that she had typed the book would be a pale reflection of the true value of her contribution.

CHAPTER ONE

Beginnings

'No. You're not to throw him out. Keep Jack there and get him to teach the youngest,' was the request to the Sunday school mistress from Canon Meyer; his seven-year-old son, Jack, was duly set to teach a class of three and four year olds. By his later admission, they certainly heard some rather interesting variations on the Bible stories, for even then he realized that some means had to be found to keep children's attention.

His father's suggestion was in reply to an apologetic letter from the Sunday school mistress, which described Jack's behaviour as becoming a little disruptive and suggested that Matins or Evensong might be a better place for him now. Being sacked from Sunday school would have meant a very uncomfortable time for the disgraced son of Canon Meyer, and there were reasons why Jack felt the reprimand was not altogether justified. His father had, of course, recited and explained the Bible stories and parables many times to his brother, Denys, sister, Constance and him, so when he heard them again at Sunday school, told in a rather simple manner, he lost no time in offering a more comprehensive explanation of loaves, fishes, talents and walking on water. For a young boy who was basically rather shy, the thought of standing in front of this class had held no terrors; with a father and grandfather in the clergy and three schoolmaster uncles, the skill was obviously in the blood.

This early sign of his future career was clearly influenced by his father's pursuits. At the turn of the century Canon Rollo Meyer occupied his first living in Clophill, Bedfordshire. It was a village of some five hundred souls, resting peacefully on the banks of the River Flit. The High Street provided the usual essentials of life: a sweet shop, grocery store, post office, public house, doctor's and a church with a large rectory where the Meyers lived. It was a sprawling, Victorian house with many rooms, servants' quarters and extensive, mature gardens. During long, hot summers it sported enormous shades over every window and portal to keep the sun out, and the interior cool. It was here that Jack was born on 15 March 1905. Little of his surroundings interested him until his second year, when a growing awareness of life's pleasures and pains obliged him

Jack 'getting his eye in' on the lawns of
Clophill Rectory in 1908

to take some part in it. As with all infants, the indignity of expulsion from the Garden of Eden was entirely unjustified, yet that expulsion was relentless. And as his eyes opened, life was invaded by ever more contrasting senses of joy or sorrow, kisses and kicks, stinging insects and sweet-smelling flowers.

Denys, his older brother by eighteen months, observed with grudging interest that even at this rather sticky age there was something unusual in the way Jack would watch a ball, and toss one so that it fell back into his cot. Also, while crawling about the lawn, he would somehow manoeuvre a crochet mallet several times his size and attempt to hit a ball with uncanny, fumbling determination. Such activity was a delight to his father, who was a particularly sporting country rector. At Cambridge he had played tennis, golf, racquets and cricket, becoming a 'Crusader' in the latter, and he was well known and liked in local cricket circles.

At a time when the domestic servants of the rectory took much responsibility for looking after the youngsters, the enjoyment of games brought the children happily closer to their father. At every opportunity they would be out on the lawn with stumps, bat and ball where he would encourage them in the importance of watching the ball and keeping a straight bat. Jack was about three and a half when coaching began, and photographs show that within the year the foundations of style and discipline were already appearing. This was despite being somewhat encumbered in those early days by being dressed – as was the Edwardian tradition with children – in smocks and rather too much clothing. Hats were always worn, otherwise the clergyman's offspring might catch the sun and be mistaken for the village children. Even meals were punctuated by enthusiastic discussions about sport when, much to Mrs Meyer's annoyance, because she was trying to teach the children some manners, her husband would spring up and grab a poker or some other object to demonstrate the finer points of using a cricket bat. The encouragement and enjoyment that Jack received so early in his life was to have far-reaching consequences in terms of pure ability during his later years. Nothing learnt later will be learnt quite so well, and what Jack gained from his father was instrumental in taking him to the brink of world-class cricket later on.

Jack's attitude to his mother at this time was something of a contrast to the relationship he enjoyed with his father. He often said that the first thing he could remember her saying was that he, Jack, needed 'a good whipping'. This was a strange revelation, for while it is probable that the boys received the odd corrective slap, none of the children ever experienced anything which could be described as 'a whipping'. Jack's unease may have been the result of his parents' very different characters. Arabella Crosbie Meyer, whom all called Ella, was perhaps rather tougher than her ever-forgiving and trusting husband, and she was also surprisingly practical considering her aristocratic background. If Jack or

Growing in confidence, aged five, at Clophill, 1910

another of the children were sent by her to their father's study for deserved chastisement, it was quite likely that they would emerge ten minutes later with a sheepish smile and an apple or humbug in their hands. Upon enquiry Ella might learn that Rollo had quite forgotten the reason why the errant child had been sent to him. It also fell to Ella to run their large house, training and guiding three servants and keeping a keen eye on the enormous garden. Notwithstanding all of this, as the rector's wife she also played her part in the activities of a busy village community, keeping in touch with the parishioners every Sunday morning at church. She helped to organize many village activities both in Clophill and at Watton-at-Stone in Hertfordshire, where they later moved, and often lectured to the Mothers' Union and Women's Institute where she was popular with both audiences and organizers. Perhaps it is not surprising, therefore, that Jack felt he and his siblings did not receive enough of their mother's precious time, and was resentful that the servants were too often delegated to look after them. Later, it became clear that there were many similarities between his own and Ella's character, particularly in their liking things to be done properly, and she was in fact enormously proud of her children, and gave them tremendous support all her life.

Jack's education commenced at what he called a dame school. Hayes End House School in Middlesex was a friendly and informal institute run by his Great Aunt Lettice and her husband, Fred Harrison, for a few well-chosen children. Little of this period is remembered save for the shocking wrench of being parted from his home and family at the tender age of five; parted also from his young friends in the village because it would not have been the done thing to have gone to their school. Here, Great Aunt Lettice instilled in her pupils the importance of completing their special assignments before going off to enjoy themselves. 'If you were on hamster duty you would attend to these blessed creatures as a sacred trust, and only after that would you be available to join your friends in kicking a ball about or whatever.' If this was not appreciated at the time, Jack later quoted it as excellent training and discipline for life.

During 1910 the Meyers moved from Clophill to the new rectory in Watton-at-Stone, some 4 miles north of Hertford. By contemporary standards the house was modern and, according to Ella, easier to run than Clophill. As far as Jack was concerned it was just as uncomfortable, having neither electricity nor central heating, and as yet no lawns to play on because the land around the rectory was still as the builder had left it. However, there were some adventures to be had in the grounds, which extended to over 3 acres and included a small wood. Of course, to Rollo and Ella the gardens proved to be a wonderful challenge, in which they were more than aided by the faithful gardener Izzard and his 'lad', who had come with them from Clophill. In a remarkably short period of under two years, new lawns were sown, borders, shrubs and trees planted and, best of all by Jack's reckoning, a new grass tennis court appeared. The croquet lawn was already in use by this time; as an outdoor game croquet rivalled tennis in popularity during the Edwardian period. As 'Master Jack' spent more time exploring his new surroundings, Izzard began to take him under his wing, introducing him to the ways of nature and identifying the many plants, trees, birds and animals to be seen in the surrounding countryside. He and his lad, being keen cricketers, would also join in the games with Rollo and the boys. A challenge to Jack's growing curiosity was provided by Denys, who had been decent enough to warn him that there was a certain place in the woods where it might be very dangerous for him to go. In fact, Denys was probably the only one who could safely venture there, and Jack could see from the look in his eye that he was quite serious. However, one sunny afternoon when there was little else to do, and Denys was visiting somebody on the other side of Watton, he thought that it would not hurt just to have a peep at this forbidden place, and perhaps discover why it was so dangerous. With some trepidation he left the beaten track and pushed through ferns that almost met over his head. Stumbling on and hoping he would remember the way back, he was startled by a sudden scratch on the back of his hand as he pushed the ferns aside, and saw immediately a cluster of sweet chestnuts, so ripe that they were popping out of their husks. Looking about him he perceived that he was at the edge of a group of laden, mature trees and with a sense of revelation realized that he had learnt another of life's lessons.

A child of the emerging twentieth century, Jack was influenced by many of its turbulent events; repercussions from the first of these were to hit the Watton-at-Stone rectory when he was only seven. As he eloquently stated later, 'Fate, tiring of the situation, re-shuffled the cards and dealt us a very different hand.' Besides the modest stipend Canon Rollo Meyer received from his living, the family also benefited from a few investments yielding a reasonable private income. An uncle who was a stockbroker advised Rollo that he should put all that he could spare into a scheme that was producing wonderful returns; it seems to have been one of those organized under the empire of Ernest Terah Hooley. Hooley had caused a sensation just before the turn of the century by buying the Dunlop Tyre Company and selling it after a few months at a £2 million profit; later, from a position of respectability as Sheriff of Cambridgeshire, he had set up schemes offering attractive fortnightly dividends targeted at small regular investors, often country clergymen. But following Hooley's visit to the Old Bailey in 1912, Rollo and all the other investors lost everything.

Being reduced to the stipend of a village parson called for some fairly drastic trimming – the first economies involved the domestic servants, who were reduced to one. The gardener stayed because by now the vegetable plots were highly productive and young apple, pear and plum trees had begun to bear fruit.

The effect of the calamity on the children was initially one of some confusion as their parents became preoccupied with the situation. However, as the old order crumbled away the new stringencies actually brought the family closer together, and for Jack nothing could have been more welcome. Now it was all hands to the pump, and that included the children; even though the eldest, Denys, was just under nine they were all expected to do their regular share of the chores to keep the house going. There was no lack of example from Ella who, with the remaining domestic, became housemaid, gardener, charlady and cook and set a rigorous new timetable for the rectory, beginning at six o'clock each morning with the lighting of the stove to heat the water. At about half past six Rollo would bathe in water which was not much warmer than icy cold. Denys and Jack were next, when it was about tepid, followed by Constance, who might have warm water. Having cooked breakfast Ella was at last entitled to a hot bath after which she came down to her breakfast, which consisted of porridge, and fishcakes or sausages, with the children waiting upon her. According to Jack, after breakfast the slavery would begin in earnest, starting with stripping and airing the beds prior to making them properly later. Then it was: 'Please clear the breakfast, boys, then you can wash up, then you can peel the potatoes, Jack, and Denys, it's your turn to sweep the floor. Constance, would you get the things ready for our blackberry and apple pie and later I want you to help me turn out and clean the guest room, so don't go and get lost in the garden.' Having completed the early morning chores the brothers would normally attempt to steal quietly away.

During school holidays the three children attended the village Sunday school where Jack's over-enthusiasm had been channelled into his first teaching post. He learnt much from this school, which was run by good, down-to-earth folk from the village. Although it was in contrast to his own enthusiasm, he remembered later with not a little respect the unaffected way the baker's daughter gave her lesson. Also the clink-clink of pennies falling as they collected for the blind during the hymns. Patriotism was another virtue frequently referred to in church and school; to children in 1912 it seemed to mean that they could be proud of their country while that country expected a certain standard of behaviour from them in the way of politeness, punctuality, working hard at lessons and even washing. In church and school they would sing 'What can I do for England, who's

done so much for me? One of her faithful servants I can and I will be.'
They also unashamedly thought of themselves as English, 'and the British
were actually English, but with the Scots, Irish and Welsh too'.

The new regime at Watton-at-Stone rectory suited Jack well for all its
chores. It enabled him to get closer to his parents and form an easier
relationship with his mother than might have been possible had they
been surrounded by servants. But as in any relationship where familiarity
exists, a rough and a smooth side have to be accepted, and Jack was
fascinated by watching the different temperaments of his parents.
Although Ella had been obliged to do more than double the housework,
her practical nature and sense of duty had come to her assistance. That is
not to say that she buckled down with the meekness of a nun. Worrying
about money and doing long, hard hours often put her on a rather short
fuse, sometimes carelessly lit by Rollo's unworldly generosity. 'Well now
dear,' he would say, 'things might work out for the better.' 'You stupid so-
and-so!' she would snap and a plate of porridge would fly across the
breakfast table, with Rollo using every ounce of his sporting instinct to
duck as it smashed through a kitchen window. Detailed as part of their
morning chores to clear up the mess, Jack and Denys found a dead
sparrow among the splintered glass and porridge. Although in retrospect
it was probably a victim of the cat, to a family accustomed to shooting for
the pot, bringing down a sparrow at ten yards with a plate of porridge was
a feat that enhanced their mother's reputation for some time. However, it
was about this time that family ties were to be reinforced even more, for
Ella disclosed that her fourth child was on its way. Christened Derek, her
new son was to be Jack's junior by eight years.

The family's financial upset was not the only major event of 1912; it was
also the year when Denys started at his prep school. Rollo Meyer was
anxious to provide a good education for his son, and was fortunate to
find Stratheden House in Blackheath, where a relative used his influence
to get half-fees for the country parson in reduced circumstances.
Fortunately Denys worked hard and behaved himself there and having
received the same coaching on the rectory lawn as Jack, distinguished
himself at cricket. Nothing could have been more pleasing to the
headmaster, of whom Jack said, 'The most important things in Herbert
Lyon's life were Christianity, classics and cricket, but I think I might have
just stated them in the wrong order.' Therefore when Lyon received
another application from the Meyer family to take the younger brother
about a year later, he was pleased to do so, again on favourable terms. In
order to save even more money the new boy was to live with an aunt and
uncle, initially attending Stratheden as a day boy. Although Blackheath is
less than 40 miles from Watton-at-Stone, Jack, at the age of eight, felt it to

be something like a million. It was certainly one of the longer train journeys he had made, and the meadows and woodlands tumbling past made an almost incomprehensible contrast to London's smoky back-to-back houses seen from his carriage. Climbing from the railway station up to Blackheath village he was immediately struck by how busy and bustling it was compared with Clophill or Watton, and so was relieved at the open spaces they passed on the way to Stratheden House in the new motor bus.

Herbert Lyon was without doubt the best master that Jack had throughout his schooldays. He never seemed to lack energy and enthusiasm, often the first virtue to be eroded when facing the same children day after day. Not only did he seem to teach every lesson there was, but during each break would be out with the boys playing football or cricket. During the summer these periods became special coaching sessions for those who showed promise at cricket, and soon put the young team in a very strong position when playing matches against other prep schools. Even at the age of ten Jack had six good years of batting experience behind him and went straight into the school's First XI during the summer term of 1915. Although he had come to expect a high standard of play from Denys, and looked forward to no less from Jack, Herbert Lyon could not resist writing to Canon Meyer the day after the opening school match against Brightlands:

> We lost four good wickets cheaply against inferior bowling for twenty-four, when he came in and stayed until we retired 108 for six. He got thirty-nine not out, a very stylish innings with not a bad stroke in it. He watched the ball like a hawk and was particularly strong on the leg side, but he was not afraid to jump in and lift the half-volleys, in fact the judgment the young monkey showed was very remarkable.

With Old Lyon's coaching it was not surprising that Stratheden won nearly all of its cricket matches, except for the fact that during their cricket practice they were never allowed to hit a ball hard to the leg side. This was often frustrating, for they were certainly encouraged to punish the outfield and hit firmly right through the ball. But the reason was a practical one – a potential six hit to leg from the nets would clear the school avenue on its way to rows of houses, when it was a question of whether it might hit the first, second or, for a very good shot, third greenhouse. On the subject of these cricket practices, Jack related that on one glorious day:

> Old Lyon bowled a pretty fast Yorker to me which hadn't left his hand long before I could see the middle stump address on it. Attempting to

return the challenge I gave an almighty swing off the back foot and sent the ball soaring straight over his head and on and on and on, but my elation evaporated with the sound of tinkling glass from the rifle range window. I shall never forget it. I thought I'd had it when Old Lyon said, 'Come here. Come here, you young monkey! That's the first time I've seen that done since I've been here. Take this' – two shillings, golly! – 'and buy yourself some sweets, and I don't want to see you during the next lesson.'

So with a very unusual mixture of pleasure, remorse and relief, that was precisely what he did.

However, missing one of Herbert Lyon's lessons was not altogether a treat for Jack because he had come to respect him, and was curious to know how someone so energetic and keen on the sports field could apparently apply the same enthusiasm to a subject as awful as Latin! The explanation, when it emerged, proved to be one of the foundations of the educational practices which Jack was himself to apply many years later. Lyon, a classics scholar, was convinced that a reasonable command of Latin was an absolute necessity to anyone who wished to consider himself educated or educable. And what was really important, according to him, was that having mastered Latin the real pillars of wisdom were within sight when the students could start to learn Greek.

I'll give you two years to try and find out if you've got any brains. If you have any intelligence you'll be able to read Homer like a comic. If you can't it proves you're pretty stupid and you'll have to make do with geography or something like that.

This was a pretty tall order for a lively young group of boys. It would have been easy to have fluffed through Latin, reluctantly doing just enough work not to get into trouble. But Lyon, who knew his subject, could see through this in an instant, and life would be made suitably uncomfortable for any boy who was not doing his best. If he ever saw Jack floundering he would say, 'Goodness gracious. Is this the same boy who put forty-three runs on the board in half an hour against Dulwich last Wednesday? You shouldn't be having any trouble with Caesar!' At the age of eleven, Jack was none too confident of the comparison. But Old Lyon knew better. He had watched the shy new boy, and seen his confidence grow, cricket bringing the respect and friendship of others. Slowly the master's message began to penetrate as he used the boys' interests and abilities to erode any doubts they might have about their competence in other studies.

Soon Jack left his aunt and uncle's house to become a full boarder at Stratheden. He departed rather more quickly than perhaps some had expected, because there arose a difficult clash of personality between him and his aunt. Whenever he or Holly, his cousin, had committed a sin, she would sit them on her knee and deliver an interminable, righteous sermon, after which they felt as guilty as the famous murderer Dr Crippen, who not long before had been arrested in mid-Atlantic. On one occasion she thought that Jack had told her a lie when in fact he had not. With Jack seated upon her rather plump, soft knee in a haze of rosewater perfume, his aunt began to pick over his soul:

Dear, darling Jack, darling boy. I want to talk to you about your father who loves you so much. How very disappointed he'll be when he hears that this boy who he loves so much has told auntie a lie. Don't you think it will make him so unhappy that he'll cry too? Our Heavenly Father who looks down on us can see everything, and you can never run away from Him or tell untruths. He wants to love you, but unless you always tell the truth . . .

By this time Jack, in tears, was ready to admit to just about anything to escape further suffocation from this maternal righteousness.

It was a relationship in which he often managed to put a foot wrong without the slightest intention of doing so. In general he was a well-behaved boy, properly brought up to consider others and to be generous. His skill with ball games and good progress at bookwork made him notable and popular, but he did have a streak of independence. If he thought that a particular course of action was necessary and reasonably within the rules, he would take it with or without the support of his peers. What he had noticed was that even in a home like his, the enjoyment of kicking or throwing a ball about seemed to attract more than average chastisement. The odd thing was that whether the 'crime' was partly intentional or wholly accidental didn't seem to matter when judged by the somewhat arbitrary punishments handed out by adults, but no punishment was worse for Jack than the stratagem employed by his well-meaning, Christian aunt. On another occasion she decided that some art appreciation would be useful and brought down one of the Italian Madonnas that usually hung on her bedroom wall:

'Perhaps the most beautiful picture that was ever painted. Tell us Jack, why do you think it's so beautiful?'

'Well, actually I don't think she is as pretty as my cousin.'

'Blasphemy. That is blasphemy. You mustn't talk like that. Go to your room immediately!'

Although the dormitory Jack soon occupied at Stratheden held few of the dainty comforts of his aunt's home, he was far happier to be among his friends, and easily became accustomed to the necessary routine.

Britain had declared war on Germany on 14 August 1914, a few weeks before Jack came to Stratheden, and initially this had had little impact on the school. Naturally enough for boys of his age the world did not extend much further than the horizons of the *Boy's Own Paper*, and to have got that far was sometimes exceptional. But many of the pupils had older brothers who were keen to join up in what seemed a marvellous adventure. It was going to clear away all those things that mothers and fathers had been discussing rather angrily for so long, so it seemed entirely appropriate that one should go over there and jolly well sort things out. However, most of these schoolboys were far less excited by the war than by an argument over how many runs Jack Hobbs had made that year, or a discussion on what C.B. Fry had said about rugby. Through the remarkable variety of sports he played, and his ability to write so well about them all, C.B. had become something of a hero, though none suspected that in ten years or so he would be writing about a certain R.J.O. Meyer.

Early in August the first British Expeditionary Force landed in France, as the Germans swept through Brussels and on into northern France with catastrophic and bloody efficiency. Inexorably, while Government and press ensured that the news at home was 'good', the death toll accelerated. As the letters to Rollo Meyer show, the school always kept in touch with families, and also had a very good Old Boys' network. Many of the pupils who had left Stratheden House four or five years earlier were being commissioned in the forces. One of the boys had a small photo of his brother, who had recently become an army officer. He had often spoken about him, boasting how good he was at rugger or fishing, and describing many of his practical jokes. There seemed little of this joviality in the treasured photograph: the brother's eyes were hidden under the broad peak of his cap, he sported rather a new-looking moustache and had a stiffness of posture induced by an unforgiving uniform, having belts, buckles and hooks for unimaginable purposes. All the boy's chums loved to look at it and he rationed them accordingly. Then, after a month or two, they realized they had not seen it for some time; in fact they never saw it again, just as their friend would never again see his brother.

It soon became too painful to read out the names of the latest casualties during the school assembly. And as the war proceeded the younger staff, caretakers and garden boys also enlisted to satisfy the demands of the conflict. Now the school was beginning to feel the effects of the war: all sweets and confectionery disappeared and the food became simple and monotonous, much of it tasting rather old. The boys were always hungry and as a result tempers easily frayed as Old Lyon fought to preserve some semblance of fairness and learning. Sports and games of any type became an important diversion, luckily maintained at Stratheden by the games field not being entirely dug over for potatoes, which was the current fate of so many playing fields and open spaces. As the war proceeded many pupils left school, sometimes through enforced changes in parents' circumstances, sometimes because boys were moved from Blackheath, only a few miles from the city, for safety's sake. In fact in August 1915 five Zeppelins raided London, and did a great deal of psychological if not much physical damage.

With food now severely rationed and of dismal quality, the general health at Stratheden House deteriorated despite the enthusiasm for all outdoor activities; when measles took hold the effects were appalling. It seems that at least three boys died in one term, among them, sadly, Old Lyon's nephew. Jack, under the delirious influence of the virus, was unfortunately instrumental in hastening one of these poor boys back to his maker. There were so many who were ill that they were moved to a special dormitory normally used by the youngest. As Jack was already quite tall his feet stuck out of the bottom of the bed, and in his confused state he became convinced that the bed next to his was larger, although it was actually occupied by a smaller boy. With the little strength he had left he turfed the unfortunate lad out and crawled into his bed. Instead of getting into Jack's bed, the boy slept on the floor, caught pneumonia and soon died. Because of his illness it was some time before the impact of what had happened dawned on Jack, and even then it was too awful to contemplate, and the complete antithesis of his Christian values. A damning and incredible feature of this attack of measles was that no medication was available, and the doctor's advice upon seeing Jack was that he should be kept warm and drink only barley water. In the circumstances the advice was almost worse than useless because there certainly was no barley water available, and as a prolonged fever seemed to be part of the illness, keeping warm when one already had a temperature of 104° seemed a ridiculous notion. As it happened, trying to keep cool was almost the end of Jack. The fever gave the boys a continuous and terrible thirst, and as the stringencies of the war effort had caused the tap water to be declared unfit for drinking, clean water was provided for the dormitory in several jugs. In a desperate bid to try to get cool Jack emptied one of these all over himself. In his wretched state the shock was too much for him and he collapsed, saturated, onto the dormitory floor. However he was more fortunate than his companion because he was found, dried off and returned to his bed by the matron.

By 1918, Jack's last year at Stratheden House, the First World War had reduced the roll of the school to about thirty boys. From this small number a Cricket XI was selected in an attempt to maintain some of the prestige the school had earned over the previous three or so years. By this time Denys had moved on to Haileybury College, and having lost such a fine cricketer the school looked towards Jack and a few others to put runs on the board. During July, Herbert Lyon wrote to Rollo Meyer trying to persuade him to play in the parents' match and commenting on Jack's efforts: 'Jack is in great form with both bat and ball, and his 105 not out against Abbey School particularly pleased one by the judgment he showed, apart from its being a very sound and stylish innings.'

That year arrangements were being made for Jack to follow Denys to Haileybury. Despite the war this school had maintained a generous disposition to the clergy of the country, allowing their sons to be educated on half fees. However, even with this benevolence Rollo Meyer's small annual stipend of £550 made it imperative that Jack should sit for one of the scholarships on offer, because his father also had to find the school fees for Constance and Denys, and their young brother, Derek, was now of a size where hand-me-down clothes were running out. The examination included a Latin paper that Jack thought he should be able to manage quite reasonably. However, in his anxiety to get started he translated the introduction into Latin, instead of translating the Latin set piece into English. It appears that he managed this piece of stupidity quite well, because with a few generous words of recommendation from Old Lyon he won his scholarship, and looked forward to Haileybury the following term.

CHAPTER TWO

Haileybury

The contrast between Stratheden House and Haileybury College couldn't have been greater. At Jack's prep school the roll had diminished to about twenty-five; Haileybury was vast, with 521 boys, and sported the biggest quadrangle of any school or university in the country, bordered by buildings of austere grandeur. A Greek portico and columns opposed the enormous chapel of Byzantine solidity, which dominated the whole school and the landscape for miles around.

Haileybury College had always had strong links with the services and a fine Officer Training Corps, and as early as the autumn term of 1914 thirty boys left the school to enlist for the war. They were joined by masters and college servants, and for the duration the college continued to give willingly and bravely, considerably extending and intensifying the activities of its OTC. The effect of the war upon the college was devastating; what had been a flamboyant and lively institution before the conflict was now cast into sombre mood. Each day the names of casualties were posted on a Roll of Honour for all to see, something that must have cast fearful doubt for those approaching their eighteenth birthdays. By the end of the war over two thousand eight hundred men and boys from Haileybury had fought for King and country. During leave many of them, now young officers, would visit the school and take comfort from its familiar surroundings. But by the time peace came 586 young Haileyburians had lost their lives. At least half the strength of the staff joined up, and this left the school with the difficult problem of filling their places. In common with other schools, to prevent the educational system from collapsing altogether, they were replaced by venerable, elderly retired teachers, prised from their favourite armchairs and put back into service with varying degrees of reluctance for the duration. Despite the college's efforts, it was inevitable that the sadly nicknamed 'Dug-outs' caused the great flame of knowledge to become somewhat dimmed by a little deafness here, short-sightedness there and much stiffness everywhere. But beyond the unkindness of old age was a greater anguish; many of those who had retired from the college only a few years previously returned to see the familiar names of the boys they had taught appearing day after day as casualties on the Roll of Honour.

New boys were understandably given little attention and made to settle in quickly with Haileybury's austere regime. Above all, they were expected to prove themselves worthy of their brothers making a supreme sacrifice at the Front. Jack could not easily appreciate what the school had been through since 1914, and there was little in his experience, even after Stratheden, to help him come to terms with what he found. Those already there who knew of the dreadful realities bore their feelings stoically, and they were not a topic for discussion save with contemporaries.

Jack found the situation at Haileybury crushing. It seemed to him that the Dug-outs mostly ignored the pupils altogether, or only spoke when a ticking-off was apparently required. He thought the remarks would be more appropriate to the barracks, and felt insulted because they were remorseless and too often unjustified. Jack also learnt that the use of the cane was quite common, but this didn't worry him too much because he knew that he would probably not do anything bad enough to merit that degree of punishment. However, floggings were mostly applied by the all-seeing prefects and not the arthritic Dug-outs, and could be as easily earned for the comparatively innocent crime of ignorance as for misbehaviour. During his first few weeks at the school the imposing regime seemed to turn Jack into someone either timid or stupid. His problem was that although he had been presented with a timetable of his lessons, he somehow remained completely ignorant of where to find the classrooms. The ridiculous situation was further damned by the rebuff experienced when asking another boy for directions. 'Who the hell do you think you're talking to?' was the reply nine times out of ten because he had broken a school rule introduced for obscure reasons, that new boys did not speak to older boys. Wandering sheeplike through the endless corridors, in order to escape further retribution he timidly spent the larger part of several of those early days hiding in the toilets. He was even too embarrassed to ask his brother Denys where he should go. Obviously it was a situation that couldn't continue, so one morning he just went into the first classroom he found, braved the Beak's (master's) insults and sat down, apologizing for his lateness. The subject seemed to be geography and the Beak pointed to him and barked, 'You boy. Open your Euripides and start.'

Fumbling with the stiff new atlas he mumbled, 'Sir, I'm sorry sir. I can't find Europe.'

'What do you mean "Europe" boy? I said Eurip——— What are you doing here anyhow?'

'I don't know sir. I think – I don't know . . .'

'Get out! Get out!'

He was a little tearful and pretty angry by this time so he knocked on any classroom door he could find, but related that it was not until the third or fourth that someone would help him.

When Jack came to the school the Master was Frederick Blagden Malim. As a man he did not readily exhibit a character which boys found immediately attractive, being of rather diminutive stature and stern countenance. However, as an educationalist he was quite outstanding, providing the academic structure of Haileybury and introducing the Oxford and Cambridge Board for Higher and School Certificates. In doing so he brought particular benefits to those who sought university places. Furthermore, this Master of sombre appearance did much with the assistance of his wife for the arts, music and literature, making their study more accessible to all. The First World War dealt a savage blow to these enlightened innovations, and the Master and his bursar used all their resources to maintain the school in the face of progressive hardship. They were remarkably successful, but the necessities required for the complicated task of running a boarding school were now vastly more expensive and strictly rationed. It was remarkable in such circumstances that Haileybury still extended the hand of benevolence to the sons of clergy, and fortunate for Jack Meyer that it did so.

The high point during his first term at Haileybury was the declaration of peace on 11 November 1918. On the morning of Armistice Day a thanksgiving service was held in the Quad around the flagstaff. Most of the boys were in the OTC and their khaki uniforms made two opposite sides of a large, open square. On the south side in front of the Chapel stood the remainder of the boys, and opposite them staff, college servants and their families. The cold November morning seemed to mirror the awful conflict of emotions as all stood there to reflect on the last four years. There was, of course, enormous relief at victory, but it had been at an appalling cost. There was a feeling that all deserved some part in the celebrations. A few days earlier many seniors had quite expected to be sent off to the Front to face its appalling life and death lottery. Many of these went into Hertford, visiting two or three hostelries which seemed to throw their doors open wide to anyone during the days following the Armistice. Exhibiting the buffoonery of lads not knowing how to hold rather too much drink, they eventually made their way back to Haileybury, where there had also been celebrations. Odd things had been thrown into the swimming pool, chamberpots miraculously appeared on chimney stacks, practically every light in the college was on and there was the odd bit of singing and laughter wafting on the evening air from different places around the Quad. The same air also bore a strangely acrid smell; it was learnt later that someone had attempted to set fire to part of the college. Some of the seniors who had, only a few hours earlier been especially enthusiastic in their merrymaking, now appeared somewhat the worse for wear, others were really frightfully ill. This seemed rather too much for the Master, who had already tolerated hours of behaviour that would normally have merited summary punishment. He decreed that the culprits would receive a beating on the following day.

News of the punishments caused great indignation among the boys, and Jack, who had a sense of fair play, was united in adversity with others in the house whom he would previously not have dared address. When the dreadful hour arrived the head prefects took their canes and waited outside Bradby Hall, where a crowd of boys had already congregated. The revellers were cheered both as they went in and rather uncomfortably came out, and a short while afterwards the head prefects emerged to be greeted by loud boos. Already embarrassed by the episode, this proved to be the last straw and they ordered the mob back to their houses and told them to expect a beating for their impudence. At that time the head of Batten, Jack's house, was Howard Marshall, who went on to become a war correspondent and well-known BBC sports commentator. He was very unhappy at the situation and after assembling the boys said, 'You booed the prefects and this is justice, but any of you boys got anything to say for yourselves? Were any of you by any chance not there?'

Three were not because they had been in the sanatorium and then another spoke up and said, 'Please, I was there but I didn't boo.'

'Really?' said Marshall, hackles rising. 'Really? Well, do you know I think I shall need all my energy to explain to this boy what a worm he is, and as I shan't have the strength to beat the rest of you, you can all get out. Now!'

This impressed Jack, who later thought that here were the beginnings of justice and leadership.

As if the mortality of the First World War had been insufficient, a near global epidemic of influenza reached its European zenith during the winter of 1918/19. It was to kill twice as many as had the four years of conflict. Many in the college caught it and found its severity debilitating; Jack was one of them. In fact he was so ill that it was thought better to send him home, as Haileybury was only a few miles from Watton-at-Stone. Although terribly weakened by the fever which accompanied the 'flu, he was quietly pleased at the curtailment of term and the prospect of being nursed by his mother. There was a slightly awkward moment when she tried to find his food ration book, to learn that naturally enough the school had taken a first charge on the coupons. The scarcity of food was still an acute problem for all and although produce from the rectory gardens had been harvested and stored, items like meat and butter required a ration book.

As Jack's strength returned he began to take a little more interest in the things going on around him. Ella had bought a second-hand table-top snooker set and he and Denys soon mastered the game. Also Denys had become an ardent card player and when he began collecting volunteers for games it was as well to appear deeply involved in some other occupation if one couldn't face several hours passing and shuffling cards across the green baize. However, any occupation could be interrupted by Izzard's lad, Bertie, reporting to the rectory that he had seen a covey of partridge land in the Glebe. Rollo had shooting rights, and the others would attempt to circle round the birds and send them towards him. Jack was becoming quite a shot himself and knew every inch of the land. He would take the gun out with Bertie when Rollo was away. Any one of these forays could stock the larder for a few days and was of great value to the family. Jack later rather regretted his lack of discrimination in shooting practically anything. He once received an irate letter from Ella, some three weeks after returning to Haileybury; she had traced an appalling stench in his bedroom to an old jacket whose pockets were full of very dead sparrows and very much alive maggots. Thereafter she made it a rule to go through the boys' pockets as soon as they had departed for the new term.

Jack's parents were naturally interested to know how he had done in his first term at Haileybury and Rollo detected that there were things that seemed to make him rather unhappy. His father's reply to what Jack considered to be 'injustices' rather surprised him:

> Without injustice there cannot really be justice because it's what one seeks after something has gone wrong. In life, things do go wrong, just look at the last terrible few years. We sent you to Haileybury because it is the best school which we could afford, so it's your best hope. If you suffer an injustice right it if you can, but if you can't you just have to accept it because it really is a part of life. Mind you, you must not behave badly to others, but do be prepared to live with the odd bit of injustice.

It may not have been the answer for which Jack was looking, but he could sense that his father was being realistic and certainly practical. A few weeks after his return to school it seemed that Jack was really going to put that advice to the test. He was hauled out of his dormitory bed one night after lights-out and promptly beaten for hiding a prefect's bath sponges. His anger at the indignity of it all was multiplied by the certainty of his innocence, and after a short time it also became clear to the prefect that Jack could not have been the guilty party. He was instructed to go to Howard Marshall's study where the prefect surprised him by

Canon Rollo Meyer, Jack's father

saying, 'Look Meyer, a terrible thing has happened, I've beaten you when I should not have done. I heard from another prefect that it couldn't possibly have been you, so I had to report myself to the Headmaster this morning for having beaten you – among others who richly deserved it – and I'm wondering if we could square it. Look, here's a whole tin of biscuits. I haven't touched them. Would that do?'

'Them – to eat? All of them?' Jack couldn't believe it.

'Well if that's alright we'll shake hands on it and here you are. Now the point is I haven't bribed you to say nothing. You can speak to the Housemaster and tell him that it was unjust. I'm sorry about it but tell him I did my best to square it.'

Jack didn't go to the Housemaster, because what had just happened was of far greater importance to him than any satisfaction he might get from whining.

Conditions at Haileybury were still pretty tough as the cold winter of 1919 turned into a rather bleak spring. *The Haileyburian* was still full of war despatches and memorials, the college was cold and the boys were hungry. Efforts to supplement their diet were later described by F.M. Heywood, who was both pupil then assistant master.

A boy was lounging on the 'soft-arse' in the corner by a gas ring, frying sardines on the top of an inverted biscuit tin, and conveying it to his mouth on the end of a ruler. Over a gas light another boy was roasting a mole, stuck on a pen.

However, the Dug-outs were leaving and some masters returned, recognized by the older boys who remembered them. There were also new masters who had come from the Services. Despite the unpleasantness of war their self-discipline, honour and ability to give instruction made them excellent teachers, bringing a breath of fresh air into the school.

The XX Acre field, which had been cultivated for potatoes, was returned to its rugby football status, but for a sportsman Jack had a curious aversion to this game. Being rather tall, when he ran his action was rather gangling and, as some remarked, certainly not pretty, but like everyone else he found himself on the rugby pitch. What he lacked in style he made up for with effort which unfortunately resulted in a deeply cut knee from a stone buried in the soft turf. It seems that he reported to the sanatorium only to be told to come back when it was open. The wound turned septic and he bore the scar of that deep and ill-attended injury for the rest of his life, and swore that he would never play rugby again.

At last the summer term came round and Jack looked forward to taking part in the college's cricket, and pitching himself against new and stronger opposition than he had found at Stratheden. At Batten House cricket trials his bowling fairly carved through the batsmen: he took about six wickets for two runs. Since it was a trial situation Jack was not necessarily playing against good cricketers, so the result was predictable, but he was pleased that things had gone well. While he was waiting to bat a house prefect came along and asked in a rather bored voice, 'Anything happened here?'

'Yes! Some ghastly new boy has taken six for two and absolutely ruined the game.'

'Oh God. Not one of those.'

Jack hardly knew what to make of this attitude, but it turned out that neither of the seniors were much in the way of sportsmen, and he later noted with some satisfaction that they were none too keen to be near a bat when there was a chance of him bowling. However, Jack's performance was promising enough to get him into the House team, together with Denys, who had represented them for some time.

The next cricketing highlight was to be selected for the College Colts against St Paul's Colts. Because the visitors arrived late Haileybury found themselves with only one hour in which to make ninety-five runs for a win. After the fall of three wickets Jack and the other batsman found themselves passing the total in just over three-quarters of an hour. Those who represent their school have a special camaraderie and Jack started to regain some of the self-respect which had been somewhat dented during his first term. Once again his sporting ability was strengthening his confidence even though there was no-one quite like Old Lyon to support him, and as soon as Jack began to demonstrate his ability and enthusiasm there were several masters who took a concerned interest in his cricket. P.H. Latham, who had been a Cambridge captain, had come to Haileybury before the turn of the century as an assistant to take over cricket coaching. Until then the college had been principally a rugby playing school, but soon cricket pitches sprang up everywhere and it was not unusual to see up to six games of cricket all going on at the same time on the Terrace Field, an enormous expanse of ground on the south side of the school. This was also the site for an interesting entertainment called 'skying' which was reserved for Saturday evenings. It consisted of three or four of the first team players, and sometimes Latham himself, hitting sixes to about two hundred boys in the field. Jack certainly finished his first year at Haileybury in a far more positive frame of mind than he had started it, and his academic studies were also beginning to improve. This new enthusiasm was maintained during the summer holidays when his favourite occupations seemed to be sitting in his father's chair in the study lost in a book, or playing cricket. Even when there were no other boys to play with he would go to a special place in a nearby field where he had made his own pitch and would practise bowling for hour upon hour.

Although new boys arrived each term at Haileybury the intake during the autumn term was usually slightly larger and Jack, from his elevated position as a second-year pupil, surveyed them with some sympathy. This compassion was part of a personality that had some way to go towards maturity of course, and anyone later knowing the charismatic figure of the man would hardly have recognized the retiring fourteen year old until he saw him pick up a cricket bat. Also, upon close scrutiny, he might have recognized an emerging single-mindedness that was to carry Jack into and through storm and success later on. During the first term of 1920 Jack began to show the remarkable coordination that made him such a formidable squash, racquets and fives player. From almost nowhere he came first in the college competition for the Lower Squash Set, but the game that had already caught his imagination was racquets. A new racquets coach, Gerald Barnes, had been employed by the college from Princes and Queens Clubs, Cambridge, and he soon recognized Jack's potential ability. With little match experience Jack and an older boy, D.H. Marlow, beat all-comers to win the Junior Racquets college competition. As if this was not enough of a high note he also ended the term by carrying off the form prize for his academic studies.

As much as Jack loved being at home, the holidays at that time made him a little impatient to get back to Haileybury and whatever sport he was playing. On one occasion the feeling was exacerbated by some rather well-off friends who had organized a dance in their large house. Jack hated dancing. It was not an aversion that lasted for long and probably had more to do with his awkward time of life, still prevailing natural shyness and the overwhelming fact that his older brother was an excellent dancer. None of the excuses he invented cut any ice with his parents, and he was duly ordered into his best suit and stiff collar, polished boots and regulation parting. Being in the country the fashions were a little behind the times; there was certainly no jazz or 'shimmying' but plenty of good old hesitation-waltzes, foxtrots and one-steps. Jack was hopeless at the lot; as far as he could see all dances came under the heading of slow shuffle or quick shuffle, and he just could not understand why all these awful women wanted to dance with him. With one clammy hand extended to his left, the other held his partner's waist, confused by the hard corset moving strangely beneath the silky floral print-stuff. Observers noted that he appeared to dance with a slight stoop, but did not understand that this was caused by gently trying to avoid the sensuous nudge of a bosom, at which he perspired with embarrassment. The announcement of supper was a blessing and the guests retired to an excellent buffet in the dining room, many ladies promising Jack another dance – for which he had not asked – after refreshments. Suitably invigorated with fizzy drinks and an exotic *soupçon* of this and that they made their way back to the hall, a Young Thing having promised to show them what was 'it' in town, only to find that all the new-fangled electric lights had gone out. Closer inspection soon revealed that every electric light bulb in the place had actually disappeared – and so had Jack.

Jack's development as a sportsman continued and in the new year of 1921 he heard that he was to play racquets for the college. This was an honour indeed and confirmation of his ability and growing strength, for in this fast and vigorous sport he was partnering C.E.J. Evers, who was a good three years older and Haileybury's racquets captain. Although naturally determined to show his worth, his first college match against Tonbridge presented him with more opportunity than he really wanted, because Evers was slightly off-colour and Jack carried a somewhat ragged match to a 4–2 win for Haileybury. The next contest was against Harrow and the most formidable pair on the public school's racquet scene, C.S. and L.G. Crawley. Their appearance was mature compared with the Haileybury pair and Jack, only just turned sixteen, had to contend with the knowledge that the last time the schools had met, Harrow had won 4–0. Although designated a 'friendly' match the game turned out to be the most exciting of the term. The Crawleys swept away the first two games but the college pair threw themselves into the match with blistering serves and brilliant finishes to rallies. The Harrow pair were clearly disconcerted by Haileybury levelling 3–3, but having greater depth to their play, managed to hang on in the last game while Haileybury, still fighting but fatigued, let slip a few loose strokes and gave them the match. However, it was a tremendous game and a valuable experience resulting in Jack being awarded his Racquets Pair.

Early in 1921 Denys left Watton and the college to go into business. The rather sad prospect of his departure was alleviated to some extent for Jack by the wonderful gift of a Rigby & Co. sidelock shotgun. His shooting had become something of a legend, and his contributions to the rectory larder were both necessary and respected, so a local landowner had made him a generous gift of this classic shotgun. Izzard the gardener remarked with his usual objectivity that if the thing were sold they could feed the family for half the year without setting foot on the Glebe, but this idea was quite alien to Jack, who kept the gun for the rest of his life, though there were times when he certainly could have done with the cash its sale could have produced.

Returning to Haileybury alone, Jack was considerably cheered to find that he had been picked to play for the college cricket XI. He and his friend, R.E.H. Hudson, were the two youngsters in the side, but were soon given the chance of proving their abilities in a close match against Fitzwilliam Hall. A stand of fifty runs was ended when Jack clean bowled their highest scorer, and by taking two wickets he felt that he had earned his keep and provided justification for his selection. A week later, playing against the Old Wykehamists, he didn't bowl but made a stand with Hudson, who scored a magnificent 168 not out, Jack just passing the half-century. Besides P.H. Latham, Haileybury also had a professional cricket coach. George Bean was well known to the Sussex XI and at Lord's for his famous coaching classes during the Easter holidays. The results of such good coaching combined with plenty of serious practice improved Jack's game considerably, and there was another, perhaps more philosophical side to the game that began to interest him. He had always loved talking about cricket and often did so until his companions in the dormitory actually fell asleep, but during the last year or so he had also developed a liking for experimentation. This was not done purely for its own sake, but out of genuine curiosity and love of the game. Often something might occur to him and whether it be a practice in the nets or even during a match he would take the opportunity of trying something new. It was not easy to reconcile the activity with a sense of fairness towards team members, or even with his purposeful intention of winning, because experiments can go wrong.

To play at Lord's has to be a schoolboy's dream come true, and when Jack was selected to play there for the college against Cheltenham it was wonderfully exciting. What impressed him more than the pavilion, Tavern and grandstand in pristine white was the immaculate condition of the pitch and outfield. It seemed so perfect that it felt like a crime to set foot on it, but there was a match to be played and such considerations and the awe of the place had to be forgotten. It was during this game that Jack met K.S. Duleepsinhji. Rain during the night had made the wicket slow, and this was to be to Jack's advantage as he pitched the ball well up, making it break suddenly. This caused Duleepsinhji to offer a dolly-catch for a duck. However, the young Cheltenham player took ample revenge, his slow leg breaks taking the wickets of Jack, Hudson and Seabrook, the Haileybury team's three best batsmen. A week later Jack returned to Lord's to play in a one-day match for Mr C.S. Tufnell's XI against the Lord's XI. Both teams consisted of boys selected from the leading public school XIs and he was the only one from Haileybury. He was given the opportunity to bowl and took four wickets for five runs in the first innings, thus playing a substantial part in Mr Tufnell's XI's victory. An important aspect of playing at Lord's was that many of the matches were reported in *The Times* or *Morning Post* by writers who really knew their cricket. This meant that any schoolboy whose form looked promising would very soon be a topic of discussion at county club bars or university ground pavilions.

Harrow, with the Crawleys, still loomed large in the racquets' fixture list for the new season in 1922, and Jack, now captain of racquets, had formed a new pair with R.E.H. Hudson. During that season victory in the Harrow match had gone to Meyer and Hudson 15–12. Jack had also been made a House Prefect and an NCO in the Officer Training Corps. The latter enabled him to indulge in rifle shooting, for which he later won the college's Trethewy Individual Cup, scoring 80 out of 85. With the experience of shooting on the Glebe at home combined with excellent sight and control, he had taken to target shooting like the proverbial duck to water, quickly equalling and then bettering the scores of the college team. With such a demanding timetable of sporting activities he had to keep a very close eye on the academic ball, because examinations had to be passed if any kind of living were to be made and he still had at the back of his mind the wish to become a teacher. In the two terms leading up to important examinations he had become almost madly active with his sports, and with matches home

The Haileybury Racquets Pair, 1922. 'Reggie' Hudson, Jack and the coach, Gerald Barnes, after the victory over Harrow

and away there was little free time available. During the previous term he had come first in the Open Racquets, Handicap Racquets, Open Squash, Open Bat Fives and second in the handicap Squash; he also contributed towards the winning of the Inter-house Racquets Cup and won the Racquets Singles Cup. On top of this, of course, were the college racquets matches with Hudson. The summer term brought no relaxation from sporting activities, because again apart from regular school matches there were cricket house matches, for which he was Batten's captain, and also the recently introduced tennis house matches on the four new hard courts. One can see with some sympathy that time easily and quickly slipped by before his July Oxford and Cambridge School Certificate Exam.

During 1922 a new Master, John Talbot, arrived. Quite different in character to Malim, he was a real 'John Bull' in appearance, but approachable and friendly with very many interests that he would discuss with any master or boy. Despite the dominance of his sporting activities Jack's interests and outlook were broadening, thanks to his wide, voracious reading. There was much that impressed him about the heroes of the past: those who did not go with the crowd but forged their own path, initially perhaps against the counsel of those who knew better, or were in authority.

As Jack and the other boys grew older they began to take a healthy interest in girls. The college did make some attempt to explain the facts of life, and it was done on a manly one-to-one basis. The elderly master detailed to enlighten the maturing pupil on the issue of the birds and the bees provided little in the way of revelation for Jack.

Meyer, I must talk to you seriously. You know about women I'm sure – but there are some women you simply have to keep clear of because – well, I don't have to talk to you about that because you're far too good a boy to get mixed up with that. But the unfortunate thing is, there are some charming girls, nice girls, good girls and if you get interested in them, then – well you might get too interested. Then you're – you're bound to get married. Then there will be children and masters like myself will have to sacrifice our lives dealing with your indulgence. You understand? You understand Meyer?

And off he went.

If the teaching of the facts of life left a little to be desired, the college did attempt to imbue the boys with some of the social graces to help them in their future lives. With one look at the young lady from the local village who had come to teach the boys their steps, Jack's prejudice against dancing disappeared. Practically everyone fell in love with her, and it was not long before her classes became very popular, with all the boys putting on their smartest clothes for them. She certainly brightened up the lengthening evenings of the autumn term. Being quite tall, Jack seemed to receive quite a lot of attention from the dancing mistress, and could not avoid perspiring terribly at the excitement of being near her. With two other friends he got to know her quite well and they used their privileges to take her out to tea. Then one awful day she told them that she was engaged to be married and wanted them to meet her fiancé. They were appalled, because as far as they could see she had become engaged to a fat old man. Afterwards they got together and being very concerned about the situation Jack said, 'Chaps, there is only one thing to do. One of us has got to rescue her. Obviously she wouldn't marry him if she could marry one of us, so we'll pool our money, draw lots and see which one of us packs it in here, gets a job and marries her.' Jack won the draw and his friends patted him on the back and promised him their full support, speculating that there was little doubt that their fathers would want someone like him in their business. After the next dancing lesson Jack managed to get the mistress on her own, plucked up his courage and nobly explained the plan. The poor girl burst into tears and cried, 'But my dear boy, I don't think you understand, it's sweet of you but I do happen to love him.'

'But you can't love a fat old man!'

'Good gracious, he's not really fat.'

'Fat and bald he is!'

'. . . and he's only twenty-seven you know.'

'But twenty-seven!'

When Jack related the story to his friends they could hardly believe their ears, but she went out of her way to arrange another meeting between them and her fiancé and Jack eventually admitted that he was a perfectly reasonable sort of fellow. This experience made him feel that there were a few things that he did not yet understand about women, in fact there were actually quite a lot. Some time afterwards the boys were talking over the incident and one of them claimed to have actually kissed their beautiful dancing mistress. The others let him off lightly with a warning that he would be beaten up if he ever mentioned it again.

With the beginning of his final year at Haileybury the question of Jack's future had to be considered. He was still interested in a teaching career based on his strongest academic subjects of history and English. Being a Cambridge man, Rollo knew that a place at one of the colleges would suit Jack's further education ideally, and his cricket, but at that time the fees to study there were astronomical, and would have taken about half his stipend. However, Haileybury considered that with Jack's sporting prowess and reasonable academic qualifications, Cambridge was certainly in sight, and notwithstanding the family's financial situation they proceeded with the administration for the application. To enter Cambridge students were normally required to sit a 'Previous Examination' but he was excused because of the level of marks he had achieved in his School Certificate, although he still needed Latin, which he had to sit for in Michaelmas 1922.

Under the influence of Old Lyon at Stratheden, Jack had been reasonably competent in classics, but these studies had not advanced greatly at Haileybury. Consequently there was a lot of ground to cover in a very short time for the Michaelmas exam. Because of the demanding syllabus Jack was allowed the option of doing prose and translations for which he could use his books, and in preparation he was given a crib and told to get on with it. Horace's *Odes* absolutely fascinated him and without any persuasion he went through all the poems, scoring a very high pass. This caught the eye of a stern and rather critical Latin master with whom he was able to share his new enthusiasm for Horace.

With this obstacle surmounted, the application to Cambridge

proceeded and Jack threw himself back into college life. He was made a School Prefect, and the responsibility helped him to see things from the angle of those who have to govern. House matches and college matches again took much of his time and energy for he was now captain of racquets and fives. In the college competitions he came first in the Open Fives, Bat Fives, Open Squash and Open Racquets and again won the Racquets Singles Cup. Despite his gangling style he came fourteenth out of seventy in the college steeplechase and managed to throw a cricket ball further, at 85 yd, than anyone else. Toward the end of the spring term in 1923 he was delighted to learn that he was to be Haileybury's First XI cricket captain. One of the early matches was against Hertfordshire Club and Ground and brought Jack up against the formidable batsman C.H. (Titch) Titchmarsh. Although only 5 ft 2 in, Titchmarsh seemed to know every stroke in the book and improvized others with a sure eye. There were many fine games that summer, a few of them being very tough ones indeed, and Haileybury, though not a strong side, lacked nothing in fighting spirit. A typical match was the one against I Zingari, in its report of which *The Times* described him as 'R.J.O. Meyer, possibly the finest public schools racquets player who may make history, played a fine innings before luncheon – he apparently had much time to spare when playing his strokes.' And later, when he was bowling:

> Meyer had two catches missed off his bowling in one over – enough to break the heart of any ordinary boy. Meyer, however was not heartbroken and although he was not lucky at any time last Saturday the I Zingari – as they would – paid generous tribute to both his bowling and his sense in keeping himself on as the last hope of winning the match.

This term presented Jack with one of the great turning points of his life when he heard that he had been offered a place at Pembroke College, Cambridge, to read for History Honours. The excitement of the offer was bitterly tempered by the difficulty of funding. Although on half fees, twice in his Haileyburian career he had almost had to leave because of financial difficulties, the college giving the Meyers wonderful support by securing donations from various religious charities. Two or three weeks after Jack had received the news from Pembroke he led his side in the college's annual fixture against Wellington and tried to forget the anxiety over his Cambridge offer. At the previous year's match the college had beaten Wellington by an innings and four runs but Jack had heard that they were a stronger side now. After they won the toss and elected to bat he found out just how true that was. The first innings concluded with

Wellington's score charging to 306 and Jack knew that he had another good scrap on his hands. He wanted to do reasonably well because Rollo and Ella had come to watch him play. There was another spectator who was taking a keen interest, G.S. Pawle, whose family name had long been associated with Haileybury and its cricket. He had attended the school in 1868 and many of his sons had followed. His enthusiasm was based on a very sound judgment of the game and he had been watching the progress of Haileybury's current captain for some years. He sought out the Meyers among the spectators and made his way over to them at the end of Wellington's strong first innings. Having introduced himself, Pawle congratulated them on Jack's offer from Pembroke, but mentioned most tactfully that he had heard that there was some obstacle to his accepting. Rollo, a little surprised, admitted that there was and Pawle, turning to the match in hand, observed that what Haileybury needed now was runs, and indicated that if Jack contributed fifty of them he would provide the necessary assistance to get him through his first year. Poor Rollo was almost speechless, the anguish of the situation now seeming more acute by the possibility of its resolution. 'Good gracious Mr Pawle. My goodness' was all he could say for several minutes, so his benefactor concluded, 'Well, I expect we'll meet at tea, and we shall certainly meet tomorrow at the end of the match.'

At lunch Rollo disappeared, but Jack joined his mother to catch up on the news from Watton-at-Stone. Instead, he was somewhat bemused by her sudden interest in cricket for reasons she dared not mention for fear of upsetting his game.

'Look darling, do try to make some runs this afternoon, your father would be so pleased.'

'Mother, you know I'm really more of a bowler than a batsman. I just get sixes or out.'

'Yes Jack, but today is rather special and we may not see you play at Haileybury again, and it would be wonderful to see you make some runs. Please trust your mother.'

'Mother, I trust you for anything other than cricket, but of course I'll have a go,' was his irritable reply.

The Haileybury innings started badly but Jack hung on for the rest of the day and the following morning. He was starting to slash away and was into his thirties, missing rather a lot of balls while his parents' hearts missed beats. Then he was out to a fine slip catch for forty. The bottom seemed to drop out of Ella's world, but was quickly restored by Rollo explaining that Jack would almost certainly bat again in Haileybury's second innings. But after Wellington's second, Haileybury needed to make an impossible 195 in one-and-a-half hours to win. Jack changed the batting order to have a go at it, but two wickets went quickly and cheaply. Rollo could not bear to stay in his seat, knowing that Jack was next in. Playing a forcing game he scattered balls around the ground, but Wellington's fielding had risen to the occasion and they were as keen as mustard. So was Ella, perched dangerously on the edge of her folding chair and adding Jack's erratic ones and twos to the first innings score of forty. The bowler was sending down lobs again and Jack flashed an on-drive to one that dropped a little short, the two runs bringing him up to forty-nine. Moving up the wicket he hooked the next lob off his shoulder. Returned very smartly from deep square-leg it made only one run possible and rather curtailed the traditional applause for the half-century. After a single he was back at the crease and repeated the stroke, but this time the lob had turned into a quicker fuller toss and he skied it to a fielder whose hands clapped around the spinning ball for the captain's wicket. 'Damn it!' he thought and turned for the pavilion. Approaching the spectators he looked up sheepishly to where his parents were sitting. He noticed that his father was missing and was about to give some kind of apologetic shrug to his mother when he stopped in his tracks, saw that she was looking very flushed, smiling from ear to ear, crying and blowing kisses. He wondered what on earth could be the matter with her, and felt a little embarrassed, getting out with a cow-shot like that was certainly nothing to celebrate. Running out of time the college had made eighty-eight, so the victory went to Wellington. Jack was still pondering on how Haileybury had let them run away in the first innings for 306, when at last Rollo appeared. He looked dreadful, and Jack later learnt that he had been in the Chapel praying, but had had to leave because he started to feel very ill with apprehension. In fact on returning to the cricket ground he was forced to make a detour behind the pavilion where he was very sick. 'I say dad, you don't look too well. Pity about my last innings, I hope you didn't see it.'

'Don't trouble yourself about that, old boy. The thing is you got your fifty and you're going up to Pembroke. It's all settled.'

'What's that? Really?!'

CHAPTER THREE

Cambridge

I loved Cambridge and those days were the best, unquestionably the best. The reason was that we were free – absolutely free to make of it what we would. Nobody pushed us or pressed us. If you failed, you failed but anything you were successful at you achieved yourself and no barriers were put in your way.

So Jack summed up what he found at Pembroke College, Cambridge. Here, at last, was a place that easily accepted his independent character and where he was free to work or play as he wished. Work in this case encompassed all that he needed to qualify for his History degree, and play was essentially cricket. The degree was necessary for his teaching career, which would in turn support more cricket. It was as well for him that he came up to Cambridge during the autumn of 1923; it gave him a term or two to settle down before his first hectic cricket season began.

Although confident that he could justify his place, Jack had little doubt about his good fortune in achieving his heart's desire. He also acknowledged later that no small part had been played by Pembroke's admissions tutor, H.G. Comber, MA. Having noted Jack's career and the comments of Pelham 'Plum' Warner, *The Times*'s Special Correspondent, he had been in touch with Talbot, Haileybury's Master, concerning young Meyer's future. In Jack he saw a potential Blue who also had reasonable academic standards, and at that time Pembroke was a particularly sporting college, with men in the University boat, rugby XV and cricket XI.

Inevitably Jack was already well known to Hertfordshire Cricket Club before he left Haileybury, and played for them during the summer before going up to Cambridge. Life will always sort out the men from the boys, sometimes gently over the years but at other times at a great deal more forced a pace, such as during the few hours of a cricket match. If, like Jack in 1923, you were neither one nor yet the other the forcing was often obligatory. During a match at Watford Cricket Week against Oxfordshire, a varsity county, Jack was allowed a few overs and although he did not take a wicket, Oxford could only claim five runs from him.

Jack started to bat well and was soon into double figures when suddenly:

> I came face-to-face with Biveas-Burrows, who bowled in a way which I'd
> never seen before. He bowled bouncers, very fast balls which arrive at
> about head height. I played 'schoolboy' forward to the first and back to
> the second ball. As neither seemed effective I went down to Titchmarsh
> to get some advice and enquired in a stage whisper whether Biveas-
> Burrows had bloody well killed anyone yet. He said 'Keep out of the
> way until I get down your end. It's easy when you know how. So don't
> worry.' Titch, who was only 5 ft 2 in, proceeded to hook him off his
> eyebrows all over the field.

Jack had a few minutes to watch him, then about a second to get it right
as he faced Biveas-Burrows. If his heart was missing beats, the press
seemed quite relaxed about it all.

> Meyer gave a delightful exhibition of hard hitting, and was only three
> short of his half-century when he was clean bowled by Burrows, the
> famous Army fast bowler, considered by many experts to have one of the
> fastest deliveries in the country. Meyer hit him for six and many fours.

As Jack settled into Cambridge he recognized many Haileybury faces,
and was extremely fortunate to have as his tutor Aubrey Attwater, a
lecturer in English, the College Praelector and as true a Pembroke man
as there could be. Attwater had many interests and high among these was
sport. At first, conversations with Jack were almost always about cricket,
but through his great learning and scholarship he began to show him
that there were other worlds which could provide nourishing food for
thought. His study was crammed with books which he would lend freely
to any undergraduate who showed interest. Another of Jack's tutors was
the Master of Pembroke, William Sheldon Hadley. His association with
the college had begun as a Scholar in 1878 and he had become Master
during 1912. Jack felt that his being there for nearly half a century had
something to do with the way he lectured, because Hadley did not seem
to notice whether he had any students present or not. Jack's opinions
were, however, quite contrary to what others thought of Hadley, but
typical perhaps of a fresh undergraduate with emancipation in sight.

With the close of the spring term thoughts were turning towards cricket,
and Jack was delighted to receive a card from the secretary of the
Pembroke Cricket Club inviting him to take part in a two-day trial. Then,
at the beginning of May, he was invited to play in the Freshman's Match at
Fenners, the famous Cambridge ground. This match was always a notable

annual event, with detailed reports in *The Times, Morning Post, The Field* and, of course, *The Cricketer*. Jack retired from batting after making his half-century and took four wickets for forty-four when bowling. He was both relieved and pleased that he had made a useful contribution, and Cambridge responded quickly by inviting him to play for the university against Lancashire. The elation that Jack felt after his Freshman successes was soon tempered, for he was now in the company of first-class cricketers and county players. There were several Blues already in the Cambridge side and their strength, experience and match performance could make Jack's contribution look fairly ordinary. Meeting Lancashire for this first match he experienced again what he knew about the first-class game. There was no 'give and take', the level of skill was uniformly high and, irrespective of its pace, the game was played with a consistent intensity that was both exhilarating and slightly formidable to the tyro. A few days later Cambridge met Yorkshire and Jack met the legendary Herbert Sutcliffe. The *Morning Post* reported that the general verdict of the Yorkshire batsmen was that 'R.J.O. Meyer, the Freshman, should develop into one of the best bowlers the university has had in recent years.'

The frequency of cricket matches in Jack's first Cambridge season certainly took its toll on his academic studies. During May there had been five first-class games since the Freshman's match, all over a period of two or three days, and many of them involved travel. However, for this nineteen year old there was little more that life could offer, or that he would have demanded. While his cricket and physique both progressed, he was still comparatively immature, and it says much for the Cambridge team, who were a pretty tough lot, that they were usually sympathetic to his inexperience. There were three or so Australians in the side and the captain, T.C. Lowry, was a New Zealander; Jack learnt something of his attitude when he heard an ex-Eton player suggest with some justification that the university side could do with some fielding practice. The reply was typical. 'Look, you silly young bugger, if you didn't learn to field when you were taking your mother's milk, you're no bloody good to me. Get the hell out of here and stay out!'

Jack also received some unpleasant attention when he was careless enough to arrive late for a match with only half his kit. He managed to borrow most things to make up his shortage except socks. Lowry was totally unsympathetic and annoyed at Jack's poor punctuality. He arrived on the field in his stiff canvas cricket boots and Lowry asked him to bowl – and kept him bowling until his feet bled.

It was as well that Jack had his full kit when he played in the university's match against the South African touring side, because Tom Lowry asked of him a feat of considerable endurance. The Cambridge team had been weakened because several of its strongest members, including their best bowler, were sitting their exams. Before the match Tom Lowry had said, 'Jack you will be on the far end and you're going to stay there for some time so you had better get used to it.' The score stood at only forty-six when Jack started to bowl and he was still at it some two hundred runs later. In fact he was bowling for most of the day, which rapidly became one in the batsman's favour, because as the pitch dried out the ball moved less and less, and Jack felt that he was being hit all over the field. The papers commented on his remarkable endurance and slightly chastised the skipper:

> Mr Lowry, whose methods were nothing if not drastic, gave him as a Freshman such work as might have cracked an apparently stronger physique and most certainly have broken any but a very stout heart.

Back in the pavilion changing-room Jack was despondent at the result of his day's labour. Lowry came along and asked, 'What are you looking so bloody miserable about?'

'Well, it wasn't a particularly good day for me, was it?'

'Wasn't it? I'll tell you what sort of day it was, it was the best one we could manage, now you'd better go and get your Blue stuff.'

'I don't understand. Are you being funny?' Jack asked.

'Look, you silly young bugger, don't think you can bowl or you bloody well never will, but I've got to have somebody on the side who doesn't mind trying – even in the rain. So now go and get your bloody Blue things.'

So Jack learnt through the usual series of insults that he had been awarded his Blue. Congratulations poured in, particularly from Cecil Perkin, who wrote: 'Readers will remember that I tipped this Freshman, and I beg to offer him my heartiest congratulations.' Jack admired Lowry as a captain, and said that he was the best of the three he had at Cambridge, but he was an extraordinarily tough character.

Jack was the junior of the side, most of whom were twenty-two or twenty-three and in their second or third Cambridge season, but they looked after him well, particularly during tours, when their behaviour off the pitch was, to put it mildly, fairly wild. The usual procedure for away matches was to stay in a hotel, and for a small establishment this could mean virtually taking it over. The ensuing payments for breakages, necessary letters of apology and enormous drinks bills were valid indication of the normal fun and games. However, Jack was not usually allowed to stay in the same place, but billeted out with some trustworthy acquaintance in the area. This didn't seem to upset him at all, not because he was in any way dull, but he never liked strong drink, an essential for the riot, and he had practically no experience with girls, which made it rather awkward when picking up women. He only stayed in the team's hotel once that first season, and the experience was enough to convince him that the company of the 'trustworthy acquaintance' was infinitely preferable.

On the first night he was dragged out of bed at around four in the morning. His presence was vital, absolutely vital, because three of the fielders had already passed out. Through bleary eyes, shielded against the harsh light of the corridor, Jack could see that those who were still standing, or at least leaning, were engaged in a bizarre game of cricket with three magnums of champagne for stumps. This was not immediately clear because the wicketkeeper had just made an enormous effort to stump the batsman and had passed out on the bottles. He was unceremoniously dragged down the corridor and heaped in a 'long stop' position where he might still be of some use. Jack was to be wicketkeeper. The 'home rules' applying designated that for the fall of each wicket all should have 'a jolly good swig of champers'. Dragged from bed again at ten past eleven that morning, Jack just got on the field in time. He couldn't see the ball, couldn't bowl and dropped a catch. That evening's entertainment was a visit to the Palais de Dance with some local girls. Because the dance finished at about two in the morning Jack was determined to have a quiet time on the third evening. Lowry had reached the same conclusion in the light of his poor performance and more or less commanded him to spend the evening in a local funfair and then get an early night. Apart from a lot of rather silly girls to watch there was little at the fair to interest him until he came to the shooting booth. It took two or three rounds to see that the rifle was aiming an inch or so to the left and below the target; then Jack was able to compensate and hit the bull every time. He was seen off the fairground by some fairly dangerous looking chaps with beery breath, but managed to hang on to the fifteen alarm clocks he had won. He arrived back at the hotel at about nine to find the rest of the team having a drink prior to the evening's entertainment. After the inevitable hilarity at Jack's sharpshooting, Lowry was suddenly smitten by an idea and asked him if he could borrow the clocks. Apart from Jack, the only member of the team to remain in the hotel was Leonard Crawley, who was senior enough to insist on taking an early night no matter what the skipper thought. The following morning he was very late for breakfast, and when he did turn up he looked dreadful. A few of the team cheerfully greeted him with 'Good morning Leonard. How are you? Have a good night?'

'You bastards! You bastards!' was his rather strong reply which seemed to render the team helpless with laughter. The mystery was resolved for

Jack with the explanation that the alarm clocks had been hidden all over Crawley's bedroom and set to go off at one-hour intervals through the night. With pranks like this it was perhaps inevitable that Cambridge had lost five out of the six first-class matches so far that season.

The last match for Cambridge was the annual Varsity contest against Oxford at Lord's. Cambridge were a superior side in most respects and deserved to win, but Jack didn't have a particularly outstanding game because he was anxious about the end of term and year exams. However, he made his presence felt by hitting his first ball for six into the Tavern. With only a few days between each match he had put in a whole series of all-night revision sessions to get his work up to standard. He was particularly anxious to achieve a decent pass, since his History tutor was the college principal, and he had a private desire to justify the generous support of G.S. Pawle. During the course of Dr Hadley's lectures which, according to Jack, consisted mostly of reading over his old essays, many valuable references were quoted from his doctoral thesis on the Star Chamber. Jack's idea was to look up all of these and do a little extra research off his own bat to produce a reasonable paper. The work paid off very well, and Dr Hadley sent him a letter:

> I must write to you, my dear Meyer, just to congratulate you. Your papers are some of the best that I have seen from any cricketer for many, many years. There are passages which are quite outstanding. I am therefore writing to your father to suggest that you sit for a scholarship because I am sure that we can't afford to lose you.

The latter remark was a reference to the necessity of finding fees for the second year at Pembroke. However, the idea of sitting for a scholarship worried Jack considerably, much to Rollo's disappointment. 'I cannot sit for a scholarship because I am a fraud, they'll find me out. I told you how I did the Mays paper Dad.'

Rollo tried to convince him that there was nothing dishonest in the way he had researched and written it. 'But I'm not first-class honours material. I'm sure I can get my degree and perhaps get a reasonably good one, but I am certainly not sitting for a scholarship.'

Therefore, rather to Dr Hadley's surprise, the scholarship suggestion was not taken up, but a grant did appear from somewhere – quite a decent one – so the way was clear for a very fortunate Jack to enter his second year.

Hertfordshire were waiting with open arms as Jack arrived from Cambridge for the beginning of Stevenage cricket week. Skipper Les Reid and 'Titch' Titchmarsh noted a very different young man to the lean schoolboy they had signed on the previous year. He was about 6 ft tall and had put on plenty of muscle, and was certainly a far harder player. The week opened with Hertfordshire playing Bedfordshire. Jack came in at eighth man and opened his innings with a staggering succession of five fours. It wasn't long before most of the field were on the boundary, but this seemed not to trouble him as he carved his way to a wonderful 109. The highlight of the vacation cricket was meeting the South Africans at Norwich, where Jack was playing for the Minor Counties. Runs came slowly on a difficult wicket and the Counties were fortunate to make 196 in their first innings. In fact, as the press reported, Jack came in at seventh man to stop the rot caused by some very accurate bowling. He managed this by demoralizing their fastest bowlers, hitting them for a six and four fours. South Africa could only reply with 149, very much as a result of Jack taking six wickets for sixty runs. The match finished as the paper said with a 'major victory for the Minor Counties', some even referring to it as 'sensational'. The 1924 season ended for Jack with the 'Cricket Festival' in Blackpool where he played for the Gentlemen against the Players. In this match he certainly marked himself as a bowler more than a batsman: he took a magnificent eight wickets for only thirty-eight runs, but got ducks in both the Gentlemen's innings.

The autumn term of 1924 eased the pressure from cricket and Jack was able to take rather more interest in the social life of Cambridge. He had certainly had a few corners knocked off by his captain, Lowry, and after the success of his Mays exams the uncertainty regarding his academic ability had gone; also to be offered a scholarship was a feather in his cap even when he felt unable to accept. If he grew physically during his first year, perhaps it was his confidence that progressed in the second. However, like many young men his attitude seemed to move from one extreme to another, as Rollo was to discover when invited to Pembroke to discuss his son's progress. Tweaking the nose of authority was emerging as something of a pastime, but Jack rather overdid it when he commenced a set essay with 'The Peace of Paris passeth all understanding.' To impress any Cambridge don, the wit has to be of a rather higher order. So were their expectations, as Jack found when he received a summons to see his tutor. 'Ah, Mr Meyer do come in. I feel that I really ought to have a chat with you. You know that Professor Elliott – a very able lecturer from Jesus College on Constitutional History, is on your lecture list, and we recommended that you see him. Well now, we have a report that not even on one occasion have you honoured the Professor with your presence. Now what I want to tell you is this. There is of course no compulsion about it, but don't you think that as a matter of courtesy perhaps, when we advise you – purely for your own benefit – to attend a few lectures. You understand my meaning?'

'Oh yes, of course sir.'

'So you'll . . .'

'Of course.'

'Right. Good. Come on Jack, let's go and have a round of golf.'

Women were beginning to play some part in the social round, but initially, perhaps because of Lowry's tuition and Jack's naivety, he was no judge of feminine character or suitability. Persuaded somewhat against his wishes he played in a few rugby matches for the college and inevitably had to follow the teams into pubs to celebrate or commiserate. Visiting pubs was not generally to his liking because he rather disliked beer and the normal run of pub company. One of the exciting aspects of university was that no matter how obscure one's interest or reading, sooner or later one could find a fellow soul to share enthusiams. Jack found that this rarely happened in pubs, where the conversation hit lower and louder levels as the pints flowed. However, he was rather obliged to accompany his fellow players and waste away yet more evenings. Leaning on the bar once, and then leaning on him with mascara, bosoms and all was Flossie Roberts. 'Hallo dearie, what you gonna drink? Would you like to buy me one?'

'Yes, of course I will,' and she leant on him a bit more.

Well before closing time Jack was asking, 'Flossie, can I see you . . . ?' and within the fortnight as far as he was concerned they were well on the way to becoming engaged. His parents were somewhat more than astounded by the news but had to agree to meet the young lady, so Jack borrowed a motor cycle and chugged down to Watton one weekend with Flossie on the pillion. According to Jack his mother passed out, or at least rapidly disappeared, Rollo explaining, 'I'm afraid your mother isn't very well today, but how nice of you to bring your friend along.' Then addressing Flossie, 'Now your name is Mrs? Oh Miss, I see. I see, do forgive me. Tell me how many children . . . Ah, I'm so sorry I can't get this into my head. It's Miss Roberts of course.'

'She's only twenty-five, Dad,' Jack whispered.

'Really, only twenty-five, remarkable, remarkable. A charming woman like yourself. One would have thought that you'd have been marr——, well now, all the men in Cambridge must be blind.'

Rollo understood the reality of the situation immediately. Flossie was well past thirty-five, let alone twenty-five, and was rather on the make, suspecting that by his general manner Jack was from an aristocratic or rich family. Jack could see none of this, and to him she was a very pure young lady. There had certainly been no leaping about in haystacks. At the end of an extremely awkward afternoon Rollo, ever a gentleman, said, 'Jack, dear boy, you are quite right to bring your friends home, they are always welcome. So nice to have met you Mrs . . . Oh, Miss Roberts . . . I beg your pardon.'

The moment Jack was out of the drive Ella's health suddenly revived and she galvanized Rollo into action. He knew which pub they had met in and spoke to the landlord, explaining the situation. In turn, the landlord got in touch with Jack, asking him to pop along during an afternoon because he had something important to say. 'Look here Sir, I've got to tell you. Your father wants me to tell you that our Flossie, well, she's a nice enough girl, but she ain't quite, ahem! she ain't quite what she ought to be, Sir. You only come here with the team, but you come along tonight Sir and just 'ave a look.'

Jack was mystified because she had said that the only times she came to the pub were when he was there. However, he determined to come back later that evening to see if there was anything in what this landlord said. Knowing that he could get a look at the bar through a particular window, he had a stealthy peep before entering. There she was of course, lipstick grin from ear to ear, draped over some other chap. Jack was really heartbroken, as only the naïve can be. He went for a long walk by the Cam, threw his bike in from despair and, as he said, damned nearly threw himself in.

The Cambridge team for 1925 was very different from the previous year's. Tom Lowry had gone and of the five bowlers only one remained, that was Jack. He was not particularly impressed by the new captain, C.T. Bennett, who had not found a great deal of form the previous year, but was pleased that K.S. Duleepsinhji had come up from Cheltenham. They had not played together since the Lord's Schools match during August 1923, and like Jack he was a great all-rounder. Stalwarts from the previous year included Enthoven, always strong, fit and cheerful, and Leo Crawley, who kept wicket. 'Eddie' Dawson remained also, and had become a particular friend and admirer of Jack's. Giving an interesting insight into Jack's character at the time, he said that while everybody liked him, he had a curious way of going off to follow his own interests, often forgetting that some important meeting or presentation demanded his attendance.

The season started well for Cambridge and for Jack, with victories over Sussex, Lancashire and Leicestershire. The *Daily Mail* commented that 'Meyer bowled with conspicuous success, and county batsmen never played him with confidence.' He was making a useful number of runs too, but the bowling was outstanding. At around this time there had been some speculation in the press about Jack being selected for England. The possible source was a quotation from Wilfred Rhodes, England's greatest

Jack (standing centre) and Kumar Duleepsinhji in the 1925 Cambridge XI

all-rounder, who said that he thought Jack should be an England bowler. Jack's batting was always spectacular, it could as easily be brilliant as disastrous. He often had some theory as to how he would tackle a particular bowler, which was all very sensible, but could never resist the temptation of flashing at a ball for a possible six at the same time. For this reason, he was always tremendously entertaining to watch, but it became the custom that when Jack got padded up the next man in would immediately do the same, not knowing if he would meet him at the pavilion gate in one minute or later that afternoon. What could not be denied, however, was his sustained contribution to Cambridge's success.

As usual the cricket season also brought with it the college exams, and the two were as incompatible as ever, particularly this year when Jack had rather found his feet socially. To be a Cambridge cricketer meant letting the game almost take over one's life. Since four other players in the side were also Pembroke men, including the captain, Bennett, Jack was in the world of cricket and cricketing company most of the time. He knew the importance of these exams and was rigorously burning the midnight oil, because despite the matches and social life he had tried to work more conscientiously since his tutor's gentle encouragement. However, with the after-effects from 'flu it was all too much for him, and he was rather dramatically carried out of the hall during his Historical Tripos. The crisis necessitated a reassessment of his college ambitions, and he was awarded an aegrotat for his Part I and after much consideration and advice decided to go for an ordinary degree in English during his third year, instead of the History Honours he had been pursuing. Since the special subject was to be nineteenth-century literature, the course suited his interest well.

With Jack playing for Hertfordshire again during the vacation there occurred one of those legendary incidents for which he was well known. Hertfordshire were playing Cambridge (Minor Counties, not the university), who opened the batting, when one of the umpires revealed a particular liking for the no-ball rule, and would yell out as soon as the bowler's foot was anywhere near the crease as he delivered the ball. Jack had been asked to bowl after lunch and several players remarked that he ought to watch that umpire. This he did, when during his first delivery he put his foot a good 18 in the wrong side of the crease, delivering a full toss to the batsman. 'No-ball!' bellowed the umpire whose attention was suddenly taken by the odd behaviour of the batsman and wicketkeeper, who seemed to be wiping something off their whites. 'Actually it wasn't "no-ball" umpire, because it was a lemon.' The umpire was dumb-struck, signalling 'no-ball' again to the confusion of the scorers. But Jack hadn't finished. Opening the bowling after the break he walked past the same umpire furiously polishing an orange. The umpire couldn't believe his eyes and looked fit to burst, screeching 'no-ball' even before Jack had let the thing go. 'No, no my dear chap. Here's the orange in my pocket.'

The great excitement for cricket lovers during 1926 was the Australian Tour and the papers were full of speculation. The early part of May again saw Cambridge playing Sussex, Lancashire and Leicestershire, but the growing civil unrest, now on a national scale, caused havoc to the preparations Enthoven's team were making for their meeting with the Australians on 19 May. During the General Strike, which started on 14 May, Jack volunteered for the Civil Constabulary Reserve, for which Pembroke granted him leave of absence. His duties ceased on the first day of the Australian match, so he and many in the side had lost valuable practice for this important event. The crowds flocked to Fenners and the Varsity side batted first, soon becoming aware of the power of their opponents. Three wickets went down for not much when Albion came to the rescue with a protracted downpour and play was abandoned. The following day was bright and sunny, the wicket not suffering too much from the deluge. Cambridge, however, continued to suffer from the Australians, managing to add only twenty-eight runs in the hour and a half before lunch. Batsmen were falling fast. Jack attempted to stop the rot by hitting out, and skied the ball. When nine wickets were down Enthoven changed his cautious tactics and in forty minutes had made forty-five runs, later receiving some comment from the press for not opening out earlier. His intention, however, had been to stay in and give his other batsmen a chance of making a stand. It certainly wasn't that Cambridge men were dropping like flies, they all fought hard, winning the congratulations of Plum Warner for the first innings total of 212.

The Australians started badly, the second batsman being caught off Enthoven's bowling, and Jack clean-bowled Collins, the captain and opening batsman, who had made only eight runs. Jack was clearly in good form, the enforced rest from cricket, courtesy of the General Strike, may have been what he needed. He had Macartney caught for twenty-nine and then removed Ponsford lbw. The Cambridge fielding was very tight and Enthoven saw to it that the visitors had to fight for every run of a tremendously exciting match; they finished the day with 165 for four wickets. The following morning Woodfull and Andrews faced the bowling of Jack and his skipper, Enthoven, and only eleven new runs were on the board when Jack had Andrews out lbw. A few overs later he made an extraordinarily athletic catch from his position of short leg, juggling full length on the ground to get a ball from Ryder. The Australian total was 189, six wickets were down and Jack's bowling had taken four of them and this last catch the fifth. The excitement mounted because Cambridge were achieving all this against one of the best teams in the world. Richardson came on – he had a reputation as a great hitter – but never got going, for Jack had him caught with the total at 207. The sports editor of the *Evening News* described the atmosphere wonderfully:

> Every Australian, as he came to the wicket, seemed anxious to get something on the score-sheet, but Woodfall had been there long enough to know that risky runs were not to be made – Meyer was the hero of the Cambridge attack. His figures of 65 for 6 were quite as good as they looked on paper.

The press certainly gave Jack the hero treatment, sandwich boards and headlines alike blazing '65 for 6', and the later editions began to speculate about the England versus Australia Test Match – 'Mr Meyer must catch the selectors' eye as a possible Test Match player.'; 'Cantab takes 8 Australian wickets for 70 runs.'; 'R.J.O. Meyer's bid for place in Test team.'

Notwithstanding what the papers had to say, there was a serious conflict in Jack's mind regarding the possibility of selection. This was the time of his final exams, and his studies, although familiar with disruption from cricket, also had voluntary duties to contend with as a result of the General Strike. So when, immediately after this match, he was invited to

MAY 21, 1926.

6 FOR 65 AGAINST AUSTRALIANS

EVENING NEWS 6.30

Jack hits the headlines with his bowling for Cambridge against the Australian tourists, 21 May 1926 play for the South of England against the tourists at Bristol a few days later, he felt that he had to take a more responsible attitude to his studies. The conflict between cricket and studies had been one for which he had received much counselling from his tutor, Aubrey Attwater. That guidance was never more needed than now. Attwater spoke to one of the examiners about Jack's dilemma and there was no doubt of his views. 'Oh Aubrey. Aubrey. Have these boys today got their priorities in order? It makes no sense at all. Don't they know that for every thousand people who can pass the examination there is only one who can bowl the Australians out?'

So the issue was settled and off Jack and Duleepsinhji went to Bristol. Because of the strike they eventually arrived on a milk train at 6.15 a.m. It was far too late, or early, to go to bed so they played snooker on an old table in the clubhouse. After a game or two Jack said, 'Hey Duleep, watch this, it's possible I'm the only man in the country who can ——' Shooting the cue with tremendous force the white ricocheted off the table hitting Duleep in the eye. Bandaged, he took to the field and one of the most promising batsmen made a duck. Jack fared little better with seven runs and not much bowling and afterwards there was a stony silence in the changing-room. A shortish man in his early fifties came in and addressed Jack. 'Mr Meyer, I don't want to worry you too much. There's always room for a bloody fool, I've always said.' Jack's anger was soon mortified when he learnt that this was none other than Gilbert Jessop, England's greatest and most devastating batsman up to the First World War.

Even as this game was being played on 26 May the press were publishing the England selectors' choice for the next trial a week later to be played at Lord's; neither Jack's nor any other Cambridge name featured in the England XI or The Rest. Perhaps having tipped him rather too strongly the press covered its tracks by stating that 'At this time of year you cannot ask men from the university to waste their time playing in Test Trials', and 'Consequently, the two teams, England and The Rest have been selected rather from past reputations than from present performances.' The situation having resolved itself, Jack threw himself into the very necessary revision for these important exams.

During the year he had been trying to give some thought to the future. Somehow it had to involve cricket and the means of keeping a roof over his head between matches, and his interests still seemed to be best served by the original intention of pursuing a teaching career. At that time there was no training in the techniques of teaching; of more importance in terms of getting a decent job was a man's academic status and background. His outstanding performance as a Cambridge bowler had made his name, and he hardly had to apply anywhere or even write an application form to be invited to a school for an interview. In all he received invitations to teach at twenty-nine of them and only one, Charterhouse, where an approach was made on his behalf by a friend, turned him down, the Master stating:

Tell Mr Meyer that if he has first class honours in whatever subject he has been reading, I am prepared to ignore the fact that it is probably not in Classics, and that he does seem to spend an inordinate amount of time hitting balls about.

However, the attitudes of those two great schools Eton and Harrow were somewhat different.

'Good morning Mr Meyer, sorry I'm late,' said the Master of Harrow. 'Now there are one or two questions I would like to ask you before we get down to business. Tell me about the modern high jump – I think it's all wrong, don't you? Why should you run sideways and be allowed to jump that way?'

'To be frank I know little about it, I never got beyond 3 ft 6 in.'

'Oh no, of course not. You're a cricketer and racquets player aren't you. We could certainly do with a cricketer here, and I know that you came here playing racquets from Haileybury, you met the Crawleys I imagine. Now, there is a thing called the School Certificate, which is an up and coming thing and our boys who want to get into university, Oxford or Cambridge I mean, really ought to have it. I assume you sat Cambridge's previous exam – you didn't? – you had a scholarship? – Oh I see, a clergyman's award, well never mind about that, what we need here are people with a bit of drive. We've some pretty idle rogues here, nice boys but they never open a book if they can help it, and they need a little inspiration. Now, what subjects are you able to teach?'

'Well Sir, English would be my main one.'

'English? Oh good gracious! Everybody teaches English here, and quite a few of the Classics people.'

'Well sir, history?'

'Oh no no no. We've far too many historians.' Jack felt that the attractions of Harrow were beginning to fade. The Master continued, 'What about geography?'

'Well Sir, I haven't learned much geography since my prep school, but I remember being rather good at the names of English county towns and the rivers of Europe.'

'German?'

'I think I know six words.'

'Biology perhaps?'

'That's a subject which has always interested me. Perhaps I could cope with natural history because I am an ornithologist of sorts and I know where to find eels and tadpoles, and also the difference between a crow and a rook.'

'Do you, what is it then?'

'Well, if you see a bunch of birds you think are crows, they're not, they're rooks, and if you see a rook alone, it's not, because it's a crow.'

'Oh very good, very good. Now I've been thinking, we need a bright young chap like you. What you could do, and we could help you here, is pop over to Germany during the vacation and take some of our language books and some School Certificate biology books as well.'

'Well. Yes. Exactly. I suppose I could.'

'Excellent. Excellent. Well thank you Meyer, I have enjoyed talking to you. Goodbye my boy. See you in September.'

The Eton interview went much the same, although there was the opportunity of teaching some history there. However, he found the place rather intimidating, with the boys' black suits and starched high collars. During the interview he answered 'Yes Sir' to everything, including the offer of a post. Now, therefore, he found himself in the happy and completely naïve position of having a job at Eton and another at Harrow. He was somewhat reticent when Rollo asked him how things had gone.

Time was passing rapidly with the approach of the university's last game, the Varsity Match, and Jack was still the man with two jobs. After his exam he had agreed to coach racquets at Harrow, and while watching them play at Queens Club he bumped into an acquaintance, Gerry Weigall, who was a Kent cricketer. According to Jack, Weigall was a bit of a busybody who always loved to be 'in the know'. They met when he told Jack that he'd better do alright in some particular match, because he had put ten pounds on him getting six wickets. Weigall approached him and said, 'What are you up to after you pack it in at Cambridge, Jack?' As far as he knew Weigall had no Eton connections so he said, 'Well, I've more or less committed myself to teaching these chaps at Harrow.'

'Schoolmaster eh? That's going to be a bit stuffy after what I heard about you lot at Pembroke.'

'Well, teaching is something I've always felt I could do.'

'Well fair enough then. The thing is, I've got a friend who's looking for a good bowler – a good Cambridge bowler to go out to Bombay. He's actually a cotton broker with stacks of cash who's a great supporter of the Europeans, and they are all pretty damned keen cricketers out there as I expect you know.'

This Jack did know, the Europeans was a team of around county standard who played in the 'Quadrangular', one of India's best series.

'The idea is that this bowler will train to be a cotton broker too, and it's a marvellous job. If you play your cards right you can retire after about ten years and live off your interest. It's a very good salary. Anyway, have you got a bowler at Cambridge?'

'Gerry, there's only one bowler at Cambridge, and that's me.'

'Well come along and meet this chap Travers.' So he did, and heard about the life in Bombay:

Lots of British people, plenty of parties and a great social life. The going is always firm on any race track, cricket's never rained off and they are all mad on it, you'll be a celebrity. Three months' leave after two years, and you can pop home for Christmas, and yes a very generous salary that can only increase if you play your cards right, and there's no doubt that a smart chap like you will do just that.

To go 'Out East' was quite common in those days, and the sporting press often lamented that fact when promising players disappeared after university to go overseas with the Army or some business concern. By the time the Varsity Match came up a few days later the deal was signed and sealed and he was to leave for Bombay in August. Jack felt bad about Eton and Harrow but he had not signed anything to commit himself to either, and at least something rather more positive had happened. However, while still writing letters in his head to the respective Masters, explaining why he had to go in such a way that they would still think he was a jolly decent chap, fate took a hand and moved things on a little. In Jack's own words:

And so when it came to the Varsity Match I was already signed on as a cotton broker to go out the following month to India. I went to the nets at Lord's and as I came back I noticed the headmaster of Eton with two satellites in their white clothes, and the headmaster of Harrow and his little party both converging on me. I bolted through the Tavern gate and out to the street, then back in the pavilion via the main gate. I haven't seen either of them to this day.

CHAPTER FOUR

Bombay

It would not be altogether unkind to observe that Jack had little idea of the consequences of his decision to go to India. That his immediate problems were solved was clear; there was going to be plenty of cricket and, apparently, plenty of money and he could avoid the ignominious position of having two jobs. However, there were sacrifices. The likelihood was that another year or so of play, perhaps with a first-class side, would have put him in a favourable position to be selected for England. Instead he had to cut his links with the county, MCC, and Test cricket world, without knowing when they would be restored. The dominance of cricket in Jack's life hardly needs underlining, for not only was he committed to success within the game, but it had been his lifeline to secure a respectable education. And what of his wish to become a teacher? The abandonment of teaching posts at the country's leading schools might indicate a change of direction, but perhaps it was the thought of going back into the closed society of a Harrow or Eton after three years of freedom and fun that made him put aside these opportunities. Whatever the reasons for his departure, one clear thing is that he had a mind of his own and took no small pleasure in using it. There was, after all, the novelty of making a personal decision that would, for the first time, influence the path of his own life.

The Indian years provided vital foundations upon which he built the rest of his career, but there could have been none of this on his mind on 27 August 1926 when he departed for Bombay. Instead he had to bear the knowledge that he had almost broken his father's heart. Rollo's devotion to Jack and his cricket had been remarkable by any father's standards, from when he first coached him at the age of three and a half on the rectory lawn to support from the boundary of every Cambridge and Hertfordshire match he was able to attend. What was more, Jack would be the second son to depart for the Indian subcontinent, because business interests had already taken Denys to Calcutta. Jack's outlook on cricket at this time seems to have been one of impatience. The Bristol game had been a fiasco; then, despite a successful spell against the MCC and his remarkable performance in the Australian match, he was once again overlooked for the Gentlemen versus Players game. There was more than a suspicion that the MCC greybeards, while applauding his achievements, quietly thought him a bit of a 'Johnny-come-lately'.

Party after party and packing up at Cambridge had been exciting and sad as Jack collected odd bits of paper with friends' addresses and faithful promises to keep in touch. Then followed the last games with Hertfordshire, which included a couple of matches during Watford Cricket Week. He had to miss the last one as it was only a few days before his departure, and he made painful goodbyes to great mentors like 'Titch' Titchmarsh and Hylton-Stewart. Above all he spent as much time as possible at home with his family before leaving, and began to feel the weighty significance of his decision to go. While he was writing to his aunts, uncles and cousins, ancient parishioners would totter up to the rectory to give Jack a little advice from their days in India fifty-odd years before. They completely forgot that Jack had neither servants nor even bearers to carry his own thunder-box. But that was all behind him, receding like the Isle of Wight over the stern of the liner. As he headed out into the English Channel Jack felt the apron-strings slipping and a certain sense of relief to be free of the difficult emotions of the past three or four weeks.

The clamour and energy of Bombay caused him to suspect that he must have arrived during a celebration or public holiday, but he was assured that this was typical. Disembarking in the harbour, one of the largest and finest natural shelters in the world, he could survey the eleven-mile long sprawl of the city built on an island, dominated by the Apollo Bunder, a colonial Indian version of a triumphal arch. Used as part of the pomp and ceremony to welcome visiting kings, princes or viceroys, it was clear to see why it was called the Gateway to India. The city was like a beehive and seemed to have people from every Asian and European country. In fact over sixty languages and dialects could be heard in the bazaars and wrangling between buyers and sellers often seemed about to break into violence, but rarely did.

Most Europeans lived in the older quarter of the city which had grown up around the ancient Fort, and this was where Jack was taken first. He rather expected to buckle down to his duties immediately, whatever they were, but Guy Travers, the cricketing partner of the firm for which Jack was to work, had other ideas. It was he who had come to England to find just such a person as Jack to bolster the fortunes of the Europeans cricket team who were one of four strong sides, the others being Parsi, Muslim and Hindu, known as the Quadrangular. Rivalry was keen and the Europeans had not been doing too well for some time; their prestige had been rather well dented to the mostly polite, but obvious delight of the Indians.

Upon arriving in Bombay on 17 September Jack had only a matter of
hours to sort himself out before being whisked off to Poona for the first
match. This did not please the other partner in the firm of Gibb & Co.,
and made for a somewhat awkward introduction. 'Meyer. Presumably
you've come out here to learn about business, not to teach us how to play
cricket. I cannot see that you are making a particularly auspicious start to
your relationship with the Company. However, you may go, although I
shall expect something rather special in the way of progress when you
return.' The feeling of chastisement was not altogether dispelled by
Travers commenting that it was nothing to get worried about. With more
important things on his mind he told Jack, 'You're staying with me to get
you started, so the driver will pop you home and you'll need enough
clothes for a week'.

'We'll be away for a whole week?'

'Yes, a couple of important matches. I'll tell you all about it on the way
there.'

'Well, I hope I have a job to come back to.'

''Course you will. Course you will. What else did you expect the old
chap to say? But he'll be as chuffed as anything if we start winning, and
all his chums will be patting him on the back, don't you worry.'

Although somewhat fatigued by so much that was new, Jack's eyes were
all about him on the journey to Poona. Running through the various
players, Jack was delighted to hear the name of R.E.H. Hudson, the great
Haileybury batsman and his racquets partner. Hudson had left
Haileybury a year before Jack to join the army, hence his reappearance in
India. Poona was a wonderful place, much cooler than Bombay, and the
traditional hot weather residence of the Governor. In fact the first match
was a single innings, twelve-a-side game between His Excellency Sir Leslie
Wilson's team and the Poona Gymkhana for whom Jack was playing. Jack
was given a bungalow to stay in which belonged to Governor Wilson, and
a Rolls Royce with a driver to take him about. The Governor's aide-de-
camp was also available to ensure his wellbeing and passed on some
significant information in the form of an introduction to the Poona
Racecourse. There was a day to spare before His Excellency's match on
Sunday, and it happily coincided with a ten-horse programme at the
races. Not knowing any form, Jack had intended to go more as an
observer, with the possibility of a flutter if something looked probable.
However, the ADC seemed to know all the Arab trainers, who happily
discussed the day's prospects. The result was that Jack backed a winner in
eight out of ten races, and made about £15 grow into about £320.

So I was a rich man, richer than I had ever been in my life. I'd never more than, you know, seven quid in my pocket – usually it was a ten quid overdraft at Barclays Bank, so I was well under way.

It was certainly an auspicious overture to his new life as a 'colonial boy'.

Naturally enough Jack was in an excellent frame of mind for his first cricket match in India. Travers had warned him not to expect too much from this game, but to consider it more as an opportunity to acclimatize to the heat and hard pitches in preparation for the important Quadrangular Cricket Tournament Final between the Hindus and Europeans. It emerged that His Excellency had selected a very strong batting side and it was clear that a fair amount of effort would be required to make a game of it. They took to the field first and Jack opened the bowling. With the total standing at over 100, His Excellency took guard. Jack's first ball was a full toss to the leg side which he hit into the square leg's hands – who promptly dropped it. Not quite believing what he had seen, Jack delivered the next ball fast and straight and had His Excellency plumb lbw.

'How's that?'

'No ball!' the umpire shouted at the top of his voice. Then, more quietly, 'Bloody fool, what the hell do you think you are doing?'

'What's that? Oh – I see – I get the message.' His Excellency was, of course, a great benefactor on many levels of public and private life, and his inclusion on his own side owed little to his prowess at cricket. He was allowed to notch up twenty-one runs before his stumps were unavoidably, but quite gently splayed, and having made a respectable little contribution to the game he retired to the pavilion and the cool drinks. Introduced to Sir Leslie Wilson later, Jack's verdict was, 'He was nice enough and very kind to me, but people who were sent out to govern were often failed politicians who were given soft jobs. He was one of the "Sir, you have disappointed us, go out and govern New South Wales" type, who actually became Governor of Queensland later.'

Jack had little idea of the standard of cricket to expect before this match. At the Final of the Quadrangular Tournament there were thousands of spectators sitting, standing, up in the trees and anywhere else from where they might see the pitch. The Indian love of cricket was more like fanaticism, and a day's play reported in *The Times of India* could easily cover a whole broadsheet page as it was described almost ball by ball. The Europeans had never won the Quadrangular and there was much interest in the Cambridge Blue. During the voyage out Jack had picked up that unwritten, certainly unspoken, yet pervasive sense that as a colonial, there was some kind of responsibility to teach these Indians what civilization was all about. He was aware of a similar feeling on the cricket pitch, but found that even the most casual glance through the score book indicated little that the Europeans could teach their hosts about the game, and in this Final the Hindus were once again victorious.

The return to Bombay and the office was a decided anticlimax to the Poona experience, and started something of the Jekyll and Hyde existence that pervaded Jack's life as a cotton broker. He had to check the books and various accounts to ensure that they were accurate, sign for new blotting paper or stationery and open the mail. He also had to decode telegrams – American business was always in code – and answer the phones when the bosses were out. His company was both cotton merchant and broker and so the business was quite complicated, but he could already see that it was lucrative, and the bosses had a very grand life style. They owned several thoroughbreds and followed them to racecourses on Wednesday and Saturday afternoons. On one of these occasions Jack found himself left on his own in charge of the business. The phone rang and a Japanese client asked him to purchase 5,000 bales at the best price and send a contract note. Feeling rather important he chatted away to Mr Toyamaka about this and that, but on putting the phone down began to feel very uncomfortable because it dawned on him that he hadn't a clue what to do next. The bosses were at the races and probably impossible to find so he phoned a friend to see if he had any ideas. Jack was advised to phone down to the market and find out what the best price was before purchasing, but as it was Saturday there was probably little point in sending the contract note until Monday. Arriving at the office on Monday morning Travers asked Jack if there had been any activity over the weekend.

'Yes, quite a nice order from Mr Toyamaka.'

'Oh splendid. How much was on the contract note?'

'Well, I was just about to write it out if you can tell me where they are.'

'What?'

'A contract note, can I have one?'

'You mean you haven't bloody well sent it yet?'

'Well, ahem, no. I thought it would . . .'

'For heaven's sake man. We're supposed to be dealing, and I mean dealing in cotton. It's not like buying a packet of fags you know. Get on to the market now and find out what the price is.'

Sure enough the prices had slipped because it was the beginning of the week, with not much happening. What could have been a profit of several hundred pounds to Gibb & Co. if the customer had received the contract note had disappeared into thin air. 'Get the contract written out now and you can damn well take it round to Toyamaka yourself. He'll be bloody pleased to see you I'm sure.'

Feeling somewhat chastened by all this Jack sheepishly presented Mr Toyamaka with the contract, but to his surprise he insisted on paying the

Saturday price because that was when the deal had been made. Thereafter Jack always had confidence in making a bargain with the Japanese. Another benefit issuing from the affair was that Gibb & Co. realized that it was about time they showed their new cricketer the ropes.

Cricket was always just around the corner when office routine began to stifle a lively mind. Jack was invited to play for the Bombay Gymkhana side against Rallis Bros, who were another European firm. By this time he had been in India around a month and a half and was a little more acclimatized to the way Indians played cricket, which certainly had a flamboyant edge on the British game and was much to Jack's liking. In the Rallis match he knocked out a stylish sixty-seven, finding the boundary five times in his first seven scoring strokes. He was also in deadly form with the ball. From his ten overs he took seven wickets for twenty-two, and got five maidens into the bargain. A few weeks later he found himself travelling from one side of the subcontinent to the other to meet the MCC Tourists in Calcutta. By now any qualms about leaving the office to play cricket had evaporated, and Guy Travers, his boss and fellow-player, was pretty optimistic about the new Cambridge Blue. The team were on board the train for days, but a first-class carriage made life reasonably bearable. The visit to Calcutta gave Jack the opportunity to meet Denys, and they had a lot of catching up to do as Jack had seen little of him during the Cambridge years. During their conversation it became clear that Denys's attitude to business was somewhat more mature than Jack's. One piece of news he had was that Ella and Rollo might bring Constance out to India next year for her twenty-first birthday. Jack met the MCC three times because he was selected to play for the Bombay Presidency XI, the Europeans in the East and All India, this last being regarded as an unofficial Test Match. The MCC were victorious on all three occasions and were a very strong side, having players like the famous Maurice Tate.

The New Year of 1927 saw Jack settling down a little better to his new life, and there was much in India which he adored, most of it on the sporting side. He was coping easily with cotton-broking, although still somewhat impatient with necessary office routine. His social life had certainly taken off, because he was now a well-known cricketer, and this suited his gregarious nature. Outside the office there could never be a moment of boredom. He was sharing a bungalow with three other young men who seemed to be kindred spirits. Under a system known as 'chummery' they would dig into their pockets once a week for the rent. If they had enough it would get paid, if not, philosophy took over. Knowing they were in trouble the trend of thought seemed to be that they might as well stick the lot on a reliable-looking horse, with the possibility of trebling the cash, paying the rent and having enough left for a drink or two over the rest of the weekend. It sometimes worked, and when it didn't it was still a lot better than sitting around broke, feeling sorry for themselves and being unable to take out the lady friends they shared.

Jack got to know a Jewish family by the name of Raymond. Mr Raymond was a businessman and keen poker player who enjoyed a hand or two with Jack. One day while sailing in Bombay harbour Mr Raymond's son, Joseph, somehow fell overboard. He started to drift away from the boat and it was obvious he was no swimmer. Without pausing to think, Jack plunged in, managed to support Joseph and fought his way back to the boat. By this time he was pretty exhausted and all he could manage was one arm round Joseph with the other clinging to the yacht, which fortunately drifted to the shore where help awaited. 'It wasn't gallant, it wasn't anything at all but they made a hell of a fuss about it and gave me this party. I wasn't expecting to die for it.' They presented him with a gold watch and asked if there was anything he wanted or anything they could do for him. By this time the champagne had put the party on the friendliest of terms and Jack asked, 'There is one thing I'd like to know, if it doesn't upset your scruples to tell me – I don't want to offend.'

'My dear boy, you couldn't offend us.'

'Well, what I want to know is why you Jews are always so rich and we Gentiles so bloody poor!' The whole party exploded into laughter, for he was in good company and the impudent question was taken as something of a compliment. Perhaps Jack asked the question because of his overdraft. Few people knew the real reason for it, and it was not until many years later that one of his 'chummery' pals explained the predicament. Jack saw some very profitable deals being made on the cotton-broking front, and understandably felt that the owners should not be the only ones to benefit. When he thought he understood how things worked, he devised a massive speculation through another brokerage, but unfortunately seemed to have taken the wrong view, which set him back. During those heady days he was known to make a bet on practically anything for the sheer fun of it. With his ebullient character he never lacked a crowd of sports to bet against him. A typical instance was a wager that he would clear the tall and majestic golf clubhouse six times with an 8 iron. Having gathered a suitable crowd – onlookers were not welcome without showing their ante – and in the teeth of apoplectic glares from the clubhouse bar window he sent the six balls soaring over the roof. Amid cheers and laughter he stuffed his pockets with the price of a good evening's entertainment. The story is not remembered for the sporting feat alone, but also for one of Jack's most endearing characteristics: in his naivety he had forgotten that on the other side of the building was the club car park.

Toward the end of the year the Quadrangular Tournament got under way again. The season was not only welcome for its cricket, but for the cessation of friction, and sometimes violence, between castes. Jack had been quite startled the first time he saw an Indian seemingly minding his own business in the street suddenly spit at another. The violence at this time was rarely directed against Europeans, and Jack gathered that the official line at home was that the British didn't want to know about it anyway. Picking up *The Times*, which in fact was about two weeks behind the times, he read with interest about the disturbances in Bombay. A question was asked in the House to which assurance was given that at about 4.00 a.m. during the night of a disturbance only one man was taken to hospital with a bleeding head. Like other able-bodied Europeans Jack volunteered to become a temporary magistrate, and on his way to the police station on the morning of the incident had counted seven bodies, with plenty of evidence of other casualties in the blood-stained, dusty sidewalks. The extraordinary thing was that this bitter and deep-seated animosity was set aside while the Quadrangular Tournament was played. In fact a Muslim would pat a Hindu on the back if a good shot was made against a Parsi or European. In his office, conversation and speculation about the matches intensified. 'Well, young Meyer, what are we going to do this year?' The biggest difference from the previous season was that he now knew the Indian game and had had far more time to acclimatize to the conditions. He had also broken with the tradition of

Some of the Quadrangular Players

playing in a topi. An insurance company told him he would die of
sunstroke and threatened to cancel his policy, to which Jack's reply was,
'I'd rather die bowling than bowl in a bloody topi.' Many other
Europeans followed his lead, possibly not always altogether advisedly; like
his Indian companions Jack had a thick mop of black hair, and when
saturated with perspiration it provided plenty of protection. The first
Europeans match was against the Hindus, winners of the Tournament for
the past two years. The match turned out to be quite dramatic,
particularly when after tea on the second day the Europeans lost half
their side for a poor total, then lost the other half for only thirty-one runs
on the following morning. Most of the damage, in a literal sense, was
done by Ramji, a fast bowler who was admonished in *The Times of India*
for 'Dangerous Hindu Bowling'. He either sent the Europeans back to
the pavilion after dismissing them, or for what the paper referred to as
'repairs'. But it was Jack who stole most of the headlines for bowling
because, almost alone, he carried the Europeans' attack. He bowled half
the overs during the first innings and was on for the whole of the second.
At one point he had taken five wickets for twelve runs and the papers
described his medium-paced swings as 'unplayable'. He took seven
wickets from the Hindus in the second innings, they were dismissed for
ninety-six and victory went to the Europeans. Celebrations broke out
everywhere and congratulations flowed in.

The Europeans played the Muslims for the third match and the
tournament. Jack was in devastating form and tore into their first innings,
dismissing seven batsmen for only twenty-eight runs, the whole side
collapsing for only fifty-nine runs to the obvious annoyance and dismay
of a partisan crowd. The Europeans replied with 217 for their first
innings and before the Muslims' second commenced, several of them
approached Jack in sheer frustration to ask, 'Oh my God Sahib, you go to
play off-drive, and ball hit you on backside. My God there's a devil in the
ball. What to do Meyer Sahib? What to do?'

'Well, what you ought to do is realize that there is a devil in the new
ball that makes it swerve and swing. Put in that big chap first – your fast
bowler – and tell him to hit the ball over the pavilion roof. The devil will
get out of the ball then because he doesn't like being hit around like
that.' Jack, who had treated the question in a fairly light-hearted manner
was interested to note that this was precisely what they did.

The crowd sensed there was something interesting afoot with the new
batting order and were giving their team – top-class cricketers who had
been dismissed for an insulting fifty-nine runs – every ounce of support
they could convey from the densely packed ground. Jack opened the
bowling as the two batsmen launched a fearless attack. The fanatical roar

of the crowd every time wood touched leather, and the too regular clank of runs multiplying on the score board gave Jack an uneasy feeling. Within a dozen overs they had knocked the devil out of the ball, and with the shine gone Jack couldn't get it to swing in anything like so devastating a manner. Instead, the compulsive teacher had to work like a devil himself in somewhere near 100° in an attempt to contain the batsmen's confidence. But the first wicket wouldn't fall until eighty-seven runs were on the board, then it was eighty-eight for two, 103 for three, 200 for four, 213 for five, 248 for six and then Abdus Salaam came in. During the first innings his contribution was six not out, but he seemed to have the devil in him too as he heaved balls out of the ground. All too soon he had got his century, the crowd were unable to contain their admiration and simultaneously from every part of the ground ran on to the pitch burying Abdus Salaam under flowers. By now Jack was pretty overheated, and seeing this lot on the wicket was the last straw. Eventually they were persuaded back to the stands and the flowers moved behind the stumps. They completely impeded his run-up, and his patience finally snapped at what he considered a ridiculous interruption. Kicking the flowers to one side he let out, 'These blessed people and their damn flowers, what the hell have they got to do with cricket?' Beginning almost inaudibly from the depth of the crowd, a crescendo of outrage mounted. Travers quickly spoke to one of the batsmen, Vishram, the Muslims' captain, and then to Jack: 'It'll be a couple of overs and we'll have finished for the day. At the last ball run! Vishram and Salaam will cover you.'

'Do I need covering?'

'Jack, shut up and watch it!' With the howl that went up as the last ball was delivered he realized immediately that Travers was serious, and scurried to the pavilion with his Indian escorts amid the derision of the crowd and an oft-repeated chant which, should the advice have been followed, would have been anatomically hazardous.

Jack realized that in the heat of the moment he had made a complete fool of himself and apologized to Vishram and his team. Newspaper headlines the following day made full use of the incident with such remarks as 'Meyer tramples on Indian flowers as Birkenhead tramples on our political rights'. Vishram felt that some kind of counter-action was advisable. 'Jack, we'll have morning coffee together on the pavilion verandah, and we'll stand up and shake hands to show that things have been put right.'

Jack was deeply impressed by this splendid act of gentlemanly sportsmanship. Vishram and the Muslims wanted to win the Tournament every bit as much as the Europeans, and it would have been quite understandable if they had used this incident to whip up the crowd. As it turned out play started on time the following day in an orderly atmosphere. Once again Jack was in tremendous form and quickly dismissed Abdus Salaam lbw with a beautiful inswinger, and as he turned for the pavilion the batsman sportingly acknowledged him. Jack dismissed the remaining tail-enders for a couple of runs but the Muslims' second innings score stood at an imposing 437. The Europeans needed 280 to win and after a shaky start, played some really exciting cricket. Jack knocked up his half century in forcing style and W.J. Cullen, who had made seventy-nine in the first innings, topped a triumphant 120, which to everyone's relief was much appreciated by the crowd.

With only four runs needed for victory Travers opened what should have been the last over by taking a spectacular swipe at the first ball from Abdus Salaam; he missed it, but it found his stumps. The crowd were ecstatic to see the European skipper removing himself so efficiently. Travers cursed, turned on his heel and stomped off, the four winning runs being collected by the next batsman. While everyone was shaking hands and patting each other on the back for securing the first European win since 1921, Jack made his way over to Travers: 'I say Guy, what the hell did you do that for?'

'Because I had a damned good bet on it! If I'd have won the match with a six I'd have been a hundred quid up now. And you can stop grinning because you'd have done the bloody same.'

It seems that betting was part of life for many of the Indians that Jack met in business and sport, and the British were not far behind. The Bombay Gymkhana ground was surrounded by big offices belonging to various businesses, and enormous bets seemed to be flying to and fro. The head of Rallis Bros had bet his new Sunbeam car on the result of this match. The Europeans' win provided the excuse for parties everywhere. The one at Government House was notable because His Excellency, considered by Jack to be somewhat of a stuffed shirt, distinguished himself by flying down the grand staircase at enormous speed on a silver tray. He then attempted to get the ceremonial cannons fired in the team's honour, but because the necessary red tape was by that time quite beyond him, settled for a salvo of champagne corks instead.

What struck Jack and appealed to the irreverent side of his sense of humour were some of the tactics employed during these matches. Once, when he was getting nicely settled into his batting, a small hand mirror flashed in the crowd every time the bowler was about to deliver the ball. And on another occasion a friend of his, Captain Hughes-Hallett, an old Haileyburian, batting beautifully for a draw, received a note at the end of an over. He read it and stuffed it into his pocket, but the next time he faced the bowling he seemed to throw caution to the wind, took a wild swing at the ball and was clean-bowled. He came storming into the pavilion and threw down his bat and gloves. 'That bloody captain's mad. Absolutely crackers. We've only got to stay there for a draw and he sends out this bloody note. Look at it, "Hit out or get out".'

Coming out of the changing-room, Travers, the captain, said, 'What's that? What's that about a note? Let me see it – Bastards!' However, there were experiences of a higher order, although some of them were a little disconcerting for Western doctrine. In one of his teams Jack had a fast bowler who was to play in a match against Kathiawar Province. He was a massive chap, about 6 ft tall and 18 stone according to Jack, and an important member of the Bombay Province team. Before breakfast on the opening day of the match Jack learnt that he had a badly swollen cheek and raging toothache. 'Right, you're coming along to my American dentist in Bombay – he'll drain that and take the tooth out and you'll be fine.'

Thinking that he was doing the chap a favour he was a little surprised to hear, 'Oh no, I cannot do that. I do not like dentists and I do not like Americans and I don't go to my next life without my teeth. Gardener will help me.'

'A gardener, what gardener?'

'Hari Mali the gardener, your left hand bowler.'

Although Jack had some respect for Hari Mali's skill with the ball, he knew that he was a simple man who could hardly write his name in Gujerati. 'How on earth do you think he's going to help you?'

'He will pray for me.'

'Good Lord, what does he know about prayer?'

They went out to find Hari who was not too pleased at having breakfast interrupted, but sat down by his patient and in almost a matter of fact way started to chant some incantation or other and stroke the side of his face. Jack was rather tempted to leave the patient and his quack together, but by now several people had gathered and were curious to see what was going on. After about five minutes the redness started to go from the swelling, and after ten there were clear signs that it was going down. In twenty minutes it had all but disappeared together with the pain and stiffness, and Hari and his patient demanded the breakfast so far denied them by toothache. Jack's curiosity was uncontrollable. 'Hari, what were you saying to him? That was an absolute miracle.'

'I don't know. I don't know what the words mean.'

'Well, how the devil can you cure anyone when you don't know what you're saying?'

'Oh Sahib, you are too clever, I cannot say what the words mean. They were taught to me by my father and they nearly always are working. Thank you for breakfast. I will see you at the pavilion in an hour. We shall send those Kathainwars home pretty damn quick I'm thinking.'

What Hari said, though sincere enough, certainly could not satisfy Jack's need for a rational solution. But he had to wait a few more years in India before he arrived at anything like an explanation.

Toward the end of 1928 the market prices for cotton started to fluctuate, and in the press there had been warnings about the American economy. Since the USA, as a major producer, had a marked influence on cotton prices this could not be heralded as good news, and the directors of Jack's firm began to look rather worried. Like other companies they were merchants as well as brokers, and it had been possible to buy and deal in cotton with a mere 10 per cent deposit, the balance being payable at a later date. As a result, the wealth which many seemed to accumulate and deal in began to approximate to the value of the paper used for printing the shares after prices fell. As collateral disappeared financiers required something tangible to back their clients' borrowing. The price of cotton dropped and dropped, and the phones stopped ringing. Nobody seemed to want cotton and without money passing through the business there was no business. In the normal run of things the directors used to go out in the mornings and come back with thousands of pounds worth of orders. The juniors would be sent out on afternoons to less profitable clients as part of the routine for keeping a foot in the door. But now the directors were returning empty-handed and the firm became desperate for business. Travers would slump down on his return: 'No bloody business. Absolutely nothing. It's awful. Get me a cup of tea someone – quick. Jack and you others, you'd better go out. We've got to keep trying to do something.' Jack never rated himself as a particularly good cotton broker, he certainly had all that was needed to be one and more besides, but he was under no illusions that his eye was on a rather different ball. However, in this desperate situation he stumbled on an interesting technique that owed its success more to his social and sporting life than to business. He went round to the offices of Sir Victor Sassoon, where he recognized a group of brokers from various other firms. They appeared to depart rather quicker than they arrived.

'Sorry Mr Johnston, no business today. Sorry George, nothing doing. Come back in a week or so. Mr Meyer, come in, I think the boss would like a word' – so in he went feeling the eyes of other brokers like daggers in his back.

'Ah Jack, now tell me, when are we going to have another little game of poker? You know we had a jolly good time, so when can you fix it?'

'I can probably fix it here and now if I could use your phone.' After ten minutes the party had been arranged, but before he went Jack said, 'Would you mind phoning my office and saying that I'm on my way? Otherwise I shall be in trouble for being so late.'

'Oh. You don't have to bother about that. Go and buy 10,000 bales – at a good price – and send the contract on to me. They won't bother you if you do that.'

'Well, thank you very much, and I look forward to seeing you at the bungalow on Thursday.'

Returning to the office, Travers asked 'Well Jack. Any damned luck?'

'Well yes, I think so. Sassoons want 10,000 bales.'

'What? They had that last week.'

'Well, here's the order so I'd better phone the bazaar now.'

'Why did they give it to you?'

'I don't know – perhaps it was just a late order.'

Jack was none too sure about divulging his new tactics, but realized he had hit on something of value. Next he went round to the office of Mr Toyamaka.

'Jack, very sorry but we've no business.'

'Yes I know, but could I have a word? I've heard that you have one of your directors visiting who is a very keen tennis player.'

Jack had picked up a snippet that the man was passionate about tennis, but none of the Japanese had tennis courts and to prepare nails for their coffins, the Europeans did not welcome him at their clubs.

'I'm rather embarrassed to hear about this and I would be very pleased to arrange some tennis on a private court for your visitor – singles or doubles – whatever he likes.'

'Jack, that really is most kind. He will be delighted.'

'Well, would you care to arrange it now.'

'Good idea, take a seat, Jack. I will not be long.'

When Mr Toyamaka returned Jack asked, 'Do you think I could phone the office, because I shall be rather late getting back?'

'Of course, please do, and I think we can raise a little business for you. Could you get 5,000 bales for us when you get back?'

Back at the office, Jack received an abrupt welcome from Travers. 'Where the hell have you been? Get any business.'

'Only a little I'm afraid, 5,000 bales.'

'Not bad. Not good. Where did you get it?'

'Mr Toyamaka.'

'Come off it, I was there myself this morning, and there was definitely nothing doing. What have you been up to? Why give it to you?'

'Well, Guy, I really can't say – perhaps it was a late order after your visit.'

'You don't say!'

A couple of days later Jack visited Rallis Bros.

'Morning Jack. Hope you're not after any business because you know how things are.'

'Yes, I know only too well how things are.'

'Before we boot you out I think Sammy wants a word – is that why you've come?'

'Yes, it is,' said Jack, sensing that he was on fertile ground.

'Ah Jack, come into the office, I want a quiet word. Look, we want to know what's going on with that Parsi's horses this Saturday. He's got two running, the favourite and an outsider. You know what crooks these people are, can you pop down to the stables and see what's going on? Don't telegraph. I want to keep this quiet.'

Sure enough the Parsi was going for even money and it was ten to one on Kapapi. Returning to Rallis Bros: 'Yes Jack, come in, come in. Any news?'

'Well, yes there is, but Sammy said there might be a chance for a little business so could I see him?'

'He's busy for half an hour but he'll phone you at Gibbs – that'll look more impressive. Right, what's this horse going to do?'

Back at the office the phone went: 'Travers here. Hello Sammy, anything doing? No? You want to talk to Mr Meyer? Here he is.' Jack picked up the receiver, his heart beating slightly quicker because Travers had no intention of this being a private call. 'Good morning, Sir. Yes, Sir. 5,000 bales. Of course, we'll send the contract note over this afternoon. Thank you very much.'

'Jack, as delighted as I am to have any business at all, what the hell is going on?'

After the explanation Travers was clearly impressed by Jack's ingenuity, but wasn't going to let on too much in front of the conventional staff. 'Good, that's quite clever, quite good.'

There was no respite from the worsening financial climate in 1929 and many firms like Jack's could not preserve the reasonable standards of pay to which they had been accustomed. Trade was essential to the European's presence in India and the income generated supported the opulent life style that many enjoyed. Jack had long been aware that an Indian clerk seemed to live very comfortably on a fraction of the income which his British counterpart required. The gathering gloom had unhappy repercussions for the city of Bombay where so many of its people worked in the cotton mills. However, Jack was nearing the end of his first term of work for Gibb & Co., and after two and a half years was looking forward to his leave in England. As he prepared to go in late

February it became clear that the future of Gibb & Co. was very uncertain, and while he was contracted to return to Bombay after his break, Guy Travers had to admit that he could offer no reassurance for the future. He indicated that if Jack found some other avenue he would release him from his contract and not put any obstacles in his way.

Although Jack was looking forward to seeing his family and old friends he was disappointed at the possibility of leaving India, where he had enjoyed such marvellous cricket and company. So as he embarked for the voyage home he felt unsettled, and did not know whether his goodbyes were for a few months or for life. He was also at a low ebb physically. Never having cared much about food or drink at the best of times, a mild bout of malaria and recent circumstances seemed to have resulted in a certain amount of malnourishment, accompanied by very uncomfortable boils.

It is extraordinary that when Jack's life was at such a low ebb – health prospects and financial security having deserted him – there occurred the most important turning point of his whole career. On that same ship was the Maharaja of Jam Sahib of Nawanagar, better known as Ranjitsinhji or 'Ranji' to his friends. He still ranks as one of the finest batsmen of all time, and played for Cambridge University, Sussex and England. When Jack met him his playing days were over at the age of fifty-seven, and he was Chancellor to the Indian Council of Princes and a delegate to the League of Nations. He was also Duleepsinhji's uncle, so Jack and he had a great deal to talk over, but it didn't take long for Ranji to comment, 'Jack, you mustn't mind my saying this, but you look pretty awful. What is wrong with you?' So Jack recounted what had been happening in the cotton-broking business and what he'd been up to over the last couple of years. While Ranji knew all about the cricketing exploits he had known little about how Jack was making a living, and being a man of unusual intelligence and wisdom, recognized that Jack had been completely wasting the intellectual side of his character.

'You know, you really shouldn't be doing this anyway. Look, how would you like to come up country and do some teaching? A friend of mine needs a private tutor for his grandson who wants to get into Eton, and after that, there's a little school in Jamnagar which you might be interested in.'

'Well, I think I would rather like to do that.'

'I'm going to spend some time fishing in Ireland, why don't you come over and we can talk about it.'

So here, in the middle of the Arabian Sea, suddenly appeared the opportunity to start teaching, and surely wherever Ranji was, a cricket pitch couldn't be far away.

CHAPTER FIVE

Dhrangadhra

'He was murdering them, but when I asked if he would teach me he said "No. Find out the same as I did, find out yourself!"' This was the abrupt rebuff from Sydney Barnes, the bowler whom Jack considered the best of all time. Both men had been asked to play for Minor Counties against the South African touring side in June 1929 at the Oval. Barnes demolished the batsmen and had taken eight wickets for twenty-nine runs by lunch on the first day. He seemed to have absolute control over the ball, and from a medium-fast delivery deceived the batsmen with every type of ball in the book and several that were not.

Jack had been delighted to be asked to play cricket during his leave, and was particularly honoured to be selected for the MCC against Wales and the visiting Indian Gymkhana. This gave him the opportunity to be on the receiving end of Barnes's bowling.

> I was playing for the MCC and he was playing for Wales on an absolutely perfect wicket. He was almost unplayable; he never bowled a bad ball. I made five runs in almost three hours, and the previous day I'd been hitting sixes into the pavilion without any trouble at all, this astonishing man not only had me playing badly for most of the game, but the ball seemed to spin off my bat. When I tried to drive I was getting full tosses, half volleys and good length balls swinging and breaking in any fashion but the one I expected.

Typically Jack omitted to say when recalling the match that he made the highest score of eighty-nine during the second innings, taking quite a few runs off Barnes, and that he also took seven wickets, as did Barnes. It was after this match that he made his request, but the tall and aloof bowler rather brushed him aside. The following day Jack was back at Lord's to meet the Indian Gymkhana and it was just possible that he knew something about Indian bowling that other MCC players did not, as he fought his way to a double century, in fact 225 not out at a spectacular rate of 81 runs per hour.

He made contact in Ireland with Ranji who had, as promised, arranged an attractive deal for Jack to become private tutor for some friends of his.

There was something special about India that removed hesitation about leaving his own country and family again for an indefinite period. The prospect of working for Maharajas was also intriguing because he would be nearer the real tradition of India than he could ever have been when working in the commercial areas. There was of course some regret at leaving the cricket scene at home again where he had been so openly welcome, and had knocked up some excellent scores including his 89 and 225 for the MCC, and 148 for Hertfordshire against Buckinghamshire. He was also invited to go on the MCC Tour of the West Indies, but because this would have meant going to India two months later he declined. There was little doubt that Ranji would have let him go, but Jack didn't even make the request. Ranji had said: 'You can start by being a private tutor for one of my friends. He urgently requires some tuition for his grandson who is down for Eton. Then there is a school in Jamnagar which you can take over.' Duly replenished by Ella's cooking, he embarked on his second trip to India.

For someone travelling halfway around the world his instructions for arrival were precise. 'I was told that I would report at 2.30 p.m. on Monday 1 September to the Palace, and I just managed to get there with half an hour to spare – in time to have a bath and change.' Jack let it be known that he was ready to be presented to the Maharaja of Limbdi, only to be told that he was out hunting, but should be back later. Several hours later he enquired whether the Maharaja was ready to see him. 'No. No. No. He won't be back until Friday.' This didn't impress Jack much and he began to regret declining the MCC's offer. Eventually the Maharaja's eldest son, whose own son Jack was to teach, came to see him. According to Jack he was very fat, very lazy but very polished and charming. He learnt later that this prince had put his clocks back first half an hour, then one hour, then two hours and finally two days – so that he was never actually late for anything. 'Yes, it is very important that my father sees you because he has had my son down for Eton for many years.' As the details emerged it appeared that young Tikan had been entered even before conception.

'Really, he has to be born you know.'

'Oh. It is all arranged. He has provisional acceptance.'

'Well,' said Jack, 'It seems that he has around two and a half years before he should go so we ought to get cracking.'

In time Jack met the Maharaja's other sons; one was a brilliant businessman with an excellent Cambridge degree, the other was a delightful character who did not appear to do much work because he was prone to epileptic attacks. Instead he was said to spend most of the day making love to his wife. Like all the others, his was an arranged marriage and he confided: 'She's not very beautiful but I can always kiss her mouth into a nice shape.'

A week after he arrived Jack was taken to meet the Maharaja – he was getting used to the Indian way of doing things. But imagine his dismay when he found himself in a large chamber full of supplicants waiting to have their cases heard. The Maharaja was a father to them all, and a very good one, as Jack later discovered. From his throne he listened patiently to each one, and they always took his word as law. Jack had arrived at six in the morning and by nine he seemed no nearer to being introduced. He was getting a little restless and hungry. One of the princes said, 'Jack if you want to go and have something to eat, I could arrange it for you.'

'That would be marvellous, but couldn't I just have a whisper in his ear about Tikan.'

'No, you must not do that. I am the only one who is allowed to mention the princeling's name.'

Three days later Jack found himself talking to the Maharaja about the formalities of getting a place at Eton. It took about twelve minutes.

So Jack began his teaching career in a Palace in Limbdi with the Maharaja's grandson, who for some time was his only pupil. However, Jack's obvious talent and attractive ways of teaching meant that soon other princes were attending his classes. The education which they had previously received was of a very uneven standard and Jack had to spend some time in sorting out what they did and did not know. Often a great deal had been learnt parrot-fashion without any understanding of the meaning of what they had been taught. Jack knew that real learning could not begin until he had got back to a level where there was proper comprehension. At this stage the idea of teaching in separate subjects was left behind. However, what was most surprising for Jack was the discovery of his own capacity and enjoyment of this occupation. Ranji had been quite correct because teaching required a mental capacity that had been somewhat dormant since he had left Cambridge.

Jack was asked to take the boys on a visit to the Maharaja of Porbandar to see their cousins. Their palace was on the coast of the Arabian Sea and was magnificently set amid palm trees and beautiful gardens. As it happened, Jack knew the Maharaja because he was a great cricketer and captained India on the tour to England. While Jack was in Porbandar he was given the most splendid tent to live in. It had many rooms and magnificent carpets, and he had bearers to look after him. The place was normally used by important visitors like politicians or high-ranking officers from the services. It overlooked the sea and was like nothing Jack had ever seen before. The Maharaja had a club where friends, guests and those that worked for him could spend a social evening. Naturally, when he was free Jack would always be there, chatting away to everyone.

He asked a friend, 'Who's that bit of fluff on the tennis court?'

'I don't know. I think they've just come out from school to stay with their parents.'

There was something about one of the girls that caught Jack's eye. This young lady was still very much on his mind when he should have been concentrating on the cue ball during the customary billiards session that evening. In a hushed corner of the club, risking interruption after a prolonged bridge hand, Joyce asked, 'Mummy, there's a man playing billiards with Daddy who looks so poor. I don't think he's eaten for weeks and his toes are sticking out of his shoes. Can we ask him to dinner tonight?'

Hoping that her partner would give her rather more support during the next hand she replied dismissively, 'Oh yes dear, if you want.'

As another who was looking for slightly better form to avoid a snooker, Jack's heart stopped dead as the 'little bit of fluff' appeared and whispered a message to his opponent who related, 'It seems that you have an invitation to dinner, if you'd care to join us.'

'Oh yes, I'd be absolutely delighted.'

It was not long before Jack, at his most charming and engaging, was telling Sydney and Daisy Symons about what he had been up to, all the time trying not to stare at Joyce, but everything he had imagined about her at a distance on the tennis court was true, and more than true.

Mr and Mrs Symons were a remarkable couple. Sydney was a globe-trotting troubleshooter who, as an engineer, had entrepreneurial skills and was working on a project for the Maharaja of Porbandar. His manner was relaxed and belied the breadth of his experience. Daisy was a contrast. Her family name of Selfe could be traced back to 1011, and she was rather sharp and would never suffer fools. Daisy cast a rather disdainful eye over the state of Jack's dress, but had no idea at the time that he had more interesting things to do with money than buy food and clothing. While he was telling them about teaching the princes he let slip that he was living in a tent. An image of something used by Boy Scouts came into Daisy's mind and she immediately offered, 'Would you like a bed in the house for a few days as a change from the tent?'

Jack tried to hesitate but the answer was, of course, yes. Notwithstanding his good fortune, Jack did little to disguise his interest in Joyce. They talked endlessly, played tennis and went for walks; he was infatuated. Three days after coming to stay he proposed, but although no positive answer was forthcoming, there was no rebuff either. Several proposals later he enquired how old she was. Quickly and very quietly Joyce replied, 'Oh, I shall be twenty.' This pleased Jack, because she did look rather young. What Joyce had said was quite true, or at least would become true in three years' time.

There could hardly have been a more romantic setting for yet another proposal than the brilliant moon setting on a placid ocean, as the couple walked hand in hand across the beach and between the palm trees of Porbandar. Approaching the Maharaja's club, an old friend to both of them, one of the Maharaja of Limbdi's sons, asked Jack secretively, 'Did you propose to her?' to which he replied that he had. 'Oh good,' he said and disappeared into the club. The moment they entered the Maharaja got to his feet. 'Ladies and Gentlemen, may I have your attention for a moment. The champagne's on its way round because I am pleased to announce the engagement of Jack Meyer and Joyce Symons.'

Amid cheers and congratulations, Sydney and Daisy Symons were absolutely stunned, they had known nothing of this and the announcement was as much of a shock to them as it was to poor Joyce. Whether or not Jack had any part in setting this up will never be known, but it was certainly a spectacular beginning to his pursuit. Sydney had a long talk with Jack later on, and put him straight about Joyce's age, said that she was going back to school anyway and from there to a Swiss finishing school. For his part, Jack apologized, for he had genuinely not realized that Joyce was only seventeen. However, this did not prevent them from accepting the Maharaja of Porbandar's engagement present of a panther shoot.

Joyce and Jack with the Maharaja of Porbandar's engagement present, 1931

That should have been the end of it all, but Sydney and Daisy could see that with or without apologies Jack was no less captivated by Joyce. They therefore decided to separate them, and took Joyce away to Hyderabad the following day, so that the lovers were separated by several hundred miles. However, situations like this never had, nor would spell defeat for Jack. The effect was quite the opposite; with the aid of Prince Ghanshamsinghi he discovered where they had gone, then borrowed the Maharaja's royal train complete with royal carriages, coats of arms and monograms. But his first destination was to see the Governor General's agent, because he had learnt from the prince that he might be able to get a special marriage licence, and he thought there was a possibility that if he showed this to Sydney he might give his permission. Having tracked down the agent Jack managed to get an early interview. When he explained the purpose of his visit the agent was sympathetic, but after he asked Joyce's age he had to say, 'I'm so sorry, but you see she is a minor, she is under age and I can't possibly give you the licence without her parents' consent.'

However, Jack had seen this coming, and it posed no problem for the man who could outwit the Australians or conjure cotton orders out of thin air during the depression. Sydney had written him a very formal letter before departing, explaining in the clearest terms that marriage to Joyce was out of the question. 'Oh that's alright. I've got his letter right here,' he replied, exposing just enough of Sydney's letter so that the agent could see the notepaper heading and Sydney's signature. Fate smiled – the agent didn't bother to read the letter and filled in the special licence. Jack found the place in Hyderabad where the Symons were staying and stuck his head into the lion's den. Joyce was sent to her room and said that she had never seen anyone so angry as her father. Her parents stayed up all night talking to Jack and reason should have produced some solution to the extraordinary circumstances. But instead, Jack told them very firmly that he was going to stay there until they gave their permission, no matter how long it took. They were almost speechless with disbelief. The atmosphere was appalling and the parents would not speak to him at all, except to say 'No!'.

One week and three days later they said 'Yes'. Jack's immediate reaction was to say that he wanted to get married straightaway, so tempers, already on a short fuse, flared again. Joyce's parents thought that this would be precipitous because she might change her mind. Sydney proposed that she should return to England to complete her education, then, if they both still felt the same way about each other, the marriage could be properly arranged there. Also it might give Jack more time to sort out some better prospects than the rather casual tutoring he

was presently engaged in. But Jack would hear no more of it. He wanted
to get married as soon as possible and knew of an attractive little church
on a hill at Malabar just outside Bombay. Jack's resolve seemed
irresistible, and although the parents were terribly uneasy about the
whole thing, they boarded the train for the two-day journey to Bombay.

Joyce and her parents stayed at the Taj Mahal Hotel and preparations
for the wedding got under way at a furious pace, with Jack arranging
everything. Daisy Symons did not put an announcement in the Bombay
newspapers because she still felt unhappy about the whole affair. But in
no time the word got around because Jack had so many friends there,
and it soon became clear that the church at Malabar would be far too
small, and the wedding was arranged for St Thomas's Cathedral instead.
The next problem to overcome was to find a suitable wedding dress and
trousseau, but the period of time available to get this arranged was very
limited. At this point Daisy must have despaired that her future son-in-law
was completely mad, because when Joyce should have been having
fittings for the dress there was a cricket match which Jack didn't want to
miss, and of course it was very important that Joyce came to see him play.

'But what's going to happen about her clothes?' Daisy pleaded. 'She's
got to go for a fitting.'

'Well, I'm not marrying her for her clothes. Surely Eileen could do
that, couldn't she?'

So Joyce's dress was cut to fit her sister Eileen, who was luckily a similar
size, and Joyce never even saw the thing until the day before the wedding.

Joyce was learning too that when there was a target in sight, red tape,
convention or regulations were no barrier to Jack. She had been swept
through this extraordinary affair at breakneck speed and no schoolgirl
could have imagined anything more exciting, dangerous and romantic.
For Jack, love had released powers within him he had not experienced
before. How could he, a gentleman, sensitive to the feelings of others and
brought up with real Christian values, have put such genuine, kindly
people as Sydney and Daisy through such an awful time? Even then the
surprises were far from over, because halfway through his bachelor party
Jack decided that they should all visit the women. Admonishments about
breaking tradition were of little interest, because all admitted that the
party was then much more fun. As if to ensure that there were no rules
left, when Joyce and her family took breakfast on their hotel balcony
before the wedding, who should turn up again but Jack. The service was a
magnificent affair, with a cathedral full of friends including several
Maharajas – each with their entourages – many Indians and Europeans
from his cricketing world, Government officials and old friends from the
cotton-broking days.

Jack was very fond of Poona and chose it for their short honeymoon. An important part of that attraction lay in its delightful racecourse where he had been so lucky before. It comes as no surprise to learn that the day after their arrival coincided with some important races, so off they went. For Joyce it was to be another of the new experiences crowded into the few weeks during which she had known Jack. However, he was just a little patronizing: 'Well, it's pretty serious stuff this racing, and I'll tell you all about it sometime but not at the moment. Now you go and amuse yourself and I'll see you in the grandstand before the races begin.' Patting her on the head like a small girl, Jack gave her five rupees with which to 'amuse herself'. Of course she knew nothing about betting. Instead she walked around the paddock selecting the prettiest colours, a good-looking horse or a jockey with a nice smile. The extraordinary thing was that Jack, who had ferreted out some very useful information, lost every race whereas Joyce won all six, each time betting her winnings on the next horse. Luckily for Jack she thought that it was all marvellous and paid the hotel bill with her winnings, somewhat to his grateful embarrassment.

After two or three days they had to return to Limbdi and boarded the train for the long trek up from Poona. The journey provided a little time to take stock of the extraordinary events that had just passed. Joyce thought about her parents and prayed that they would come to care for Jack as she did. Looking out of the window as they approached their destination Jack turned and said, 'Good Lord. I think this is for us.' Awaiting their arrival was a traditional Indian wedding procession with cheering, dancing people and lots of music played on instruments and drums Joyce had never seen before. The whole procession was on carts pulled by enormous white bullocks completely covered in flowers. They were greeted and garlanded, and the procession lumbered out of the station and through the town, being showered with more flowers and petals all the time. Finally the procession drew up to a palace, admittedly a minor palace, by the standards of the Maharaja of Limbdi, but nonetheless a palace, which was to be home for Jack and Joyce. It provided an unbelievable, fairy story ending to the events of the previous month. 'If only Mummy and Daddy could see it.'

Jack resumed his teaching and was one of the happiest men in the world with his new bride and a palace to keep her in. But the combination of Jack and India seemed to brew up constant change prompted by the possibility of things settling down. Amid this new found happiness tragedy struck when Jack's first pupil, Tikan Sahib, died of appendicitis. It was a great shock for everyone and when the funeral and mourning was over it was quickly arranged that Jack and Joyce should go to teach at a princes' school in a palace belonging to the Maharaja Ghanshyamsingh of Dhrangadhra.

Having spent some time living in England, the Maharaja was quite an Anglophile. While there the Maharaja took an unusual interest in how public works were organized, and also wanted to know all about how the police worked. He had a remarkable breadth of knowledge and ruled his part of the State with intelligence and fairness. What he wanted was a good education for his family and relations. Normally they would have gone to a princes' college, but he did not consider the standards high enough for the world he knew his sons would be entering. Principally he wanted them to be educated to the level where they could enter British public schools or universities.

Jack was given a bungalow to live in and a 30 yd long classroom at the top of the palace from which he ran the Dhrangadhra Palace School. Soon the numbers were swelled with nieces and nephews and the children of friends of the Maharaja. The assessment ideas Jack had started to use in Limbdi came into operation again and he settled down to teach once more. Perhaps deciding that he needed to seek validity for some of his educational innovations, he started to read widely around the subject. What particularly interested him was the disparity between different rates of learning, especially between children who seemed to be equally intelligent and lively. He was particularly impressed at the work of Professor Byrt on learning difficulties and word blindness.

He seemed to regard many of the children, princes and commoners alike, as being rather soft, and learnt that in other 'schools' there was someone like a retired colonel to clean their shoes, look after their ponies and even, according to Jack, do their homework for them. He couldn't see that much of this was character-building stuff, and conveyed his concern to the Maharaja in typically colourful manner. 'Your Highness. The princes' grandmothers went out fighting on elephants, but their grandchildren have been brought up playing with a soft ball. They dare not even jump off a chair.' So Jack devised a few little diversions that he thought the children might find entertaining, and to watch the fun he invited their royal parents to view the exercise from the Palace windows.

'On the word of command you will "right turn" and follow me – follow your leader. Now we go up this big tree which has branches like a ladder and on to the top of the wall. Run along the wall for about thirty paces – it's quite safe because it's 3 ft wide. Drop onto the garden hut roof and slide down to the edge where you can climb down the gutter and fall in over there in front of me.'

It was the same sort of thing that Denys and he had done at the rectory about twenty years earlier and the squeals of excitement amply demonstrated that these children, liberated to behave in the same way for the first time, were having just as much fun. After about ten minutes most of them had completed the regal assault course, but word came down from on high that his presence was required. 'The Master may do anything with my children – but this is disgraceful.'

'Well, Your Highness, I did tell you what I intended to do. They need these experiences. Even when they are on their ponies they are led at never any more than a walk, and they dare not ever jump through a hedge unless someone looks the other side for them to see if there is a snake there first.'

But the Maharaja said, 'Jack, I must tell you something. That is not done to see if there are any snakes but to make sure there is no-one with a rifle waiting to shoot my son – to assassinate him.'

'But surely, Your Highness, – this is 1931.'

'Yes, and it was in 1929 that my eldest son was shot by his uncle, just at the place you are talking about.'

'Oh dear. Your Highness. I'm so terribly sorry. I had no idea . . .'

'Okay, Jack – you're a good man.'

As the news got around about the school its popularity grew, and several new children, with fathers in the Army, came along, but that was definitely not to the liking of the Maharanis who said, 'Why were my children made to play with the dirty hobbledehoys from the bazaar?' This was an awkward situation, because Jack could see that many of the army children were helping the young princes, especially in terms of getting them to play games. There were other conventions Jack wanted changed. When the princes and princesses entered a schoolroom, it was the custom for the teacher to stand out of respect. But Jack felt that this was fundamentally wrong because in order to learn anything the children had to be working for him, so when he entered the room, they had to stand. One princess was rather upset about this and made a complaint which was related to the Maharaja. In his typical and sensible manner he visited the schoolroom and spoke to the pupils. 'Children, understand that here it is Meyer Sahib's kingdom – he is King here – even I am not King here, but he is. Outside this room he knows that I am King and he gives me respect, but in here you must do as he tells you.'

In Dhrangadhra, unlike Bombay, where people from so many nations lived and worked together, Joyce and Jack were almost the only English people. Joyce's life style was extraordinary. During the day she was often taken to the zenana where Maharinis and their children would spend

Joyce and Jack in Indian dress, Christmas 1934

their time. Although she could not speak their language she was made welcome, and had an insight into other lives and customs which would have been impossible to gain elsewhere. She was dressed in the most marvellous clothes and decked with priceless jewels. The Maharinis and Princesses often asked Joyce to go for a drive with them. Rolls-Royce limousines with darkened windows and an armed guard would take them to a temple or garden. Walking around the formal gardens was always a great pleasure, but before getting out of the cars a whistle was blown and any lesser mortals enjoying the flowers and borders knew they had to leave to guarantee the royal visitors their privacy. As far as Joyce could see it was all they used to have in the way of exercise.

When he had time Jack would go off with his gun. Of course the Maharaja organized many grand shooting and hunting parties, and splendid things they were, but like many shooters, Jack liked a bit of solitude, wandering around and taking pot luck. One evening he drove out to a few ponds near some outlying village. It was very quiet and still and there was very little about that would make a reasonable meal. As the light was going – and there it got dark very quickly – he suddenly spotted a lone duck on a small pond quite near the mud-baked village building. With a sense that it was not a completely wasted outing he put the bird up and dropped it with one barrel. Suddenly the whole village erupted, and everyone seemed to be angry and shouting as they ran towards him. Obviously he had no idea as to what they were saying, but if, as he began to suspect, this was the last duck in the larder he would have been happy to hand it over. However, the villagers seemed really furious, and he reflected afterwards that the only reason he did not come to any harm was because he was still holding the gun. Above the din there was the sound of a motorbike and the village policeman or guardian arrived. Luckily he spoke English. 'You have done a very serious thing, you have shot the headman's grandmother who died last night. Now I must arrest you for your own safety and take you to the police station. I will put my hand on your shoulder to show that you have been arrested and we will go to your car.'

A mile or two from the village the policeman pulled ahead and waved Jack down: 'Okay, you can go home now, but I shouldn't come out here again. I do not know what they will do. His grandmother has nowhere to go now.'

'I'm so terribly sorry. I had no idea . . .'

'Of course, of course. How can you.'

Feeling somewhat wretched about it all Jack drove back to the bungalow.

The Maharaja of Dhrangadrha shot ducks in a rather different way.

The shoot was on an enormous lake several miles long and about a quarter of a mile wide. At one end was a great arch of reeds some 50 yd deep. The idea seemed to be that the ducks should be shot from punts which were easily hidden in the reeds. They were enormous boats, much larger than anything on the Cam, with about 2 ft of freeboard and six guns each. Each one also had a crew, who served endless whisky and sodas and kept winding up the gramophones. Tents were erected each night and the party would eat, drink and be very merry, lazing on thick rugs and cushions around the camp fire. The Maharaja declared that the food stocks were low, and while there was plenty of dinner that night, the next day was looking as if it would be on the lean side. This was what Jack wanted to hear. 'Well, let me go out before breakfast and I'll show these bargees and bird catchers that an English gentleman knows a thing or two about duck shooting.'

'Oh Jack, you do that if you want to, so long as you don't scare the ducks away from here.'

That evening he gave his Rigby a thorough cleaning, which always brought back memories of the Glebe and home. Putting it back in the case he promised it plenty of sport in the morning. Up at the crack of dawn he and Joyce made ready with the bearers who were to go with them. With a look in his eye which threatened dire consequences, he hissed the impossible command in a whisper: 'You remain silent and invisible.'

'But only the Gods . . .'

'Ssh–!'

The sport was all that Jack could wish for. 'I went out and shot about thirty snipe and something like fifty ducks. It was pretty easy.' The Maharaja said: 'Well Jack, how on earth do you do it? My mouglis couldn't have done that.'

'Well of course they couldn't. They catch about a duck a week and seem rather proud of themselves. But they just don't have experience, that's what you get with the shooting people back in England.'

'Anyhow, well done and thank you, Jack. That's splendid.'

A few weeks later at a cricket match the Maharaja, whose side was opening the batting, said, 'Jack, I want to take some pictures of this match and there are one or two other things I have to do. Would you mind opening the batting for a change?'

'Well I don't usually. Ramji is one of their fastest bowlers and the wicket doesn't look too even to me. I don't want to mess things up.'

'Oh no, I'm sure you won't. Don't worry about that.'

So out Jack strode with his companion. They weathered the furious opening balls and started to ease a few runs onto the board. The wicket was matting as usual and this was on a concrete base because of the sandy soil. One of the bowlers seemed to be mistiming his delivery and put a short ball down the off side that was almost wide. The second time it happened Jack didn't resist the invitation. Stepping off the matting he delivered a flashing square cut meant for the boundary. At that instant the ground exploded around him and as he blinked to avoid the flying sand he saw a net shoot up in front of him, its draw string pulled tightly across his head as he fell to his knees. Feeling like a trussed chicken he looked up to see the Maharaja peering down at him. Amid cheers and laughter he could just make out 'Jack, anything the matter?'

'Well, I seem to have a problem here.'

'Don't worry, I will get your friends the bargees to release you. They seem to be rather pleased with themselves.'

This was typical of the Maharaja of Dhrangadhra; he didn't take umbrage or criticize Jack for getting slightly inflated over his shooting, but nevertheless he made his point with imagination and in a manner everyone could enjoy.

During 1932 Jack and Joyce went for a short holiday in Ceylon (now Sri Lanka), to seek one of the most spectacular golf courses in the world and to give Joyce a rest because she was expecting her first child. Unfortunately she contracted a mild bout of malaria and was given quinine, which caused her to go into labour. They were, as usual, miles from anywhere but Jack was told there was a retired doctor living somewhere in the area. He set off in the middle of the night, and within a short time there was no-one in the area who didn't know that he was looking for the doctor. As if the delivery of their first daughter, Gillian, was not dangerous and stressful enough, the arrival was also accompanied by the cries of bull elephants as they crashed around outside. In those days, so long as one's health was good, India was a wonderful place to be. Medical facilities were not good unless there was a city nearby. The risks were underlined a year or two later when Joyce suffered another difficult delivery in Dhrangadhra with the birth of their second daughter, Jacqueline. That both daughters grew strongly, while Joyce was determined to recover from the ordeal, revealed to Jack a strength in his wife beyond that suggested by her petite stature.

After the Third Indian conference in London at the end of 1932 a White Paper was issued. A few weeks later the Maharaja of Dhrangadhra obtained a copy. He called Jack into his office. 'I have just received this copy of a White Paper on the future of the Native States as they call us. It is very long, so will you read it please and let me know whether the British Government are going to keep the promises that Queen Victoria made to my great-grandfather, or not.'

Jack knew that there was something behind this. Although he was a very busy man with many responsibilities, the Maharaja was perfectly capable of interpreting government jargon himself. About half an hour later Jack returned to the study. 'Your Highness, I'm afraid I have some rather poor news for you. It is quite clear that they are going to let you down.'

'Right. That's what I wanted to know Jack. You see it that way too. Do you remember that we discussed having the boys educated in England? I didn't tell you at the time, but it was as an insurance against precisely this kind of thing happening. My next step is to get the boys into good schools in England, and I want you and Joyce to take charge of this. I know this can be done more easily in England, so it will be necessary to find a house over there so that you can teach and look after them. I may be able to send some more over. I have friends in the Congress and there could be a few more from there. But the first thing is to find a good house in England for them. Can you help me there Jack?'

So Jack wrote home to Rollo and Ella to tell them what the Maharaja had said, and asked them if they had any ideas about finding a suitable home for the family and the princes. They were elated at Jack's news, but had little idea of how difficult this task would be.

The Dhrangadhra Princes. Millfield's genesis, 1932

Meanwhile, teaching in the long classroom at the top of the palace was developing in some interesting ways. An almost universal fault among the young Indians was a complete lack of knowledge of the world's history and significant events. Jack felt that this was a foundation necessary for later, more specialized, subjects. Therefore along the whole length on one wall he had a continuous, illustrated frieze which stretched back to the dinosaurs at one end, and up to the present at the other where R.J.O. Meyer's latest stand of 189 for His Highness XI was recorded. Other great moments in history were marked with tags of one colour to denote important kings and rulers, and other colours to mark inventions or revolutions. The whole frieze was always being added to as Jack would set homework for his pupils to find the dates of the French Revolution, or the invention of the printing press, and become involved in the pageant of history by sticking coloured tags at the appropriate year. His own schooling, particularly what he had received at Stratheden, influenced his ideas considerably, especially the way in which Old Lyon had led enthusiasm and confidence gained in a favourite subject to spill over into areas where the pupil had been less confident. Jack extended this practice with his own experience through which he had found that any person having a real passion for something seemed somehow more confident in many other areas. This confidence went a long way to removing doubts of ability, which often thwarted a pupil's readiness to take on a new subject. Therefore he sought to find the special abilities and interests of each pupil, and having found them would do his utmost to support and encourage them further. This notion of enterprise was sometimes foreign to such privileged children, which was one of the reasons for Jack being rather keen on inviting the children of Army officers and others to join the school – much, as was recorded earlier, to the displeasure of the Maharinis, who did not want their princes and princesses mixing with this 'riff-raff'. However, these children were lively, good at games and confident and brought much to the sometimes rather protected royal children. And when all else was said and done, Jack certainly needed them to build up sufficient numbers for his cricket team.

Of course not all the children had a special interest or outstanding ability, and this was often because no person or experience had touched off that spark within them. Finding the spark became an important and significant process for Jack. As a diversity of activities emerged in the long classroom, those who were not especially interested in anything would suddenly become inspired, or find the confidence to talk about some interest which they thought others might have laughed or sneered at previously. Jack later referred to this special interest or ability as a

Staff and pupils of the Dhrangadhra Palace School, 1934

'handle' which he could use to get the rest of the machine going. That handle could also be found by talking to the pupil, and gently testing and enquiring until 'a light went on'. What he found particularly gratifying was that pecking orders, very natural to such privileged children, seemed to crumble as each became aware of others' talent. These varied interests within the room dictated that children would work on an individual basis or sometimes in small groups, and although Jack had never experienced small classes at his schools, it became clear to him that the pupils were motivated and making very good progress under this strategy.

In England, meanwhile, Rollo was looking for a suitable property to rent for the princes. He was, of course, delighted that his son was coming home at last, and this must have supported him in his quest. However, what he had not bargained for was the attitude of some owners. There were quite a few properties available, because it was the mid-1930s and the country was in a state of relative depression. However, potential landlords or their agents declined to go any further with the arrangements when they heard that foreign princes would be staying in their properties. As a result he cast his net geographically wider and wider, eventually learning of a property in a Somerset town oddly named

Street. It was owned by a family named Clark, the famous shoemakers, who were Quakers and philanthropists. Rollo was delighted to find that, unlike certain of the gentry he had met, the Quakers' 'brotherhood of man' philosophy readily accommodated Indian princes. So he made his way down to Somerset to meet Mr Roger Clark and Mr Anthony Clark and had a look at the vacant property, Millfield House.

CHAPTER SIX

Millfield

History might credit 3 May 1935 as the day that Millfield School was founded with the arrival of the Meyers and the Indian princes at the house in Street. Although the school would never have come into existence without this initiative, the aims and standards for which it strove a few years later were not on that day's orders. Instead, under Jack's management and funding by His Highness the Maharaja of Dhrangadhra the aim was to prepare the Maharaja's princes for entry into British public schools or universities. There were also two Wadhwan princes sponsored by the Government of India, the British Resident's son and daughter, a Bombay Muslim aiming to get into Oxford and two visiting American children. The Maharaja had given Jack discretion to expand the numbers at Millfield House as he saw fit, but it was still he who provided Jack's salary and the rent for the house.

Since finding Millfield House, Rollo and Ella had been working furiously to prepare it for the princes and their son's family. Just as at Watton, Ella trained some local staff who were ex-miners to take on the domestic work, and had been shifting furniture and dealing with landlords, lawyers and tradesmen. The house and grounds were in excellent order, and had been the home of the Clarks, who founded the famous shoe factory in the town of Street. Until her death in 1934 it was occupied by Alice Clark, a director of the company and pioneer of its welfare services. The house then belonged to Anthony Clark and was vacant because he preferred to stay where he was in Street. Jack signed a contract for a five-year lease at £350 a year.

Along with the house came its head gardener, Philip Taylor, who let it be known that the Clarks would not allow any bush or tree planted by their ancestors to be removed. Taylor had the greenest of green fingers and anything receiving his attention would grow bigger, faster and more beautiful than before. Jack used to say that he knew all his prize onions and chrysanthemums by their Christian names, and slept in the greenhouse when his tomatoes were sick. Taylor was a dour character with good old-fashioned standards and his friendship, or even approval, could not be won overnight. However, he saw in Rollo a fellow soul with commensurate experience and enthusiasm, and gave him much support when he laid out the new shrubs, trees and flower beds which added delightfully to Millfield's environment. Jack found that Taylor's second love in life was cricket.

Organizing the move from India to England had been an exhausting task requiring considerable logistic skill and endless patience. Added to that, the experience was almost traumatic for the young princes who were exposed to more new experiences in a month than they had had in the whole of their lives. However, Jack and the Brahmin priest who came over with them were in close attendance, and at least they were not arriving in England at the coldest time of year. In fact Somerset was coming into its greenest season, and the lush countryside provided an overwhelming contrast to Dhrangadhra.

During their first week of residence the boiler burst; showing that they could be businesslike as well as philanthropic, the Clarks gave Jack the option of either paying for it himself or putting £15 permanently on the rent. A few weeks after their arrival the Meyers were visited by Roger Clark, who had been brought up in Millfield House as a boy. In his diary he described Jack and Joyce as 'a most charming young man, serious and friendly and interesting, and she is very pleasant.' He also saw one of the Indian princes whom he likened to a Rubens cherub. Jack was busy with paperwork to ensure that he could match the boys' education to the entrance qualifications necessary for the various schools or colleges they aspired to. His parents had moved from The Bear Hotel in Street to a house in Ditcheat and were still very much involved with Millfield. There seemed a surprising amount to be done to look after less than a dozen pupils, and Joyce was learning to cope with a very different life style to that which she had enjoyed in India, where practically everything had been done for her. However, what she may have lacked in domestic training was more than made up for by her willingness to learn.

As the summer came on, the ideas which Jack had been forming at the back of his mind for some time about planting his international wards in 'England's green and pleasant land' seemed to be gently taking on a real form:

We were apparently established without causing even a ripple, although the local rector did feel called upon to mention in his welcoming address the need to pray for the heathen when the Brahmin priest accompanied the princes to church. Street, under the Quaker influence, was well disposed to foreigners and accepted the 'brotherhood of man' ideal. We settled down blissfully to work and play in the Somerset summer, getting a couple of ponies (riding is a must for Rajputs) and flattening, weeding and marling a cricket pitch, my wife being the first assistant groundsman. Our first match was against Queens, Taunton – bless them – on 1 June.

It was a sporting gesture on the part of Queens to agree to this historic first fixture at Millfield House, because the home XI consisted of all abilities and standards. The opening batsman was Philip Taylor, the head gardener, aged fifty-eight. He took his stand wearing his thick leather gaiters instead of pads.

It took a disaster to initiate the change from Millfield House into what was to become Millfield School, and the utterly improbable source of that disaster was the scheme's great benefactor, HH the Maharaja of Dranghadhra. He arrived a few days after the cricket match, thoroughly approved of all that Jack had done, but explained that the operation was now too expensive for his impoverished state after losing an enormous amount of money on a chemical works venture. He said an affectionate farewell, packed up the princes and took them to London where an uncle was to look after them. Suddenly Millfield House had the stuffing knocked out of it:

> He took with him half our total strength, all financial support which included my modest salary, rent, rates, insurance, heat, electricity, wages, boarding expenses and, apparently all hope of our survival as a viable entity and of course, 'Jerusalem in England's green and pleasant land'. A rapid assessment of our position with half a dozen miscellaneous pupils, two Hindus, one Muslim, two Brits, two Americans – short stay visitors and the rector's twins provided us with a possible income of about £60 per month, showed it to be untenable, Pandora's box was empty, and the game appeared clearly to be up.

Jack was understandably angry and frustrated. The idea had taken years to become a reality, and it had now been demolished in a matter of minutes. Some means of survival was needed and the situation at Millfield House did not seem to offer a solution; there was not even any capital to be saved from it apart from the two ponies, a few tables, chairs and beds and pots and pans in the kitchen. Jack's mind turned to an offer, repeated several times, from the heir to Ranjitsinhji, HH the Jam Sahib of Nawanagar, better known as 'Ranji', who had arranged the first teaching job at Limbdi. He was chairman of the princes' school and keen to have Jack as headmaster to this large establishment. Jack approached him and it seemed that he and Joyce would soon be sailing back to Bombay. In fact Ranji even promised to try and persuade HH Maharaja of Dhrangadhra to square up any debts incurred in quitting Millfield House.

However, the way back to India was challenged forcefully by Jack's mother, who countered his proposal on two fronts. First, she did not care to waste all the work she and Rollo had done in preparing for the return of her son, and secondly she told Jack squarely that any such move now would break his father's heart. Rollo had only seen Jack twice during his nine-year sojourn in India, and was overjoyed at his return with his wife and daughters. It was Ella who proposed starting a new school at Millfield House, to which Jack replied in forthright manner, 'My dear mother, I am as you know ready for a gamble on most events. I will gamble that a coin will land head or tails, or even that it will stand on its edge if the odds are right. But I will not gamble on a project which has no chance of success at all. We have no money, limited teaching and boarding space, only three properly fee paying pupils and in short no chance at all!'

That, in normal circumstances, would have been that, but Arabella Crosbie Meyer was no ordinary person: 'I'll build you five prefabricated classrooms. I have already held a meeting of local tradesmen who have agreed to back a gentleman like you to make good on a year's credit, and I have already heard of children in the area whose parents will be calling on you, so we are expecting you and Joyce to try and make a go of it.'

As Jack said later, 'The school should drink a toast to her memory every year on 3 May.'

However, he was now rather punchdrunk over the whole affair. A further bar to his quitting was the contract which he had made with the Indian Government to tutor the two Wadhwan boys, and they were not immediately giving in to Jack or Ranji's request to reconsider.

As there seemed nothing much to do about India except wait for developments, or anything else in hand except teach the remaining flock, and as the racehorses were running unusually favourably, I decided on a policy of masterly inactivity.

If Jack intended to be inactive, he didn't keep the intention up for very long, because in ones and twos pupils were appearing on the doorstep of Millfield House. Parents were either a little dissatisfied with present educational arrangements, or some qualification was required for entrance to higher education or a career, which was unlikely to be gained in time through normal educational channels. Here, inactivity evaporated because Jack was quite incapable of remaining uninterested when confronted with problems educational. What parents discovered in June 1935 remained true for the rest of his long life: even before they had finished explaining the difficulties their offspring might be having, the problem became Jack's, and he had an imperative moral obligation to help. It was instinctive that he should educate, and there had been no end to the observations and innovation which he had made at the palace school, Dhrangadhra. Added to this was his ability to sympathize with any young person in trouble, aided by his memory of some of the wonderful or shocking experiences he had had at Stratheden and Haileybury. Upon interviewing a parent and child his astute observation and intelligence would formulate a solution with little apparent effort well before anyone came round to enquiring if anything could be done. The authority and conviction with which he commented on a possible solution was one of the most powerful factors in the growth of the school. Remarkably, his ability as teacher and analyst were attracting pupils – albeit in a small way – during one of the worst years on record for public school closures, when there were rows of empty beds in the dormitories of even the best schools. Although few of his prospective parents equated Millfield House, set in its lush summer greenery, to an Eton or Harrow, some were hoping that their children would eventually enter such esteemed schools, and saw in Jack a method of breaching the requisite entrance exams.

A reminder of the plight of mid-1930s' public schools was brought home to him through a surprise visit from his prep school headmaster, Old Lyon, with his elder brother, now an ex-headmaster and governor of nearby King's School, Bruton. Old Lyon had been Jack's favourite teacher, and it seemed remarkable that he should meet him again when he was on the threshold of his teaching career in England. Jack said afterwards that he was never quite clear whether it was a courtesy visit from old friends, or whether they were sounding him out for a possible vacancy at Bruton, perhaps even a headmastership. They were certainly quite disparaging about the possibility of starting a new school in the prevailing economic climate. Jack also received a letter from H.D. Hake, who was senior to him at Haileybury. Hake had been outstanding at racquets and cricket as a pupil, and was then a housemaster at the college. He implored Jack to reconsider any intentions of starting a school, promising that disaster could be the only outcome when established schools were half empty. This couldn't have made things any easier for Jack. He had a dozen pupils, each requiring something different, and yielding an income nowhere near the cost of running Millfield House, let alone producing a salary for him. The only way that he was keeping his head nominally above water was by financial support from his and Joyce's parents. Added to that, and being entirely objective, here was a young man aged thirty, who had never been a schoolmaster in the accepted sense of the word, let alone headmaster, and who was being encouraged to set up a private school by his mother, father and pretty twenty-three-year-old wife. A little encouragement from an authority in the educational world would have been helpful, but Jack had just perceived that that was not to be forthcoming. A reasonable man might have telephoned Bruton to see if there was at least a part-time job as a games teacher available, but Jack didn't have to be reasonable, he was rather cleverer than that. He knew that his school experiences were not vastly different from what others had been through, and he was convinced that he had a method of education that could be vastly more effective, even if it was untried in a British school with staff and timetables.

Should Jack have been contemplating any of this, he would have been disturbed by a loud bang at the door of Millfield House. When Joyce answered there stood a retired squadron leader with his seventeen-year-old son. Being rather deaf he bellowed, 'I'm looking for a genius to teach my son.'

'Oh well, my husband is a genius,' was Joyce's reply.

'He has failed School Certificate for Sherborne three times, can't read, can't write. We've tried crammers. I've got a suitcase full of his rubbish here, every bit of work he has done since he was five. He can probably get a crummy job now, but I want to send him to Cambridge.'

Jack later described him as a 'kindly but heavily overdominating parent, the type who used to go up in his aeroplane with a bomb in one hand and a revolver in the other during the first war.'

'Mr Meyer, the boy won't read anything. I'd read the whole of Dickens by the time I was nine and Thackeray by the age of twelve.'

'Squadron Leader, I wonder if you would excuse Charles and I for a moment, we are just going to have a short walk in the garden.'

Charles had been sitting beside his bellowing father and almost trembling like a leaf. But Jack had noticed that his eyes were everywhere, and even at this early stage in Millfield's career there was evidence of Jack's multiple interests sprawled around his study. Leaving Charles outside he returned and said, 'I think you have to make up your mind what you want. I think you want someone like yourself who will spit in your eye and stand up to you. At the moment Charles will never do that, but he might shoot you in the back.'

For an instant the Squadron Leader looked as if he would like to shoot Jack. 'You've got to lay off him. He'll never get anywhere with you bawling at him. But I think I can help Charles, I don't know to what extent until I've given him a few more tests. The thing is, if he comes here it will be on one condition, and that is that you don't come near this place. That you leave him to me and you don't come near Millfield.'

It had been a lot for the Squadron Leader to take in, but he swallowed his pride and agreed to the terms. So Charles came, but a fortnight later there was another loud bang at the door. 'I want to see Mr Meyer. I got a letter from Charles – absolutely illegible, just as bad as ever!'

Jack reminded him that he had broken a promise and sent him off again. Eight months later Charles had got into Cambridge and the Squadron Leader was somewhat amazed. Speaking to Charles, Jack commented, 'You've done very well and your father is obviously very pleased about it, although he doesn't say much. For his own sake I think he needs a bit of a cure, just a little bit of a leg pull.'

Over tea the Squadron Leader said, 'Meyer, you've done a marvellous job for my boy, he only needed teaching of course, he's a bright boy but he needed teaching. Half the trouble is he never would read a book.'

'Father, that reminds me. Mr Meyer got stuck when he was talking about Thackeray. Do you remember in the book *The Newcomes* where Colonel Newcome sent for the Major? He said he couldn't explain that, but you probably could.'

'Yes of course. Delighted. Absolutely, but after tea Charles.'

'Oh no,' said Jack, 'come on, let's have it now.'

'Ahem, ah – well dammit, we're having tea!'

As he left, the Squadron Leader said, 'Dammit Meyer, you set that up didn't you!'

'I'm afraid I did, but it's really what you needed.'

'God! That boy!'

There was, however, an even more important aspect to this typical story, as Jack admitted later:

That's what started it and that man brought in customers. He told everyone about us. He'd even butt into other people's conversations if they were talking about education. Once he dragged a couple of chaps off the train at Castle Cary, the station nearest Street. 'Did I hear you say that your son was not doing well at Eton, Sir? I'll tell you what to do – I'll take you there now – we'll get out at the next station.'

Here Jack saw a means of survival. His advisers, or detractors, were probably right in that it would be unwise to try and start a conventional school, but because his teaching quickly got to the fundamental issues of where a child was, and how they could learn successfully, his methods were obviously highly suitable for solving and salvaging educational problems.

Once I was on my own – after the visit from the Maharaja there was only one thing to do and that was to live. We took everyone – most of them needing repair jobs – once we were seen to mend them better than anyone else could we were in with a fighting chance.

His local reputation for being able to do this became Millfield's salvation, and any young person from the age of twelve to around eighteen or nineteen who had a problem, or needed a particular qualification was welcome. However, there were two things that quickly emerged as being not to his liking. First, any pupil who was aspiring to or being pushed by enthusiastic parents into an exam or qualification beyond his or her reach was soon put wise to that fact, and secondly those who wanted a 'crammer' were quickly pointed back down Millfield's drive. Jack had no interest whatsoever in teaching parrots or indeed in becoming one himself. In that channel lay repetition, tedium and boredom, and boredom was never on Jack's menu. Jack taught in order that pupils could learn, not merely remember.

Thus it was that Millfield gradually emerged on the scene. There were no grand fanfares, or announcements in *The Times* or society magazines. All that happened was that Jack quietly started to provide a necessary service. Millfield could not even have been called a school in the accepted sense of the word, it was more like a coaching establishment. It was in this connection that an important local family, the Dickinsons of Kingweston House, first heard of the place. Rollo and Ella were having dinner with Captain W.F. Dickinson and his wife when it emerged that their son, Caleb, needed his School Certificate for entry into Cirencester Agricultural College. Having been to Harrow, he duly arrived at Millfield where he got his certificate. From that time a special relationship grew between these families and, as with the Squadron Leader, their recommendation produced more pupils. At Millfield, Caleb was in the good company of other ex-Harrovians, Edward (Eddy) Greenwood and Mick Noel-Buxton. Another place which was to feature largely in Millfield's development was Edgarley Hall. At this time it was occupied by the Thomas-Ferrands and their son, Hugo, a flying officer who sought a permanent RAF commission and promotion. Twelve places were available and he got in on the second or third. Jack liked to say that knowledge was only really tested when trying to teach others, but could not have applied this dictum to himself while teaching Hugo aerial navigation!

Those seeking qualifications like the School Certificate had to cover a range of subjects, and although Jack was fairly agile at keeping a page or two in front of his pupils, it became obvious that having staff with other

*A forward glance against the Australians, playing for The Gentlemen at Lords, 1938.
Meyer is batting to M.G. Waite*

disciplines was necessary. In order to rectify the situation he phoned
the educational recruitment agency Gabbitas-Thring, who said that
they had various likely people on their books and would lend Jack an
office to interview them in London. He had to admit that he could
offer practically nothing in the way of remuneration. On the morning
appointed for the interviews he arrived at Paddington station and took
a taxi to Gabbitas-Thring's offices where he saw a long queue of
people. Being a little confused by this he was unsure whether he
should join the queue or go straight in because he had an
appointment. To try and settle the affair he asked a chap in the queue
what was going on.

'Oh, haven't you heard? Some madman in Somerset has started a new
school and needs staff. He's interviewing this morning.'

But it was not for this reason he found these interviews humiliating,
it was more because the depression had thrown excellent people out of
their jobs and he was interviewing men with far greater experience and
qualifications than he himself had. By the end of 1936 Jack had five
staff teaching seventeen pupils, and this not only enabled most of their
needs to be covered, but also opened the door just wide enough to
allow him time to file his application for Somerset County Cricket
Club.

His cricketing pedigree gave him a fairly quick entry into the county side, and he was fortunate to be given a warm welcome. The regional press announced on Saturday 27 June 1936, that

R.J.O. Meyer, the Cambridge Blue, made his first appearance for Somerset, and although his figures may not appeal, believe me, he is a player of class – and will be a great asset to Somerset when he can spare the time to play.

Later, another editorial also welcomed him:

One man I should like to see playing regularly for Somerset is R.J.O. Meyer, the Cambridge Blue, who came out of the match with Yorkshire – only his second for Somerset – with 5 wickets for 111 and 43 and 32 runs.

This was the beginning of a long association with the county side and provided introductions to such notable cricketers as Harold Gimblett, Arthur Wellard, Wally Luckes and Bertie Buse – all great stalwarts of the 'Cidermen'. With the exception of a match against the MCC in which he took seven wickets, his contribution during this first season was more as batsman than bowler, and nowhere was this more evident than in the last game against Lancashire at Taunton. The visitors had made an enormous 423 first innings total, and Somerset could only reply with 253, an excellent 127 being contributed by Mitchell-Innes. Following-on for their second innings, the opening batsman again went cheaply until Mitchell-Innes stopped the rot. Jack joined him, playing himself in and reaching a century in just under three hours. He was then batting superbly with style and panache and put on a second century in about one hour, his last fifty being in under half an hour. To be fair, Lancashire did not take the game too seriously after tea because it was inevitable that Somerset could now draw the match. Accordingly, the whole side, including the wicketkeeper had a bowl.

Earlier in the year Jack had also been involved in a piece of rare excitement in the golfing world. He had always been a keen and very accomplished player and had entered the English Golf Championships at Deal. He got through the first two rounds and then met Cyril Tolley, who had twice been amateur champion. They started off fairly evenly, but Jack had his 'fluking iron' out that day, which was not to Tolley's liking. There is a tradition that if one ball is only a few inches from the hole and the other a metre or so away, the player whose ball is farthest away will concede to the other, or they might agree to 'halve' the hole depending upon the number of shots. Jack had refused an invitation

from Tolley to concede a hole when the champion's ball was 18 in
away, and Tolley, somehow having missed the put, was then in a foul
mood.

He drove straight down the middle of the fairway. I drove further –
straight into the bush. The spectators encouraged me to 'pick it up,
pick it up'. 'No. I'm going to give it one more belt', and from about
100 yd I clipped the top of the ball. It shot along the ground, cleared
the canal onto the green and went straight into the hole. He was not
amused. The next hole was 500 yd off. We both got to the edge of a
very long green together. He putted to within a couple of feet of the
hole again, I removed an enormous divot and the ball got halfway
there. I rushed up, gave it a good whack and bobble, bobble, into the
hole it went. I won't tell you what he said.

There followed the incident at the ninth hole, described by at least half
a dozen newspapers as 'disturbing' or 'uncomfortable'. Jack was now
leading by one hole and his ball was about 4 in from the ninth and
Tolley's 18 in. Offering to halve it, Jack said, 'That's good enough.'

But as Jack's caddy picked up his ball Tolley putted, sank the ball and
claimed the hole, saying, 'I didn't give you that.'

'Well you might have said so in a voice that I could hear.'

Unfortunately Jack was very upset by this behaviour and lost to Tolley
by three and two. For all his enthusiasm and ability he was a sporting
gentleman, not always happy to win, rarely surprised to lose and always
delighted to take part. This kind of behaviour he found exceedingly
distasteful and he was regrettably reported in the press as declaring it to
be his first and last championship. 'Such things don't happen in
cricket.'

It is interesting to note that few Millfield teams of that era were called
by the name of Millfield, because it didn't mean much to anybody and it
was, in any case, still uncertain how long Millfield would be around.
More often teams would go under the name of R.J.O. Meyer's XI or
R.J.O. Meyer's XV. Downside, the excellent Catholic school, was host to
R.J.O. Meyer's XI, and as usual Jack was short of players, so one of
Downside's juniors, Hugh Watts, was commandeered onto his side. Jack
was impressed with the fourteen year old's play and invited him to stay at
Millfield during the summer holidays and enjoy some cricket. From that
time Hugh Watts spent every summer at Millfield House and
commented:

In the mornings we were in the nets or would find a tennis court, and in the afternoons we would play in some cricket match somewhere in the Street or Taunton area. He was certainly the best cricket coach I ever experienced and, of course, as a net bowler he was unsurpassed. Five minutes in-swingers, five away, five of leg-breaks and five at off-breaks and then the whole lot all mixed up when we learned to watch the bowlers grip, run-up and action. I certainly learned more from Jack than anyone else.

To be gregarious by nature must be a distinct advantage for a headmaster, although in larger schools, particularly boarding schools, the remnants of privacy can become jealously guarded. However, Jack was pleased to see everybody who had an interest in Millfield; this must have been an enlightening experience for some parents who felt that their children were accepted at schools on sufferance only. Admittedly, during that early period there was a great need for new pupils, and those who came experienced what so many others did, the feeling that Jack was really interested in them. He wanted to know their likes, dislikes and what their opinions were. There was an immediate contrast to the 'seen and not heard' brigade. One of those early pupils who interested Jack so much, and to whom he later referred as 'one of the bravest men I knew', was a boy called Colin Hodgkinson. He was as courageous and pugnacious as a scholar as he was as a pilot. During one evening Jack, Joyce and some of the boys visited the traditional Tor Fair in Glastonbury where there was a boxing booth extending an invitation to one and all who might be prepared to risk their features and futures for a rather small prize. Colin was quite prepared to take on anyone and that included Jo-Jo, said to be champion of the Congo. There was little question as to who the winner was other than the professional, but Colin got his prize. Later he suffered an appalling accident training to be a pilot, and, like Douglas Bader, who later became a friend, lost both legs. However, he requalified as a pilot and distinguished himself in the Battle of Britain.

By 1937 the number of regular pupils had risen to thirty-three, and there were now ten staff to look after them. Millfield House was like a large and happy family. At the younger end of the scale Gillian and Jacqueline were romping about, and there were pupils of all ages up to nineteen who led a life which could hardly be equated with 'school' in the least. Some of them had cars, and smoking was not against the rules, though only permitted at certain times and places. The ten staff had to be very flexible about what, who and when they taught, and could expect to be roped in for the odd domestic chore at times. As numbers slowly grew, some kind of order, and even the odd rule, became desirable. Jack's outlook was rather unique. He could remember the stinging whacks for petty transgressions at Haileybury, and concluded that as a basis all should have as much freedom as they could handle. If they abused the privilege, it could soon be withdrawn. This was the ideal, and it was applied to all pupils as far as possible, although the younger ones required more looking after and so had less freedom as a result.

Within the relaxed family atmosphere was cushioned the all-important necessity of work. The fact that little of any worthwhile or lasting value came without concentrated effort was a reason for Millfield's existence, and all other disciplines were subservient to it. Jack had learnt through his own education, and from his long classroom in the palace, that to try to impose concentrated effort was a waste of energy. Pupils had to be encouraged to succeed; it was only when there was a real desire within each of them that improvement could be made. Further, this desire could only be cultivated when the pupil was helped to discover that it was quite within his or her capacity to manage a subject at which they had been failing for years. Jack found that there was only one reasonably successful way to prove to pupils that they had it in them. The first essential was to treat them like people, because that was what they were, people at a certain stage of their lives, who while fortunate to have healthy bodies and lively minds were susceptible to a few very strong influences. Parents, schools and peer groups all too quickly put them into a compartment and told them whether they were good, bad, or clever, or stupid. The effect of inappropriate teaching or insensitive handling was almost impossible for any young person to correct unaided. Jack's first steps were to find out how much they knew and how much they understood what they knew, and then he would establish the rate at which they could begin to learn. At its simplest, this was discovered by watching a pupil carefully while teaching. Signs of boredom could mean two things, either the teaching was too slow or it was too fast and pupils had lost the thread. The application of these theories, which he considered basic common sense, began to produce results which the educational world and parents looked upon with some awe. Boys began to arrive from the country's leading public schools looking for success in all manner of exams including School Certificate, service entry and university entry. Of these, 91 per cent achieved their goals. Millfield survived because it got results, so parents and others supported it.

When Millfield had only three dozen or so pupils Jack demonstrated that the school was different by reflecting one of his own passions and employing Captain Roy Hern to look after riding. Brilliant at equitation, he trained pupils and horses to the highest degree, and some who had a

Millfield boys and horses, c. *1937*

year of his stern instruction swear that they can still remember how to
ride, groom, clean tack and muck out the stables, even though they may
not have ridden since. Millfield's rugby team was one of the few
institutions to benefit as Hitler threw his weight about, because there
were increasing numbers of boys who wanted to sit the services
examinations to get into top establishments like Sandhurst, Cranwell or
Dartmouth, or at least ensure that they got a commission. This meant
that Millfield built up a team of healthy sixth formers from Britain's top
schools who wanted and expected to play rugby. Jack was delighted and
arranged fixtures by the dozen for his team who were nearly invincible.
As their formidable reputation spread Jack rather slyly referred to them
as his School XV, which was not altogether convincing because they were
knocking local sides out by anything up to fifty points to nil! This period
was also one during which Jack was able to compare his performance
with other schools, because Millfield's representatives regularly took
between 20 and 30 per cent of the limited services places for which they
entered. There was justifiable pride in an establishment that had only
seventeen staff and forty on the roll.

One of the more notable young pupils who arrived before the Second
World War was Wyndham Bailey, who will always be associated with

Millfield. His reasons for coming were typical: he had been having a rather thin time of it at his prep school, and needed assistance to gain his Common Entrance Exam to enter the next level of education. As a junior of around thirteen or fourteen years he was immediately impressed by the older pupils, although he shared little of their lives. They all seemed to own sports cars, smoked and had a very adult life style. He, on the other hand, was in a very small group of three, who were all successful in the Common Entrance. Millfield suited Wyndham, who had wider interests and abilities than many of his age, and instead of moving away to join an established school, he remained there to continue his education. Millfield provided a marvellous introduction to all the sports and the headmaster seemed to have a passion for each of them in the same way that he appeared to have a passion for following everybody's academic progress. He was apparently not content with merely scanning the mid-term or end of term tests, but seemed to both know, and wanted to know, what any pupil was doing at any point during the unpredictable twenty-four hour day.

Wyndham noted that there were quite a few pupils who would probably never be able to enjoy that recreation because they were physically handicapped. Jack saw no barrier to having them, provided that they could be properly cared for and wanted to learn. The staff who taught Wyndham appeared to him as being fairly strict and insistent upon well-written prep and exact time-keeping. In such an environment progress was inevitable, as it was virtually impossible to deviate from the straight and narrow path. 'Daddy' Fisher taught classics, Bud Atkinson French and Jim Bunbury, otherwise known as 'Jungle Jim', taught English. The reason for his nickname is obscure, but might have been something to do with his lolloping gait, or the way that this exceptionally tall man leaned on the roof beams as he mused over some didactic point or other in his teaching hut. Miss Drake was an inspired maths teacher who ruled with a rod of iron except on Sundays, when she would invite the boys to tea in her house in Street. Jack seemed to teach everything, including divinity. His approach was very relaxed, and he interpreted the Bible stories in a philosophical yet approachable manner. It seemed that he could speak of Jesus as a man as well as the Son of God. He hardly ever had a failure for the subject, and his pupils learnt that while he was certainly not going to be dictatorial concerning religion, Sunday worship was a rule and all pupils were expected to choose and practise the religion of their choice. The Church of England seemed to be popular, not only because it was one of the predominant faiths, but because after a pupil had been confirmed, devotional duties commenced with Holy Communion at the 'Tin Tabernacle' in Street at

Outdoor activities, including digging the swimming pool, c. 1947

eight on a Sunday morning, after which the remainder of the day was gloriously free.

Thursday saw a very different routine under the heading of Public Works. Like many other Millfield activities, including games, it was supervised by prefects, and the purpose was to maintain the fabric of the buildings, help in the gardens and look after the sports facilities in the grounds. All of Millfield's pupils took part and did so in good spirit because Jack was insistent that it was not to be treated as a chore or punishment. Pupils did all the things that contractors ought to have done, but no-one minded because they all got involved and did their bit, as Jack said, 'in giving something back to society'. Although it was to be hoped that none were too aware of it, Public Works saved Millfield quite a lot of money.

Public Works also played its part in attracting new pupils. Air Vice Marshall Struan Marshall bought his thirteen-year-old son to Millfield for an interview. It seemed that the boy had had the opportunity of a scholarship to Epsom, but there were some holes in his educational background that would need filling to be able to take advantage of it. The boy was a 'loner' and found Millfield attractive because he had a great love of the countryside. Unfortunately he was also a keen and competitive swimmer, which should have made the choice of a school nearer Bristol where there were excellent facilities, more logical. Having sensed that the father and boy were ready to choose Millfield, Jack was not about to have the opportunity of a precious bright new pupil lost through lack of a swimming pool.

'Well yes, swimming is of course something which we take seriously – excellent exercise for everyone. All at Millfield are encouraged to swim for exercise and pleasure and I am pleased to be able to tell you that by the time your son arrives our own pool will be well on the way to completion. There are the plans on my desk,' said Jack with an airy gesture to a heap of envelopes. The deal was struck and father and son left happily, contemplating the many benefits Millfield seemed to offer. The story was rather different for those already attending. Foraging parties were sent to scour Street and Glastonbury for every spade, shovel, bucket and wheelbarrow which could be bought, begged or borrowed. The land to the south of the house fell gently to a wooded area where there was a duck pond, and after a careful survey plans were rapidly drawn up for the new outdoor swimming pool in the same area. Then the work began in earnest as the whole of the Public Works were committed to digging and carting away soil. Even a kind of railway was constructed to carry the spoil away and Jack used every ounce of encouragement and bribery to keep the project going. The scheme was one to be proud of and made a beautiful, natural place for boys to swim, surrounded by trees and wild flowers with a view up to Millfield House. It was an important milestone for Jack, who commented:

The lesson to be learned was obvious, and we learned it thoroughly. Very early on it was clear that if you want a good school you must have better things to offer than your competitors. We decided that what parents wanted most was a good healthy atmosphere and the best teaching at all levels.

The completed pool in 1947

By 1939 Millfield's reputation had spread and there was a modest but regular trickle of new pupils who would turn up each week or two. What Jack described as the cream of the country's public schools with good brains and backgrounds were hurrying to get into the services and formed an excellent group of prefects. Although it was unlikely that they attended for longer than eighteen months, the contrast between their traditional public school regime and the realistic, responsible disciplines that they enjoyed at Millfield could not have been greater. Also their academic progress was enormously enhanced by intelligent teaching in small groups. Many years later they looked back at Millfield as 'their school', even though they spent much more time at other establishments.

However, Millfield could not ignore the gathering clouds in Europe, and reluctantly conceded with the rest of the country that a stand had to be made against those whom they had defied amidst stupefying carnage only twenty-one years before. Having just about got Millfield off the ground, Joyce and Jack had to contemplate radical changes which the conflict would inevitably bring, and they had to face the chance that they might not survive the next formidable challenge.

CHAPTER SEVEN

The War Years

On 5 September 1939, two days after the declaration of war, Jack took the seniors up to Bristol to enlist. He volunteered for the RAF and rather fancied being a pilot, and his staff were told that they were free to enlist or serve the war effort wherever they could. He had some notion of electing a caretaker headmaster to hold the fort until he returned. The senior boys trained by Jack for the Special Services Exams were immediately classed as potential officer material, and he hoped many more would be coming while hostilities continued. Initially, however, the opposite thing happened, because the importance of getting the country's fighting services trained and up to strength as quickly as possible meant that they did not have time to spend months in preparation for admission. Almost anyone who was of suitable age and fitness and turned up at a recruitment parade was in.

At the grand old age of thirty-four, Jack was advised that he was rather too old to be trained as a pilot. This he countered with evidence of his being an exceptionally good shot, to try to get a place as an aircraft rear gunner. Jack had everything packed in suitcases ready to leave for training, but the way ahead was still not clear because it was soon pointed out that as yet no aircraft gun turret was large enough to hold him. Then an order came through from a nameless officer to whom Millfield probably owed its future, because if Jack had become a rear gunner there would have been a less than sporting chance that he would have seen the end of the war. Instead he was asked to form an Air Training Corps, Squadron No. 941, and given the rank of Flying Officer. This ATC unit proved very successful and prepared many young men for the RAF. Jack ran it with Squadron Leader The Lord St Audries and liaised with RAF Western Zoyland. The gliding instructor from nearby RAF Locking was Prince Bira, the famous racing driver, who owned the fabulous ERA cars which brought him many successes. Jack also got involved with the National Defence Force and the Home Guard, and became ARP warden for Millfield. Still he was not entirely happy with his role and went about quoting Doctor Johnson, who had said: 'A man must feel meanly about himself if he hasn't at one time fought for his country.'

Joyce at leisure – a rare moment around 1937 – and as a Volunteer Nurse during the war, when she worked at Butleigh Hospital and various camps

From having the strongest rugger XV, Millfield, having lost all its seniors, was again at the bottom of the league. They lost to everyone, including Wells Cathedral School, which had only twenty boys left on the roll. What surprised Jack was that the numbers at Millfield unexpectedly rose instead of falling. In fact from 1939 to 1940 they grew from forty to fifty-eight, with nineteen on the staff, pupils mostly arriving from the Home Counties for fear of possible invasion of the South and East coasts.

Joyce bore an extraordinary workload throughout the war years, not only with her duties as mother, house mother, and confidante for Millfield, but also in many local voluntary capacities. As a VAD nurse she was trained to look after British and New Zealand casualties as well as local mothers and babies. Night duty at nearby Butleigh Hospital would be immediately followed by a sick parade at Street's Camp Reception Station and visits to evacuee children from London who were billeted in the area. When physical strength should have deserted one of such slight build, spiritual strength remained. It was certainly this that helped the healing of the people to whom she ministered. Apparently she was fondly nicknamed the 'little sergeant' and was saluted by both officers and civilians. The training she received stood Millfield in good stead for many years after the war, as did the inner strength discovered through her arduous duties. This quality was not something hard or merely tough, on the contrary it was completely feminine, and to say that she won admiration from the thousands whose lives she touched would be altogether too cool.

With the end of the 'phoney' war news soon came of Millfield's first feats and casualties in battle. Two gallant young men on Jack's staff were killed during their first week of battle. Headley Rawson and John Jarmain were both excellent teachers, keen on Millfield's unusual ways, and in them Jack had seen the future strength of the school. There had been no doubt whatsoever that they would return after the war and the tragedy of their loss brought back memories of Haileybury and some sympathy for the gouty old Dug-Outs who saw their pupils' names posted on the casualty list day after day. Jack had never dreamt that this would be happening to him. However, he had no doubts about the need to challenge Hitler, or the fact that he helped to prepare boys to do precisely that, and he was immensely proud of them all. Frank Bristowe came from Haileybury because he couldn't pass the entry exams for the Royal Marines. By the time Jack had got him ready he was about nineteen years old and enjoyed the odd pint of beer. Pubs were off limits and Frank got beaten for his first visit, or the first one that Jack heard about. Then he did it again, which put Jack into something of a quandary because technically a sacking was in order. As the Marines exams were only some two weeks away this couldn't be done, so a worse punishment was devised for this interesting and highly active young man. 'All your spare time you will spend outside my window walking about.'

After about an hour of this he knocked on the door and asked to see Jack. 'Oh for God's sake Sir, do something – surely you can beat me or something.'

The request was denied by Jack, who said that he could let him off if he gave his word not to go into a pub again while at Millfield. Many years afterwards Lieutenant Colonel Bristowe said, 'That was one of the finest lessons I learned in my life.'

Another great character was Norman Ricketts, whose father was a builder in Bristol. He wanted to get the Navy Special Entrance Exam in one year. Jack saw that he was being a little optimistic and advised him that while he applauded his aims, the first hurdle to overcome was the School Certificate, where a number of credits would be necessary. 'But sir, do I have to waste time doing the School Certificate? I want to get straight on.'

Jack assured him that he had to sit the exam.

'Oh no Sir, I think it's quite unnecessary.'

'Unnecessary? What do you mean?'

'Well Sir, all you have to do is to certify that if I sat the exam I would have passed and the Navy would accept it.'

'Tell me boy, why would you not have sat the exam?'

'Because I was ill Sir.'

'Good God. I've never heard of such a thing. I don't believe it! You expect me to give you a certificate.'

'Yes, if you would, Sir. I think there are quite a few things I could do for the school sir. I started a band at Bristol and I improved the corps. It wasn't up to standard so I got a complete set of new rifles and uniforms off the Army. Then I collected a couple of hundred around Bristol and we bought all the instruments with that.'

Jack felt that he had almost met his match, and the boy's obvious enthusiasm mollified his rising anger. 'Look, this is all very well, but I don't even know what standard you are. One thing the Navy Special Entry are fussy about is maths, so let's see where you are on that. Tell me, what are two-thirds of six.'

'Two-thirds of six? Well. I mean – a half or something is it? I don't think those things are too important, do you Sir?'

After a hardworking year Norman got his School Certificate, and during the same period he had the prefects eating out of his hand, organized the building and stocking of chicken runs to supply Millfield with precious eggs, and started a band after purchasing all the instruments with money he had raised. However, looking at the Navy Special Entrance Exam he said, 'Honestly Sir, I know I can't pass this, so really my only hope is for you to give me a note saying that I would have passed it which will get me in on a temporary basis.'

'I'm very sorry Norman, I can't do that. There's absolutely nothing doing.'

'Well, in that case Sir, I shall be leaving. I think I might be able to get a commission, preferably for the Royal Marines.'

'Well if you must, you must. I shall be sorry to lose you. You have done some magnificent work for us.'

About a week later Jack received a phone call from the officer in charge of commissions for the Royal Navy. 'Is that the headmaster of Millfield? I've got a man here named Ricketts, and he says you will vouch for him. Can you tell me what kind of chap he is?'

'Well, all I can say is that if you want someone who is capable of adding up the mess bill, the answer is "No certainly not", but if you want somebody who could be called upon to make a battleship out of a bar of soap in a week, I think you've got your man.'

Another week later Norman was a one-pip Marine. Six months later he had two pips.

Throughout the war Jack kept in touch with those who were able or inclined to write to Millfield. They had often come from the best schools, had excellent backgrounds and were determined to get on. The terms in which he wrote to one of them, John Carter, a year after he left reflect this:

My dear old John, many thanks for your very interesting letter giving us the lowdown on life at Lee-on-Solent [RN] Air Station. . . . We all, including your friend Mr Taylor, send you our best wishes for the New Year and your career – look us up when you get a chance, and keep us in touch.

Mr Taylor was, of course, the gardener. He had taken on special constable duties and one evening arrested John, Olly Brockman and others for riding their bikes without lights returning from the fish and chip shop in Street. While many Old Boys wrote, one or two others made flying visits of a distinctly exciting kind – generally at about 300 mph at chimneypot level flying a Hurricane or Spitfire. The complete disruption of lessons, though officially annoying, was excellent for morale, according to the headmaster.

It was during 1940 that we were blessed by what was certainly one of the great strokes of good fortune of all my large allotment of that very necessary ingredient of success. This was the arrival of a gifted lady cousin, Elnith Sankey and her daughters, the eldest of whom, Amothe, was to become school secretary.

There were two other sisters, Gillian, who became a nurse, and Everel, who at the age of thirteen became one of Millfield's first girl pupils. Amothe had been working in the Chamber of Commerce in Bristol and was a highly efficient and competent secretary. Although only aged about twenty when she joined Millfield, Jack immediately recognized an intelligence and orderliness that he badly needed in his expanding organization, especially for paperwork and administration. Before Amothe's arrival his office had been in the roof of the house, with the family living-room on the ground floor occasionally doubling as an interview room or a place to welcome guests. Growing stacks of administrative paperwork had taken root in the living-room, whose function slowly changed to be used more and more for schoolwork. Now that he had a full-time secretary, the living-room became even more desirable as a study, and was in a very suitable position for this function. The window and a large outside door and porch looked south and other doors opened into the hall and dining-rooms, thus putting it at the hub of Millfield House. One of Amothe's first jobs was to file and sort out a mass of papers that were in vaguely organized heaps identified as examinations, correspondence and running costs. To have all of this organized in logical fashion, and to lay hands on an important document in seconds instead of turning half the room upside-down was a revelation to Jack. Other great virtues that emerged quickly were Amothe's fidelity and loyalty, for which Jack was to be infinitely grateful. She took up her position in the corner of the study from where she heard everything and knew everything about everybody – pupils, staff and parents included – much to their everlasting respect and occasional trepidation. But in 1940 there were practical matters to be attended to, and Jack, soon becoming familiar with the very real necessity of versatility at Millfield, especially during the war, asked her to take over riding while Captain Roy Hern was away doing war service. Another small but mighty significant contribution Amothe made during her early days concerned the way that people addressed Jack. 'Sir', 'Headmaster', or 'Mr Meyer' were generally used by boys. Staff, some of whom were quite old enough to be his father, also called him 'Meyer' or 'Jack'. Amothe had seen a similar circumstance at her previous job, and a universal and respectful solution had been to refer to seniors as 'the bosses'. Therefore, because she had become the means through which memos, telephone calls and other communications got to Jack, she began to refer to him as 'the Boss', and in a short time others started to do the same.

Of Elnith Sankey, Jack said: 'She was the only entirely selfless person I have met', and of her teaching: 'she not only kept the meadows green, but helped flowers and even trees grow in the most unlikely bare, parched places.' Elnith's first task was to take over the increasing numbers of juniors who had started to come at the age of twelve to thirteen to take Common Entrance Exams for various public schools. Jack's success at this task created a valuable source of income for the school, and Elnith complemented the care of these youngsters by teaching history and scripture. He said that she made the Bible stories truly meaningful to boys of all religious beliefs. She was also a competent artist and later ran that department from a mock Swiss chalet in the garden.

The youngest Sankey, Everel, joined the juniors to gain her Common Entrance qualification. According to Wyndham Bailey, who joined her in some classes, she was also very bright, sharing her family's natural intelligence, and was also quite a 'toughy', able to take good care of herself in predominantly male company. In fact, as Jack said, 'She went along with anything the thirteen year olds got up to – mayhem of all kinds – once assisting to catapult all the windows out of one of the classrooms.'

In the war glass was very difficult to get so the crime was rather more serious than the pupils probably suspected. 'So I beat the boys hard and sent for her, but she taught me a lesson. I said "I can't beat you, you're a girl." "Why not?" she asked. "Well I can't, but I want you to know that

Elnith Sankey teaching in the Swiss Chalet, 1947. From left to right, Douglas Merrie (?), Elnith Sankey, Fabienne, Richard Bevan

what you have done is a very serious thing" – she started crying – "it is the most disgraceful thing. Wartime shortages and so on" – more crying – "now wait a minute, wait a minute" – uncontrollable weeping – "look my dear you have been very naughty but it's not that bad. Please stop crying" – she couldn't and she didn't – "I'll think of some suitable punishment for you later, but just now I am a little flummoxed, dry your eyes and have a sweet. I'll talk to you later!"'

Jack saw her to the study door which he closed with a sigh of relief. Then, outside the door he heard one of the offending boys ask, 'What happened, what did he say?'

'Ha, Ha. Silly old fool didn't say anything. Just gave me a sweet.'

Unfortunately Everel's ploy, while not being exceptional by the normal thirteen-year-old girl's standard, cut Jack to the quick, and had a profound effect upon the ideas he was forming about co-education for the next ten years or so. There had always been girls around Millfield and women on the staff because he was strongly aware that their presence had a good effect on the behaviour of boys, eliminating the sniggering side of their nature, and eventually helping them to behave more naturally in female company. He remembered a Haileybury friend telling him about his first date with a young lady after leaving. The tension was almost unbearable, and he described it as 'going out with an unexploded bomb'. Jack also remembered that his own early fancies had been fairly appalling as well. He was sure also that the 'entirely unnatural dearth of women' at Haileybury and other establishments easily led to homosexual experiments in those slightly inclined. Therefore he had long since made his mind up that girls should be at Millfield. His experience with Everel modified the experiment somewhat, and for many years there were no girls under the age of fifteen, that being the time when the Boss thought they would start acting rather more predictably. Some time later he had another encounter which should have shown him that Everel's faux pas was not as dreadful as he thought. One of Millfield's girls gave him a painting of a young girl standing on some rocks gazing out to sea, her little dress blowing in the wind. They talked about art and this painting for some time, as usual Jack imbuing the subject with various human virtues. At this the young lady said:

> Boss, I can see that you think the girl is thinking about all the wonderful things in life, the love of her parents, the flowers in the garden or her favourite doll, but she is not. She is actually wondering how she can pinch the new tennis racket her brother's got, make sure she can get enough cream buns for tea and wheedle some more pocket money out of her father. That's what people are really like Boss.

Jack was somewhat flattened by such worldliness.

The war took its dismal toll on Millfield boys and within a year Cay Dickinson from Kingweston House, Dusty Miller and Michael Stevenson were lost. Jack felt deeply that such an awful price had to be paid to keep right on one's side. Joyce felt those losses, too, with the sympathy that perhaps only a mother can. Rationing was in full swing and Amothe looked after the books with a meticulous eye to ensure that what little there was went fairly to everyone. The almost non-existent ration of meat and ghastly reconstituted, powdered egg was supplemented with vegetables and fruit from Millfield's garden.

Through the Old Haileyburian network Jack received a surprise summons to the United Universities Club, where Deputy Prime Minister Clement Attlee wished to discuss his fourteen-year-old son, Martyn. It seemed that he had been diagnosed by Doctor William Brown as having word blindness. Attlee had been advised to seek help and Millfield already had a reputation for dealing with such problems. Jack eventually got the boy into the School of Navigation in Southampton.

After dinner I was invited to the bar of the House of Commons where I met his colleagues Aneurin Bevan, Dingle Foot and a Mr Ramsbotham. What I learned that night about life behind the scenes made my hair curl and I could only hope that the girl behind the bar had taken some extra special oath of secrecy. As my name is not Spycatcher I fear that history will never be able to record it, but God knows how we ever won the war!

The last thing Jack seemed to remember of that evening was walking through the blackout with Attlee singing their old school song, 'Vivat Haileyburia', at the tops of their voices.

The Playhouse Cinema, Street, was the next meeting place for the Right Honourable C.R. Attlee and Jack. He had come to see Martyn and had been persuaded to address an audience after inspecting the Glastonbury and Street squadrons of the ATC at Strode School, Street. Since it was Sunday, the rector of Street presided over the gathering and after the audience sang 'Jerusalem' he gave a little preamble to Attlee's address. That Attlee was keen to speak was obvious because at every pause he stood to begin his oration, only to subside as the Reverend Daunton-Fear got his Sunday pennyworth in. The young gentlemen of Millfield were somewhat amused to see the way Attlee hooked his thumbs into his braces, pulling them out from under his waistcoat in workmanlike manner when making a point. He spoke about the progress of the war and the importance of maintaining the effort when it was over. He was an inspired speaker and impressed all the audience with the feeling that each one of them had a part to play. Attlee was a man with a very real social conscience and since his management of the Haileybury Boy's Club in Stepney had preached the socialist doctrine to all. He was particularly popular in Street, which Jack said was originally so left-wing that even Liberals had their windows broken. In this context it is interesting to speculate on how a place like Millfield, easily associated with something rather exclusive, could exist. Undoubtedly its association and support from the Clark family did much to foster acceptance, and also Jack's insistence that the school facilities should always be available to those living in the town. Many local children visited Millfield regularly as well as attending academic and sporting holiday courses.

During the vacations Jack still worked on Millfield's grounds, and most unfortunately he slipped a disc while attempting to start a recalcitrant motor mower. He had to bear bouts of agonizing pain for the remainder of the war years and for one or two more afterwards since there was no effective treatment, and the top medical people were all on war service.

Remarkably, the number of pupils in the school continued to grow – from 40 in 1939 to 133 in 1945. Although most boys went straight into

A group of prefects around Wyndham Bailey, Senior Prefect, in 1944. Back row, left to right: Jimmy Stockley, Brian (?) Phillips, D.C. Edwick, Michael Wainwright. Front row: Pat Richardson, Geoffery Thomas (?), Wyndham Bailey, R.C. Clayton, David Fond

the services, some still came to Millfield to ensure a sound basic education. The strongest growth in numbers was still in young people preparing for the Common Entrance Exam. In the past they had left Millfield as soon as the exam was taken, but some now decided to stay on to progress within the school to higher level exams, and Jack soon discovered the value of having pupils who had been around for a number of years. When he was barely sixteen, Wyndham Bailey was made senior prefect, Millfield's equivalent to head boy. In this capacity he was in a position to watch this new school emerging, seeing Jack every day and becoming an important liaison with the rest of Millfield. Such meetings would normally occur after Wyndham had done the necessary rounds each night to see that the house was secure, and all windows and doors locked.

I used to see Boss every night, and there he was surrounded with newspapers working on until at least two o'clock in the morning. And really all he used to tell me was what had happened that day, what was happening tomorrow, the fact that he didn't think much of what we did yesterday, that we really do need to get that lot together or what's going on with so and so? We also used to talk about Public Works when he would say that we had a problem and needed to shore up the pavilion or build up the riding jumps that had fallen down.

They would also discuss the selection of boys for various teams, or any pupils who were being a problem. The head boy or senior prefect would be responsible for conveying Jack's ideas to the prefects, and through them down to the whole school, and he therefore held a position of considerable responsibility. Surprisingly, Jack allowed the prefects to beat other boys for minor offences. In doing so they had to establish guilt and ensure that the recipient was fit to take a beating; those who were ill or under some emotional strain were never beaten. Serious cases would be handled by Jack, but he hated having to beat anyone. Corporal punishment was only used if a boy had repeatedly sinned, showed little sign of repentance or in the worst cases had been dishonest or devious. However, it still seems odd that beating was acceptable in such an educationally enlightened establishment. Generally Jack was quite inventive regarding punishments, and beating was not an automatic response. He once caught some seniors on their way back from the local pub where they had been entertaining 'Rosie', a very friendly local lady, he singled out the most responsible among them, who happened to be the head boy, and made him give a speech to the assembled school on how he had turned over a new leaf.

There was a punishment known as 'ponding', which was administered by boys, and used in exceptional circumstances where an individual had been constantly rude, selfish and uncooperative. The crime did not merit a beating because it was not serious enough at any one instance, but the cumulative effect of such unreasonable behaviour needed some kind of response. The senior prefect would go to Jack to indicate that the offender justified the 'ponding'. If Jack thought it should go ahead, he would ask when they intended to do it so that he could be out of the way. At the appointed hour the victim would be arrested and informed about what was going to happen to him and why it was going to happen. Following the sentence he was frogmarched over to the lily pond near Millfield House, stripped off and thrown in. After he got out he would be given a towel and marched down to the duck pond where he would be ceremoniously launched again. Resistance was useless because as the word went round the proceedings would be followed by at least half of the school, although girls were strictly banned. Finally the transgressor would be thrown into the swimming pool, hoiked out and dried off. The ponding was never mentioned again to the boy and no stigma was attached. According to Wyndham, recalcitrant and bloody-minded characters were quickly reformed into helpful, concerned members of Millfield's society.

The expansion in school numbers naturally required more boarding facilities because Millfield House was already severely overcrowded. Bedrooms had been created in every nook and cranny in the roof and responsible boys were billeted out in ten venues by 1945. In 1943 there were nine girls on the roll who lived in the cottage in Millfield's garden with Mrs Sankey. A billet might consist of a normal-sized house with a few boys and a master in charge. Although conditions were spartan, Jack was keen that boys should have a home life of their own where they would be secure and well looked after. Since good tuition and individual attention were to be Millfield's hallmark, more pupils also demanded more teaching rooms. Both these and billets required furniture, so Jack became a familiar figure at local house clearances and auction sales. Pupils therefore found themselves being taught on anything from kitchen stools to settees, which gave a nice homely flavour to such intense teaching. One drawback was that much of the furniture came as lots, and any objects too useless or ghastly would be abandoned on the circular lawn in front of Millfield, creating a curious exhibition of domestic flotsam from bird cages to framed pictures of Mickey Mouse. The property market was dead, and Jack managed to purchase three houses – Restholm, Orchards and Holmcroft – to board pupils and started to form that 'loyal band of servants', as Jack called them, the house parents. Prior to such houses being established desperate situations called for extraordinary solutions. One morning Wyndham was called into Jack's study. 'Wyndham, how would you like to spend the summer term in a tent? There's room for two and you can have whoever you like with you.'

In his own inimitable way Jack made the idea sound like a rare privilege, and of course it made room for two more in the roof of Millfield House. In fairness Jack did not allow himself any privileges as far as accommodation was concerned. Millfield House had always been his residence and was shared increasingly cheek by jowl with the boys. Even during the 1960s his accommodation consisted of only a first-floor living-room and bedroom, divided by and entered from a narrow passage used by boys on their way to the iron ladder taking them to dormitories in the roof. The ladder is remembered with some affection by those who had to use it several times a day. It had an incurable rattle, which was not bad unless you were scaling it at a time when you should have been sleeping peacefully.

Along with all the other shortages, it was also difficult to get good teachers during those war years. Luckily Jack had employed many older staff just before 1939 who had been stupidly retired at the age of sixty or sixty-five by their schools. Millfield, with its small groups and individual teaching, was ideal for those who wished to continue in their profession. With increasing numbers of pupils it was necessary to find even more staff, but of course any able-bodied folk had long since joined the forces unless they were involved in some important civilian role. Some of those who appeared at Millfield were either not wanted in, or had evaded both. As Chaplain, Jack appointed a parson who had come from Canada; he was so impressed by him and his references that he even persuaded the Bishop of Bath and Wells to grant him a licence to officiate in Street. After settling down the Chaplain rather surprised everyone by announcing that he was engaged to a young lady in Street. However, before nuptials could get under way there was a knock at Millfield's door and a sturdy policeman was enquiring after him. It seemed that he was already wanted for bigamy or even trigamy. Everywhere he went, and he certainly got about, the first thing he did was to get engaged. Jack was in good company, because later the same parson managed to hoodwink bishops in Oxford and as far away as Australia. More brilliant references came from a teacher who specialized in stealing textbooks, a rare and desirable commodity during the war, and then selling them to other schools. There was the odd case of the mathematician who had a phobia about his ex-wife, and actually asked the boys to look carefully under their desks and tables before starting his lesson to see if she was hiding there. An ex-Army officer also arrived, who became convinced that two other members of staff were Italian spies. He terminated his employment at Millfield by locking himself in his lodgings bedroom, throwing all the furniture out of the window and threatening his landlady and anyone else who came near the place with a rifle. It wasn't that Jack was a bad judge of character, but staff were desperately needed to keep the wheels turning and he more or less had to look at everyone who came along. Daddy Fisher certainly threatened to, or may even have, put up a notice at the school's entrance: 'All peripatetic professors welcome here'.

It was Daddy Fisher, the Classics master, to whom Jack turned when he sought a school motto to complement the newly commissioned coat of arms. From the name of the house, the heraldic device displayed the sails of a windmill, and Jack felt that the motto should reflect similar associations. After much discussion the choice had come down to either *Molire Molendo* or *Moliri Molendo* and in the end they decided upon the imperative *Molire*. In translation the general meaning was 'Succeed by Grinding', and the motto emphasized to the pupils in no uncertain terms what was expected of them. In 1945 the school's tenth anniversary came up and it was clear that Jack had found a career he enjoyed, and in which he met the kind of success which appealed to him, because it came about through the challenge of helping others to achieve goals that had been considered out of reach. There were, as can be imagined, problems still to be overcome, but already in its short life Millfield had proved itself a survivor in circumstances where no-one would have blamed Jack for quietly closing its doors, and perusing the teaching vacancies in *The Times*. Instead, the war ended with Millfield House bulging from the new intake of juniors, and with a formula for teaching which was so effective that it could be described as revolutionary.

CHAPTER EIGHT

Post-war Expansion

'We've got them. The Nissen huts, iron stoves and all and ready for use.' Jack was delighted because he had just arranged a deal with the Army for the Nissen huts erected on part of Millfield's land during the war, and used for a short time by some Americans. The end of the war had seen them vacant, and since they were first built Jack had kept an eye on them. They provided an almost instant answer to the chronic shortage of teaching space. Millfield required twenty-five classrooms to maintain its teacher-to-pupil ratio of one to five, and with Millfield House, the chicken runs, the chalet, a greenhouse, the cottage, odd summer houses, sheds and even tents, twenty-five classrooms were certainly not available.

Although rationing was still rigorously applied to food, fuel and paper the release from five years of war and tension was a great tonic for everyone. The spirit of cooperation forged by the war had not yet been subjected to the materialism experienced during the following decade. Jack sensed the surge of new life as acutely as anyone, and brought his remarkable energy and foresight to bear on Millfield's growing pains. The big headache was accommodation, a problem that had three main components (the fourth, money, did not come into this immediate category according to Jack, because it always had been, and probably always would be a problem). Of the three, the first, teaching space, was well on the way to solution with the advent of the Nissen huts. The second and third concerned boarding accommodation for the growing numbers of seniors and juniors, which Jack was right to consider a major problem, because under his leadership the senior school alone was destined to grow by an average of nearly thirty-three places for each of the next twenty-five years.

The services had requisitioned many large houses throughout the country, and when they were vacated the tough post-war economy left many question marks over their future. After their owners had joined the war effort, some making the bravest sacrifice, many of these fine houses were left half or completely empty. In 1945 Kingweston House faced some of these problems and Jack and the Dickinsons discussed its future. It had been the Dickinsons' family seat for nearly two hundred years, and the house and its grounds occupied a superb position in open, flat parkland. It was, in fact, easily superior to Millfield as a venue for a school. The two parties came to an arrangement and within a few months ten senior boys moved in. They must have rattled around merrily in the enormous house and grounds, which made an almost ludicrous contrast to the normal Millfield billet. The initial restriction on numbers was the result of lack of mains water, the house being fed from a rainwater tank in the roof. However, Jack's pleasure and good fortune in acquiring the use of Kingweston cannot be underestimated. The expansive, flat grounds easily accommodated many rugby and hockey pitches later.

The third part of the accommodation problem concerned the juniors, whose numbers were increasing to such an extent that they filled Millfield House. Here the process of de-requisitioning by the services came to Jack's rescue again. Another fine house a few miles away, snuggling in the lea of Glastonbury Tor, was Edgarley Hall. Owned by the Thomas-Ferrands, whose son had sadly died, it had two cottages, six flats and 20 acres of land, and was about to be vacated by the Red Cross who had been looking after some of the Free French. Once again Jack was fortunate to secure a lease with the option to purchase. Edgarley was the ideal place for an idea that had been growing in his mind to open a

Edgarley Hall in the lee of Glastonbury Tor

Millfield junior school, taking pupils up to the age of thirteen or fourteen and preparing them for the Common Entrance exam. To run this venture he had an ex-prep school headmaster whose own school had been requisitioned for war service. Victor Edghill came with some of his pupils to start this new venture with forty-five on the roll. Finding equipment at the end of the war was a desperate struggle because supplies were short. Labour was also almost non-existent, because no-one wanted to know too much about work if they had been lucky enough to survive five years of war. Most of the work of preparing and decorating the house was done single-handed by Everel Sankey, who was then on vacation from her medical school. In fact she stained all of the floors with a 1 in paintbrush, the only size available in the shops at that time. At least she had the assistance of an elderly gardener for moving the furniture, but it was a remarkable feat for a nineteen-year-old girl.

Almost everything was ready for the autumn term of 1945 except for the beds, which had not arrived, so Edgarley's first pupils spent a few nights with mattresses on the floor, and, incidentally, water shrimps in the taps. Among its first pupils was Jimmy (now Sir James) Goldsmith and his brother Manes. Jimmy had been something of a challenge; while based at Millfield before coming to Edgarley, according to Jack, he had somehow dynamited his housemaster's cabbages. This should have guaranteed expulsion, but anyone who had shown such ingenuity interested Jack, and he could see that Jimmy was not a bad boy, just very interesting. Jack was particularly susceptible to misbehaviour that indicated a sporting instinct. While considering a new admission to the school he had been told by the boy's mother, who was being commendably honest about her slightly unruly son, 'Mr Meyer, I'm afraid there was also some dormitory trouble.'

'Oh dear, I'm rather sorry to hear that. Would you care to elaborate?'

'It seems that he was getting everybody out of their beds after midnight to play cricket.'

'Was he? Was he? Well, you know that's not too bad. In fact it's rather encouraging.'

In his palace school in India, Jack had mixed the Indian princes and the more lowly offspring of Indian Army officers. Children learn a great deal by imitating, and their teachers can always help when they begin to imitate the wrong kind of things. Similarly, at Millfield Jack had an idea, associated with 'Jerusalem's Green and Pleasant Land', that he wished the school to be open to all nations of the world. All would benefit from knowing how others thought and lived, and he hoped that this might lead to some form of tolerance in later life. The war had made the ideal virtually impossible, and there had been, in any case, some suspicion of foreigners during this period. One distinguished visitor who entered both the country and Millfield was Endalkatchew Makonnen. Soon to be known as George, he was a kinsman of Haile Selassie of Ethiopia who had lived in this country since 1936 when his was invaded by the Italians. There is a bizarre though true story that before the war His Imperial Majesty Emperor Haile Selassie of Ethiopia stopped at the lodge, while on his way to see nearby Butleigh Court. The lodge at Millfield's entrance was occupied by the gardener, Philip Taylor. As Jack put it:

> He called in at the lodge with a request to use the facilities, a bucket which could we find it now would surely be worth a bob or two, which led much later to the admission of two members of His Royal Family.

A number of Millfield's pupils had been taken abroad during the war, and afterwards they or younger brothers returned, parents having first enquired whether the school was still in existence. Another element to expand the numbers were young men coming out of the services who wished to complete their education before going on to college or university. There were several reasons for them to choose Millfield, but the overwhelming one was that their old public schools were not flexible enough to admit them. Also they appreciated a less formal atmosphere in which to become re-acclimatized to bookwork. Having seen what life could offer and easily take away they really got down to their studies, and set a tremendous example to the other boys. Even when they passed into university their dons commented that they were the most responsive students they had ever taught. While at Millfield they also did sterling work as prefects and captains of sport, fitting easily into the pattern of responsibility with which Jack ran the school. He had always been loath to create a mass of petty restrictions such as those he had encountered at Haileybury. These were replaced by the general assumption that each pupil would enjoy as much freedom as he or she could handle, and there were plenty of staff and prefects around to see if that freedom was being abused. Jack also let it be known that when pupils were unsupervised it would always fall to the oldest to be responsible for anything that happened. When rules did have to be made, he would try to convey the reasons why they were necessary, rather than merely hand out something that pupils might find obscure, and which therefore they could not respect. With Jack it was rarely a case of 'Keep off the grass', but more commonly 'Please give the bulbs a chance'.

Rules and regulations regarding co-education had to be thought out carefully, and Jack decided early on that for serious crimes boys would be beaten, and girls expelled. There was quite a lot of debate over this question, but whichever way Jack looked at it his conclusions were the same, even though a sacking seemed far worse in the long run than a beating. Parents and offspring were acquainted with the ruling from the start of their association with the school. It is interesting to note that for eight years after the war Millfield had a total of only fourteen senior girls while the number of boys almost doubled to 242, yet Jack was convinced about the value of having girls at his school, and there were many women on the staff. It is possible that since the girls needed extra and different facilities he postponed the expansion of their numbers. Edgarley eventually welcomed day girls, but had women on the staff well before they came.

Freed from the war, and with Edgarley junior school, Kingweston House and Jack's beloved Nissen huts in place, Millfield was ready to grow, and there was never an end to the pupils who wished to join the ranks. Growing numbers and complicated administration could have meant anonymity for those new members, but Jack loved people. He could be formidable to a fourteen-year-old boy just entering his school, but what the lad did not know was that Jack was by instinct a man who gave, just like his father Rollo, 'who would give away his last shilling if he

The Nissen huts in 1952

thought there were need for it'. His principal gift was one of education, and all his energy went into delivering that precious commodity. Typical of the new intake after the war was Rosemary Coe (now Crosbie), who was interviewed in 1945. She had been informed by her previous headmistress that she was to stay down for yet another year, putting her School Certificate exam two years away with, she was promised, little hope of passing in any of the subjects. Her mother had heard about Millfield – mostly that it was unconventional, but had a growing reputation for success. If parents had heard that Jack was by normal standards a little eccentric, their first glimpse around his study must have amply confirmed the opinion. It had already, after only five years' occupation, achieved that state for which it was famous, bookcases from floor to ceiling: filing cabinets and precarious stacks of newspapers including *The Sporting Life, The Times,* and the *Daily Telegraph*; the magazine *The Cricketer*, heaps of press cuttings; various dogs; sacks of feed for the ducks with perhaps one or two recuperating ducklings; bottles of ageing sherry; and a vast assortment of sporting paraphernalia with accompanying balls tossed into any spare receptacle. The walls were covered with team photos, shelves of trophies and the odd stuffed bird. Seated snugly in one corner of this fascinating organized chaos was Amothe Sankey, who would retrieve any document relating to any topic in two or three seconds flat. After greeting parents the first thing Jack invariably had to do was make a space for them to sit down. Papers, books and golf tees were swept aside to reveal long-forgotten furniture. Rosemary said that she and her mother were immediately made to feel welcome by Jack, who spoke mostly to her, asking what she considered to be some very strange questions. The biggest surprise came at the conclusion of the interview when Jack said, 'If you would like to come here next term and you are prepared to work very hard, there is a very good chance that you will have passed your School Certificate by the summer.'

Jack's prediction turned out to be absolutely correct, and staff and others soon became used to the remarkable way in which these predictions were made and proved time after time.

Leaving Millfield could also be quite eventful, as Wyndham Bailey found during the term before Rosemary's interview. As head boy he had an excellent relationship with the Boss because he had held a responsible and supportive position during the tough years of the war. However, during his last year he had rather enjoyed himself, and perhaps took his eye off the academic ball. There was also one of Millfield's young ladies who had her eye on him. One piece of excitement was the discovery of an ancient Austin 7 tourer doing service as a hen coop on a nearby farm.

After negotiations with the farmer and a little tender loving care, the Austin was discovered to still have some spark of life. With petrol rationing there were very few cars at school, and the Austin was therefore secreted somewhere in Street. On a pleasant summer's evening three or four prefects might take a stroll into town, and be chugging out the other side in about ten minutes. All went well until one evening a car went past them, and looking at one another they said, 'Oh Lord! I think that was Amothe.'

Jack didn't beat about the bush, but admitted that there was little he could do about it. In the end he gave Wyndham permission to bring the Austin up the school drive to load his cases when he left, chugging down the drive and off home to Devon in great style.

Although only at Millfield for a couple of terms Rosemary also left the school in some style. A traditional midnight feast was planned for about a dozen leavers, three of them girls. To add real spice to the occasion the boys said they would despatch one of Boss's beloved chickens, but there was still the problem of how and where to cook it. The recently acquired Nissen huts provided the answer, they were a good distance from Millfield House and the chicken could be broiled on one of the big iron stoves. The really tricky bit for the girls, almost as dangerous as stealing the chicken, was getting out of the cottage without Mrs Sankey knowing. The problems were overcome with a certain amount of forethought, including not quite locking doors, or leaving window catches undone.

Elnith Sankey, Jack and Millfield's young ladies in 1948

Moving stealthily down the drive in pitch darkness, the girls gave the special coded knock on a Nissen hut door. It opened, followed by billows of steam from the pot on the stove, which was incandescent in the dim candlelight. The windows were covered by the blackout curtains and they ate, smoked, drank scrumpy and danced to a muffled gramophone until dawn. In fact they stayed rather too long, as it was discovered that blackout curtains kept light out as well as in!

Other interesting departures involved Jack a little more. During the war a very bright head boy at Malvern wanted to get into the Navy. And the special entry he was seeking demanded good subject passes at an advanced level. Physics and history were his strongest subjects but the timetable was so structured that they could not be taken together. History with French was possible and maths with physics, but the combination he needed was not on the menu. His mother approached Jack who said, of course, that he would appreciate having such a bright boy and that at Millfield the timetable was designed to suit the pupil, and there was none of this '4A does French, third period, Wednesday morning and that means you!' The boy was on a scholarship to Malvern and his mother warned Jack that there was very little in the kitty that might match Millfield's fees. Jack replied that he might be able to make some concession, to which the parent assured him that if that was the case, she would make up the full fees if he got into the Navy. Jack was practising his 'enlightened self-interest' again, because to have a bright ex-head boy from Malvern who had come to Millfield to get good results was excellent publicity for the school. 'Exam results speak for themselves and everyone can judge them. Teaching the duffer to write and add up does not carry the same kudos, although it is as great an achievement and can require more teaching.'

The boy came top in the special Navy exams and everyone was happy, including his mother, but when she came to collect him at the end of his time at Millfield she told Jack, 'Well, I've come to say goodbye and thank you. Of course, as you've got so much publicity out of Peter being first, you won't be asking for any more fees will you?'

This left him rather nonplussed, because he hadn't entered into any formal arrangement, and had ended up doing the family a rather larger favour than he intended. Years later the young man came to see Jack after he had left the Navy to become a very good engineer in Australia. 'Boss, I know all about my mother and the fees, so now I am going to pay them in full.'

Those attending in the immediate post-war years may not have been aware of it, but they were an important part of Millfield's development into a school in the full sense of the word. Soon pupils were coming from

Edgarley to fill the gap caused by the polarization between young pupils
looking for Common Entrance success and seniors wishing to pass into
universities or the services. The arrangement had come about through
the necessity of survival, and Jack had to fill the gaps left, and indeed
often caused, by established schools. The new pupils created an effective
middle-age range for the school and necessitated the composition of a
timetable that would still be flexible enough to enable each to have his or
her own timetable, while sharing general subjects with others. Personal
attention was still the priority for each pupil and as the school grew it was
preserved by a gift shared by Joyce, Jack and Amothe – they all had
phenomenal memories. It was a quality everyone connected with the
school commented upon. After the entry interview a pupil might not
meet Jack for one or two terms, and even then it would probably be by
chance on a rare occasion when he was walking around the school. The
chance encounter would not only bring questions about the special
compilation of subjects being taken, but comments about something that
had happened in the billet, or a new hobby the pupil had developed.
Every pupil felt that this imposing man always knew what they were
doing, which generally seemed to result in them doing the right things
better.

  Jack was pleased to see various clubs and societies flourishing. Since
variety was the spice of his life he applauded others' different interests
and activities independent of games or Public Works. The societies
included drama, fishing, choir, orchestra, stamp collecting, bird
watching, chess, gardening, radio enthusiasts, farming, aero-modelling,
debating, photography and Shakespearian reading. Foreshadowing his
political future, George Makonnen was a particularly voluble member of
the debating society. He was later to become Ethiopia's Ambassador in
London and its Prime Minister, and before his tragic murder in a
rebellion he was a favourite to succeed U Thant as UN Secretary-General.
For doers as opposed to talkers the Air Cadet Force had been joined by
the Sea Cadets, which promised the great adventure of rowing on the
River Parrott, catching eels with the locals and watching baskets being
made from withies instead of getting back and doing drill. This made it
important to remember that they had a headmaster who seemed to know
by instinct where a boy was at any time during the day. However,
sometimes his methods were detectable. On a fine early summer
afternoon two or three boys decided to skip games and have a pleasant
walk around the countryside. They looked for birds' nests, and one of
them had a cigarette. The same evening they were informed by their
house prefects that they were wanted by Boss in his study the next
morning. Meeting before the appointed hour they guessed that somehow

he had found out what they had been up to. They entered Jack's study, the accusation was tersely made, the rule was clear and the punishment no surprise. The burning question was, how had he found out where they had been, because they were absolutely sure that no-one had seen them. But soon they recalled an odd incident with an AA motor cycle. They heard something coming and were ready to hide should the vehicle be recognized as belonging to a member of staff. However, the distinctive yellow and black of the motorcycle and its squared-off sidecar, which was really a big tool chest, put them at their ease. But as it passed them they were amazed to see a figure lying full length on top of the sidecar, fingers gripping the front and feet overhanging the back. Later, the awful truth dawned that it had of course been R.J.O. Meyer, headmaster of Millfield, on that sidecar, hitching a lift to Wincanton Races because he had run out of petrol.

Skipping games during the cricket term could be expected to bring a rapid reprimand from Jack, particularly as he was building up Millfield's team again after the war. Among others Alan Synge and Jock Coutts were to become the foundation of Millfield cricket. The Somerset County side had also been reforming for the 1946 season and Jack's association with it had brought wonderful players like Arthur Wellard, Harold Gimblett and the young 'Steve' Stephenson to the school with Wally Luckes giving tips about slip fielding. Millfield also had 'Sam' Pothecary as cricket coach. The war had taken an awful toll of the young men who should have been in the county sides; some were gone for ever and others were not yet up to standard. The result was that those who made up the side were by normal standards rather elderly and, as Jack put it, 'seized up with shrapnel or arthritis'. Even he was trying to play with the spinal injury sustained a few years before when he had been trying to start a mower to trim his cricket square. 'I played through a Somerset season with this ruddy disc. But it wasn't very pleasant. I got loosened up with a combination of aspirins and bowling, and if we batted next, I'd go in early before going back into spasm.'

Even the constant pain would not kill the impish side of Jack's humour though, and it was typical that during a match in Taunton, when there had been heavy showers, Somerset eventually came out apparently one man short. The eleventh, Jack, finally came on, making his protest against the weather obvious by putting a large umbrella up and tucking his flannels into his socks. 'Bunty' Longrigg, the skipper, wasn't too amused even if the crowd were. Jack was only able to make eight appearances because of his work at Millfield, but even so came out second in the season's batting averages with 43.36, just over three under that of the illustrious Gimblett. Even at the age of forty-one, Jack was not the oldest player. Wally Luckes was forty-five but, as described in *The Cricketer Annual*, 'he again proved himself to be a wicket keeper with few superiors in England'. After the loss of four opening games Somerset had a remarkably successful season, with several innings victories and scores up in the 500s. After six long years many players seemed able to find and sometimes even better their pre-war form. As *The Cricketer* said:

> Their tails were up and future prospects seemed to be rosy, except that some of the older hands are now in the veteran stage. The main problem to be solved for next Summer will be to find a suitable successor to Longrigg for the captaincy.

That successor was to be Jack, and he had a hard act to follow with a team who were a year older when years were getting precious.

> I got much criticism, but in actual fact there was no-one else to do the job. I believe I had as good an average for batting and bowling as anybody in a somewhat aged County XI which had nine bowlers all screaming to get on and no batsman averaging twenty even by mid-June. The trouble was we were geriatric. I was forty-two and crippled, Wellard had a bad knee, Hugh Watts couldn't throw the ball because of a war wound although he was still a wonderful batsman, and Frank Lee had a double rupture. Some of them were wonderful old former players, but we were a terrible side and there was no-one else to do it. I remember the awful day that Wellard was in good form against Northants and Dennis Brookes snicked one straight to me at second slip. It was a straightforward catch but I couldn't get down to it because of my back. It was appalling.

Putting his hand in his back pocket he pulled out a pound note and walked up to the bowler: 'Sorry Arthur, here's a quid.'

Resuming his comments on that season Jack said, 'Nonetheless, we beat Middlesex who were champions twice, and we were the only team to beat Lancashire and so we didn't do too badly, finishing in joint eleventh place with eight victories.'

Although the results on paper were none too exciting, it was a delightful year for most of the team with, said *The Cricketer*, 'R.J.O. Meyer, one of the finest natural cricketers, who had theories to the point of eccentricity.' Jack was of the firm opinion that matches were to be enjoyed as well as won, and he also took great care of his men. With food rationing it was difficult to get the substantial nutrition that his team needed, especially the fast bowlers, and when on tour Jack became famous for his ability to produce meals from nowhere. So important was this to him that he once pulled a communication cord on a Manchester express train in order to find some food. He thought about every match as a captain must, and took into account the personalities and style of the strongest members of the opposing teams. He would then come up with one of his special theories. Batting orders could be stood on their head as far as Jack was concerned, particularly in the second innings. In a match against Middlesex, for example, Jack had to find a way of knocking the stuffing out of their formidable opening bowler, Laurie Gray. He put Hugh Watts in first and told him to knock the first ball for six, regardless of pace, length and direction and despite the risk of being clean bowled. Hugh politely queried the request but Jack was adamant. The opening batsman walked out and Hugh took his guard. He cut the first ball square and it went sizzling over the umpire's head – not a six but an unstoppable four. The effect on Gray was one of sheer disbelief as he stood, hands on hips, in the middle of the wicket, giving a commentary on what had just happened, every other word of which was quite unrepeatable. Then seeing a pair of strong left-arm bowlers in the Middlesex side who always posed a threat to the conventional right-hand batsman, Jack thought that he should combat like with like. So he asked Hugh Watts, a left-handed batsman, to pad up at the beginning of the innings to be ready to take to the field as soon as one of the left-hand bowlers removed a Somerset batsman. Regrettably for Hugh, the whole idea was a non-event because even when the seventh wicket fell, there was still no sign of the left-handers coming on as the next batsman went in leaving him still trussed up in his pads.

One bright young star in Somerset that year was Maurice Tremlett, destined to succeed Wellard as an effective bowler and wicket taker. He described Jack as 'much the most original and exciting captain I ever played under. He was always trying something new to outwit the opposition and he once moved every fielder into the covers in the middle of an over (to the right and forward of the batsman), and bowled long hops onto the leg stump to the bewilderment of the batsman who, mesmerized by this manoeuvre, managed to get outside the line of the third delivery and spooned it into the forest of cover point fielders.' Wally Luckes, the wicketkeeper, was often on the receiving end of Jack's theories. Although he was bowling for comparatively short spells then, Jack was still capable of sending down six balls all swinging and breaking differently. Inevitably there was often a blind spot for the keeper when the ball swung in front of the batsman, but if he knew what the bowler was doing he had every chance of predicting the break and stopping the ball if it beat the batsman. However, with six different balls Jack could beat both the batsman and keeper, despite the fact that Luckes was one of the best in the country, with a record-breaking number of dismissals. Jack later opened a fund to commemorate Luckes's achievements.

One of the last matches that Jack skippered for Somerset was the return against Middlesex at Taunton that began on 12 July 1947. Middlesex were to be champions that year but Somerset had beaten them during their first encounter and on paper had an excellent opportunity of doing so again because Edrich, Compton and Robertson were absent. They were even more unlucky when Hever, one of their bowlers, split a finger while fielding. Somerset notched up a presentable 356 runs in that first innings and Middlesex could only reply with 227. At the beginning of Somerset's second innings, Middlesex's captain, 'Robbie' Robins, asked Jack if he could bring on the twelfth man to keep wicket, thus releasing Leslie Compton, the usual keeper, to bowl. 'Not on your life,' was apparently Jack's reply.

'Right then, watch this!' Middlesex opened with Laurie Gray bowling, then after the over Leslie Compton took off his keeper's gloves and pads to bowl, replacing them for the third over. This farce was kept up for four overs, much apparently to Jack's amusement. On the face of it it does not seem that he was being very sporting, but there was a good reason for him to be rather angry with Robins, who had apparently 'instructed' him to declare by two o'clock otherwise he would 'ruin the match. Just ruin the match'. He was referring to Somerset amassing a great total which was impossible for Middlesex to chase, thereby not making much of a game of it. But Somerset were having a tough season, and needed any victory in sight. Jack replied that he certainly wasn't going to declare, and that if he ever decided to, it would be when he wanted to. The following morning Robins apparently commented to another within Jack's hearing, 'Of course this bloody Meyer won't declare so he'll ruin the whole game.'

As it was, Somerset got only 229 in that second innings, and Middlesex put up a good fight in the fourth with a total of 334. Somerset might perhaps have got more, but Jack was theorizing again. The Taunton ground was taking a lot of spin and Jack Young, the Middlesex bowler, was turning the ball beautifully, taking eight Somerset wickets during the match. Having scored fifty-five runs, Jack had enough confidence to try out one of his theories. A natural right-hander, he held the bat with a left-hander's grip with the intention of following the break of the ball and hitting it hard straight through the slips. He went through all the motions, but it did not turn at all and he was plumb lbw.

This was the year in which Jack 'captained Somerset cricket by day and ran the school by night'. While that is an overstatement he did have to commit a great deal of time to cricket, with four-day matches and tours

Somerset County Cricket XI in 1948, when Jack was captain

all round the country. His being away frequently let boys off awkward hooks if they knew about cricket. Alan Synge appeared to be an addicted pillow-fighter:

> I was once told to report to Boss for a beating, not too enticing a prospect because he had wrists like Ranji's. In the event I was told by Miss Sankey that he was busy playing Yorkshire and that I should come back when the match was over – a glance at the results decided me against this course.

Jack was especially lucky to have Amothe during that busy year because she always knew what the current thinking was on any exam, parent, teacher or pupil and certainly wrote many a letter in a very similar style to his own, leaving Jack to scrawl RJOM on the bottom line. Fortunately Amothe had got into the habit of working long hours; two in the morning was quite a normal time to finish, and through to near dawn if necessary for organizing major coups or events. To run a school like Millfield was, even in 1947 with only 170 pupils, a demanding operation. The thirty-two staff had to be efficiently directed to cater for 170 different demands, and satisfying them all rarely resulted in a timetable where things fell comfortably into place. There could not have been many men who would contemplate skippering Somerset and running a school. If there was some difficulty in serving two masters, it was one which Jack had lived with all his life, although to say 'lived with' is probably wide of the mark, as he always seemed to positively invite the situation. The end of Jack's regular playing career came in 1948, although he was still to receive various invitations to play for many a year. With pressure building up from an ever growing Millfield, and the appalling pain in his back, the end of a thirty-odd year innings did not bring too many regrets. He would, anyway, be supporting cricket from his study with as much enthusiasm as when he was approaching the crease. The game had, after all, provided him with the best education, fun and great adventure and friends who would support him for a lifetime.

Surgery for spinal injury was not a well-established art in 1948, but Jack had the option of spending the rest of his life in pain with the promise of ever more restricted movement, or submitting to a relatively untried surgical technique. He decided upon the operation and happily it was successful. If he did not fully comprehend the inherent risk in what had been undertaken it certainly came home to him when he recommended the treatment to an acquaintance with back trouble. After being approached the surgeon commented, 'I think you had better tell Mr Meyer that I killed the one before him.'

It was as well that Jack did recover, because the following year Millfield had a three-day visit from His Majesty's Inspectors, courtesy of the Ministry of Education. In general the school had a favourable report, especially when taking into consideration the then current socialist views on education. With that background they applauded the awarding of what they called 'scholarships', to ensure that the very high fees did not restrict entry to only those of very high income. The experience and qualifications of the staff were also commended but premises for both teaching and accommodation were not, and were considered 'in one or two cases taxed to the utmost'. The Nissen huts were described as dark and badly ventilated but the HMIs were not too worried after being assured that Jack had agreed with the local authorities that they should be removed in two and a half years – an interesting comment for those who were still teaching in them in the 1970s. The inspectors' description of the classrooms states that 'the teaching takes place in two sets of huts' and continues in similar vein.

Since rationing and wartime restrictions had been relaxed, Jack took full advantage of the sudden availability of building materials to purchase and refurbish any type of building that could be taught in or lived in. Teaching in small groups demanded large numbers of staff and a great number of rooms to put them in, and this certainly contributed to Millfield slowly becoming the most expensive school in Great Britain and, what was worse, being described by the media as:

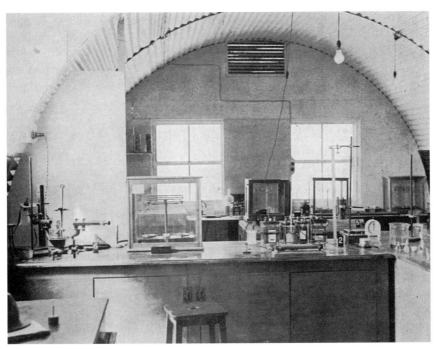

A physics laboratory in a Nissen hut, 1952

'the most exclusive' which, of course, we were not. Since personal attention often on a one-to-one basis was an essential ingredient to success, there was always a tremendous demand for more teaching room, so the pupils at this 'most expensive and exclusive school' were taught in an extraordinary array of temporary yet seemingly everlasting wooden huts.

There were now enough houses to install pupils together who had something in common, so general interests such as games, sciences or the countryside would dictate where a pupil went. Anyone who had some disability would be at Millfield House to ensure the minimum of travel, while other houses were picked to be within cycling or motor coach range. Kingweston was flourishing after mains water had been connected.

The school was becoming a big business to run, with ever-increasing sums of money coming in and flowing out. During the war W.D. Beveridge had been working on Welfare State proposals, prompted by Winston Churchill, and when, somewhat to Churchill's disappointment, a Labour Government was elected after the conflict it duly set about bringing this excellent scheme into operation. The one obvious factor which it demanded was colossal and continuous funding, and the resulting taxation placed a heavy burden on anything that looked like profit, and industry found itself paying some very hefty bills. So did Millfield. The school's bursar at this time was Brigadier Mackie who warned Jack that because of expansion, profit margins were getting smaller. During the three years up to 1952 the fee income had risen from £82,000 to £99,000, almost half of which went on salaries and wages. It is difficult to comprehend these values now, but anyone earning £15 to £20 per week at that time would have been moderately comfortable. The school only paid Jack £1,200 a year and he was not overgenerous to his forty-two staff. The Bursar's warning was graphically supported with facts: a budget forecast giving figures and a clear request for retrenchment. But according to Jack, all his signposts were facing the wrong way for the unswerving progression toward an educational ideal. He certainly noted the warning, but did not lend the poor Bursar much credit for his concern, especially because when looking for possible cuts he was rash enough to point out that in the previous year the school horses had lost around £800. However, Jack could not escape the fact that his latest profit of around £8,000 would be rather more than accounted for by current taxes.

> Having reached the decision that there was no future in being a private school if you got into more trouble when you made a profit than when you made a loss, we thought we had better try to turn the school into a charitable trust – which is exactly what we did in 1953 under the guidance of an elderly solicitor, J. Kennard of Hallet & Co., Ashford, Kent, after he had told us the correct procedure. Following the decision to form a charitable trust (or educational charity) it was necessary to elect a Board of Governors, which we did under the chairmanship of veteran JP Evan Stokes, founder and first headmaster of St Dunstan's, Burnham-on-Sea. Another was Millfield house owner J.A. (Tony) Clark as deputy chairman, J. Kennard of course, my solicitor and ever willing dogsbody, Cecil Hamilton-Miller (parent), Morley Cooper (parent and expert on insurance matters), Cedric Pritchard (valuer) and two great men and loyal friends, General Sir George Erskine and Dean of Exeter, Alexander Ross-Wallace, ex-headmaster of Sherborne who had for years fought for our recognition by the Headmasters' Conference. His conversion to the pro-Millfield-Meyer lobby was brought about mainly by the Millfield careers of the Jardine twins who came from Sherborne, where according to Ross Wallace they took turns in being bottom of everything, whereas at Millfield they passed all their service exams (including one for RNC Dartmouth and both for RMA Sandhurst where one of them won the

Sword of Honour) and both won places at the age of seventeen sailing in the Olympic Firefly team. This pair of stalwarts regularly came to my aid when issues such as 'horses and polo or not' were voted upon. The business lobby wanted horses out because 'they lost money we could ill-afford to lose'. Not only cynics understand the price of everything and the value of nothing.

What Jack had actually achieved with the help of Kennard and others was to secure the school in perpetuity.

Having become a public school it was now necessary to make a contract of service between myself and the governing body, and it was up to the expert Kennard to make me (and them) aware of my rights under official rules and my duties. They included the right to remain permanent headmaster and the one life governor if I wished, provided I remained sane – looking back I sometimes wonder how I did this or even if I did – the right to conduct operations in exactly the same financial way as I had conducted them as headmaster of a private school, the right to appoint a bursar who would work under my control rather than that of the Governors. I further insisted on continuing my 'Rendall of Winchester' method of giving financial help to parents of boys I wanted in the school.

The properties which Jack owned made him a rich man on paper, and were handed over to the school in return for half per cent debentures for twenty years. Regrettably Jack lost the value of them because he was strongly advised that their values would go down after the war as they had in 1919. However, he secured a rise in salary, and other benefits regarding accommodation and cars for Joyce and himself. Also Millfield then had the status of being a public school, which, along with its being a registered charity, opened important avenues for the future.

CHAPTER NINE

Recognition

'We do not undertake to supply brains to pupils in cases where the Almighty has made other arrangements' was a statement which Jack, feeling the need to make some qualified defence against parents demanding miracles, was obliged to enter in the Millfield Prospectus. It reflected the growing popularity of the school during the early 1950s and to some extent countered his other typically bold assertion that: 'We can start teaching anybody in any subject by next Monday morning!' The assertion that 'pupils failing their Common Entrance exams could be turned into university candidates in a few years' was coming home to roost. The 1950s was the decade when the press discovered Millfield as the result of the Hungarian crisis in 1956, when the might of the Russian Army was used in an attempt to crush the will of its neighbour. There were many refugees and Jack offered to help, accepting two boys and their families. In most aspects the broad publicity which resulted was welcomed, and ever more parents began knocking on the door. But other established public schools were not impressed, and made things difficult for Jack who was keen to join their ranks since he considered, quite rightly, that Millfield had something to offer. Initially, relationships were very friendly because Millfield was taking many of their difficult cases: boys who might not distinguish themselves academically or on the games field. When Millfield started to challenge them in both of these departments many changed their attitude to one of some disdain, and attempted to isolate the school. However, parents who had a problem or wished to get the best for their children made a beeline for Jack's study. They knew that he was successful, even though they could not understand all the reasons for his success. Far from performing miracles, he had both feet firmly on the ground when assessing a new boy's potential, which was as well, because to have promised anything to hopeful parents that was beyond their offspring's capacity would have been damaging to the school's reputation. Since Millfield would consider taking anyone, the situation was sometimes stood on its head, as with Robert Morley. 'I am told this is a very good school and that my son should do very well here.'

'I would like to support the motion,' said Jack.

'The trouble is that I did very badly at Wellington, and have done very well since then. So you see, I really want a school where Sheridan can do badly.'

Jack hoped that he was trying to be witty. 'That could be arranged, but I think it might cause disruption if others followed him down the primrose path. Goodbye.'

There were times when a pupil's potential was so obvious to Jack that he could not comprehend how other schools failed to spot it. Typical was a boy from Stowe who had been recommended by his housemaster – not without trepidation – to come to see Jack. After examining the boy, his father asked, 'Headmaster, I believe you have some surprising news for me.'

'Well, perhaps I have. Anthony's housemaster was quite clear about his ability when he spoke to me. I'm afraid he described him as the most stupid boy who had ever been in school, and was honest enough to doubt that we would be able to do anything to help him. At his age – seventeen – they thought it was probably too late to do anything for him anyway. But the truth is this. He is a boy of outstanding ability who will win a place for engineering at Cambridge and he'll get a good degree.'

After a stunned silence the father asked, 'Could you please tell me more?'

'He has a reading age of just over seven as a result of cross-literality, but he has an IQ of around 150+ and may do good work in mathematics. He is, of course, dominantly left-eyed and therefore one of the easier cases to cure. He simply has to learn to read from left to right. Surprisingly enough a good bash on the head with a coal hammer might be the quickest cure.'

'You astonish me, but do you know in my first year at Dartmouth I won all the prizes. I then fell on my head in the gym and started to do everything backwards, including writing. Even now I can write either way at will.'

'Yes, you must have been hit on the left side of your head, which damaged your right side dominance.'

If the boy's father, of high naval ranking, felt that he had been seated at the foot of some educational clairvoyant, he was delighted when all came true a couple of years later. Anthony did precisely what Jack had predicted.

There is a malaise in the business world given the rather smart title of 'innovation fatigue'. The term is self-explanatory. If it had been known at Millfield in the early 1950s, and had been a genuine condition, the whole school should have collapsed within months. It was a period of incredible growth in numbers, which were up to three hundred pupils and over fifty staff by halfway through the decade. It also saw rapid change and progress, and the quest for better systems to deliver the prize of education. To Jack, high levels of attainment, both academic and sporting, were not something to put a bit of effort into, then sit back and cross one's fingers. Opportunity to obtain the best standards was not even enough. The Millfield system had to incorporate caring and encouragement, with the expectation that each pupil would be helped to do his or her best to attain the exams needed, and which Jack thought they could achieve. Millfield's founder had always been a 'winner' and had no qualms about going for the top. The process involved challenge and that, according to Jack, was an extremely healthy state of mind. What he couldn't stand was an attitude which said: 'Come on Old Boy, do your best and afterwards I know a good little place for a beer.' It coupled with his other pet hate: 'You know how everyone says that the British are jolly decent losers – well of course we are, we've had so much damned practice!' The turbulent progress of this period was chiefly caused by Jack's realization that at last he was able to put his ideas into practice, whereas before they had been undermined by ten years of war and financial restrictions. He knew that enthusiastic involvement in any activity opened up an individual's personality, resulting in the confidence and ability to tackle other disciplines and life in general, including personal relationships. 'I have always believed and preached that if you want to survive you have got to do something – anything – better than other people can.' And he promised:

> You know, you've never lived properly if you've never tried to be first class at something. It doesn't matter what it is, cricket, physics or tiddlywinks because in getting there you will have learned something about self-discipline, dedication and achievement, and what better training for life could there be? It's not the silver cups and rosettes which are important, it's the 'trying' which makes the person, and we'll certainly help you to keep trying. If a boy wants that tennis cup he's going to have to sweat for it. We'll give him the time, the facilities and the coaching, and he'll get a hot shower and a good dinner afterwards.

These ideas, which had been born at Stratheden and shaped in Dranghadra, had to be translated into a supportive teaching strategy. 'You must always find out where a pupil "is" in any subject, though that level may be confused and the foundation shaky. Having found it you proceed to teach them at a rate which they can understand.' A new master at Millfield was once honest enough to ask Jack how that rate could be found:

> It's quite simple. If a child is losing concentration or showing signs of boredom it's your damned fault. They need a handle to keep hold of

the subject. If you're going too fast or too slow for them you are taking that handle away. If I give a boy or girl something to do which they can't manage – like quadratic equations to someone who is still learning their tables, who is the fool? Is it the pupil who can't manage them, or the person who asks him to do them?

The importance of small classes is evident from this argument. It is obviously far easier to spot a pupil who is floundering in a class of seven than in a class of twenty-seven. Shaky foundations were often one of the first problems to be dealt with for a new pupil, and with his gift for analogy Jack suggested:

If a car has broken down you can get it up the hill (through the exam) by cramming it full of facts and giving it a shove. What's better surely, is to get the engine going (by giving them that handle we mentioned) so that they can get up that hill and plenty of others as well by themselves.

From these ideas, practically all the elements typical of Millfield were in place by the mid-1950s, so what was the school they had produced like? The only valid answer can be established by starting with its pupils because, as Jack knew, without them there was no Millfield. By this time about half the intake was coming directly from prep schools like Edgarley, so Jack had successfully moved away from the polarity of very young and mature seniors that he was attracting at the end of the war. Those who joined Millfield's youngest stream provided a core who experienced and practised the way that Jack wanted things done. Short-term pupils entering the school would quickly learn the ropes from them, and they provided a stable factor that was helping to build Millfield. Some of these pupils who came for a short time were what Jack sometimes referred to as his 'repairs'. Most of them needed to pass exams in one or several subjects and roughly half of them were of average or slightly below average IQ. 'Perfectly pleasant, not a lot up top, but good reliable boys and girls and good horsemen and games players.' What they needed was a little more attention than they were receiving at their previous schools to get them through. About the same number of Jack's 'repairs' were children of high or very high IQ who were suffering from some form of learning disability, many suffering from what has been more recently referred to as dyslexia. Obvious symptoms were seemingly low ability in numeracy and literacy, and they were quite often many years behind their age groups. Typical was Sebastian Linfoot, who said, 'When I learn things from the TV and ask my teachers questions about them, they say "Boy, don't ask boring questions. Go and play footer with the other kids." Then they complain that I am no good at school. How can I learn anything?'

Jack said, 'I think we may be able to help, but first I want to find out why you failed the 11+ and why the Secondary Modern School can't teach you. Please sit down and try to answer the question on the page.'

The question was, 'Which of the following does not belong to the group – pheasant, tadpole, thrush, robin?'

Sebastian burst into tears, but when Jack read the question he said, 'The answer, I think, is something like rana, which is Latin for frog. I got that from the TV where I get all I know.'

When asked what programmes he watched his reply was, 'I'm only interested in science and maths for the sixth forms but I cannot get answers to my questions.'

Jack informed him that at Millfield questions were answered and Sebastian responded, 'Well, Sir, you know that Aston in his book on isotopes stated that if you put a mixture of gases . . . ?'

Jack awarded Sebastian a scholarship for *trying* to write the word 'cat' without crying. He was a severely handicapped dyslexic, but took 'A' grade maths and physics at thirteen, Latin and an Oxford Scholarship at fifteen, English at sixteen and, most difficult of all, French at seventeen – plus *all* his 'O' levels before he was eighteen. Jack's testing and treatment for such remedial cases also became legendary, and was developed to a fine art during the 1960s.

When new pupils came to the school a guide was selected to familiarize them with routines and the layout of the school and to tell them who was who. The guide chosen would have something in common with the new boy or girl. They would share the same house and most of the same subjects or activities. There was no punitive examination as at pre-war Haileybury whence this idea originated. The new pupils were tested, but if their knowledge was rather sketchy it was the guide who might be reprimanded and told to do his or her job with a little more enthusiasm.

Although boys and girls entering Millfield did so by way of results in the Common Entrance exam and an intelligence test, there was no rigid entrance procedure all had to satisfy; Jack would often set a specific test in a subject that was of particular interest to the pupil. The most important factor for the normal entrant was the previous or current headmaster's report on character; Jack valued this far more than any kind of academic rating. He would also assess pupils in what appeared to be a far from academic manner. A typical incident concerned a father and son who were being shown around the school. Surreptitiously, Jack took a cricket ball from his jacket pocket and tossed it gently over his shoulder. The story relates that the boy caught it and won a scholarship. It was

Lyn Lewis, in charge of remedial studies, working in the new block in 1967

more than likely that by this stage Jack had decided that the boy was coming in any case, but if he had dropped the ball or, worse still, not tried to catch it, his bursary might have been decidedly more modest. While parents were handed the *Daily Telegraph* and a cup of tea, prospective pupils would be taken outside to see if they could put a golf ball into a hole. That they may never have played golf before was unimportant; what interested Jack was the attitude they brought to the task.

By 1955 there were fourteen boarding houses for boys, ranging from Millfield and Kingweston, which were the largest, to billets with two or three and a master. To assist housemasters were echelons of prefects with the house prefect at the top. These boys held important positions and were directly responsible to housemasters and to Jack. There were twenty-one girls, who lived in the cottage in Millfield's grounds and two other houses in Street, one of them being Wraxleigh, the first substantial girls' house off the school grounds. Edgarley had grown to ninety-two pupils, and supplied Millfield with a regular supply of juniors. Pupils coming out of this school were not destined exclusively for Millfield, because they could of course choose any other school to enter.

There were fifty-two staff with weighty academic qualifications, around half being scientists or mathematicians. Because Jack actively encouraged pupils from abroad, eighteen languages besides the standard European

Jack, 'Wolf' and pupils from thirty-six nations in 1956

tongues were taught. Also, because many of these overseas pupils tended to be very intelligent and wanted to go on to British universities, there developed an active 'foreigners' English' course. Jack had also been looking for specialist staff to support remedial and very advanced studies. He was one of the first to recognize that pupils with very high IQs needed as much care and attention as severely remedial cases, and Millfield pioneered work in this field. There were between five and six pupils to each member of staff, a ratio Jack considered necessary to ensure individual care and attention to help pupils achieve the best that they could manage. Some who had not experienced such small classes were tempted to consider the teaching easy, but on the contrary it was highly concentrated, if only because the teacher was as exposed to the pupils as the pupils to the teacher. Each pupil had a timetable devised to meet his or her weak and strong points, which at junior level included art and practical subjects on a timetable that was continuously modified through an individual's school career to meet needs and aspirations. The standard period time was one hour, the minimum Jack considered necessary to cover any topic in depth. The fact that less gifted children might not be able to concentrate for that amount of time was understood; a remedial maths class might be seen throwing a ball around with a tutor halfway through the period. Regarding physical education, the 'game of the term' was compulsory up to the age of sixteen, after which it could be replaced by a pupil's personal choice. Anyone who was outstandingly gifted and enthusiastic about a particular sport would have far more time available for coaching and practice. However, not all sought excellence, like the charming young lady who chose rifle shooting and chess for her term's games. When her tutor sought an explanation she replied, ' – because I only have to move two fingers for each.' Time was also found for many other activities or hobbies which Jack applauded and encouraged, because they were an added bonus to pupils whose eyes were opened to new interests.

Jack considered monitoring pupils' progress especially important, and each would be a member of a group, having perhaps age or subject matter in common, with a group tutor in charge. There were regular weekly meetings, and the tutor was always available to sort out problems. The group tutor's first job was to arrange the pupils' timetable; this could sometimes be a headache when a number of special features had to be incorporated around block subjects like English or mathematics. Subject tutors would report to the group tutor by having a quiet word during break if problems arose, and would forward test results. All available information was passed onwards and upwards, ending in a large dossier that contained all that was known about a pupil, including information about previous schooling and hopes for the future. As the school grew, the group tutors became the guiding hand ensuring that Millfield delivered the goods Jack had promised during interviews with parents.

Small classes meant that time wasted on discipline was minimal compared with that in other schools. Jack was keen that any necessary control on behaviour outside the classroom should be the responsibility of senior pupils, and only in the last resort that of teaching staff. The chain of discipline extended from the headmaster to the head prefect, school prefects, house prefects, honorary prefects, sub prefects and monitors. The general rule was that as much freedom was available as could be properly handled, and this was linked with respect for another's freedom and property. Jack didn't refrain from beating a boy if he thought the offence serious enough, and it brought no complaint from boys at the time. The head boy held a position of responsibility and tremendous respect, he was certainly treated very courteously by members of staff. One 'freedom' that applied to all pupils was that there was no school uniform, but boys did have to wear a tie and generally dress in a conventional way, suitable for living in the country. Most of them wore sports jackets. There was a choice – albeit limited – of ties: either a Millfield tie, a games colours tie or a pupil's old school tie. This last option threw an interesting light on how Jack viewed Millfield. Some pupils would often spend only one or two years of their school lives there, so he felt it important that they had some continuity with their previous education. Similarly, the position of honorary prefect was created for boys coming from other schools where they had been prefects. Jack saw no reason why they should lose a well-earned rank by coming to him for the last year or so of schooling. Many did, after all, come to Millfield to get that last 'O' level, such as Latin or maths, which would gain them entry for the university scholarship they had been promised.

Religion had to form a part of every pupil's life, and those who came from abroad were expected to continue their devotions in whatever faith they had. Most pupils belonged to the Church of England, and confirmation classes were available and had to be attended. It was often difficult to find priests for Jews, Muslims and those practising other faiths, but such pupils were expected to read their holy books during a period reserved for devotions on Saturday or Sunday. Abstention from eating meat and other customs were also respected. After being confirmed, Church of England pupils were allowed, and even encouraged, to look at other religious traditions; Jack hoped that thereby they might gain respect and tolerance for the beliefs of others. Jack still occasionally taught divinity, and while most pupils agreed that his lessons were enlightening, some seemed to go even further. 'Sir, I certainly do believe in God now.'

'Really Harry. Why now?'

'Because He saved me when I got lost on a school outing without any money, and I prayed for help. An old lady dropped a pound note from her handbag and didn't notice. That pound got me home and I have believed in God ever since.'

'Harry, sit down and let's talk.'

The practice of what was preached in the way of caring was reflected later in the formation of a social services activity. Organized by Bryant Fell, one of Millfield's specialist remedial teachers, each week it served the elderly and needy in Street and Glastonbury, doing all manner of good works. Pupils also organized Christmas parties and mystery tours for old-age pensioners. Some of the elderly had even more surprises. One lady, whose husband was infirm, thought it was amusing to have to show her fifteen-year-old visitor how to use a spade. On her birthday he bought her a twin set and matching silk scarf. The quality of the garments was obvious, and they certainly had not been purchased locally. Initially, her feeling of apprehension at the expense of her present overcame gratitude, but her young gardener assured her that money was of no importance at all to the Crown Prince of Saudi Arabia, and it was time to rake over the plot for the carrots. The astounding wealth of some pupils rarely caused problems at Millfield, and it was often amusing to see normally scruffy individuals being whisked off at the end of term in an enormous Rolls Royce which could have belonged to Elizabeth Taylor. Collecting 'valuables' for safe keeping when boys were changing for games could mean that a master was responsible for gold watches and other possessions equivalent to half his annual salary. Often there were more subtle hints of wealth such as the time when Jenny Speirs, an art teacher, asked her pupils to draw their houses from memory. One lad looked rather despondent at the idea: 'But Miss Speirs, it'll take ages because it's a palace.'

On another occasion an older boy was apparently being rather indifferent regarding modern painting. 'Have you ever seen a Picasso?' she asked.

'Oh yes, we've got a couple hanging over the stairs.'

The fees at Millfield were high and always seemed to be getting higher. One parent who received a letter from the school notifying him of another increase 'per annus' (sic) curtly wrote back acknowledging the rise, but indicated that he would prefer to continue 'paying through the nose as usual'. There was a system whereby the age at which a pupil entered had a direct bearing on the fees; those coming for one or two years at a senior level paid some 20 per cent more than a junior who expected to be at the school for some years. Tuition formed a major part of the fees, as can be seen by the amount a day pupil paid each term – around £100 compared with a boarder's fees of £150. Transport was also a substantial factor because the pupils had to be ferried to and from Millfield each day from outlying houses by a fleet of coaches. Possibly a quarter of the pupils paid reduced fees or even no fees. These were young people whom Jack thought deserved a chance in life, perhaps because they had some ability – occasionally outstanding ability that he took it upon himself to foster. He was also generous to the children of clergy, members of the services and all teachers, not only those on his staff. He was only too aware of the generosity of the schools and individuals like G.S. Pawle, who had paid for his own education, and if he had not said 'thank you' enough at the time he was certainly doing so then by extending his hand to others. He was also very sympathetic to those who approached him who had been unlucky enough to lose a parent and whose education might therefore be curtailed. Many pupils who came on reduced fees were to repay Millfield handsomely in terms of achievement, both academic and sporting.

Those of outstanding ability could encourage others in the school by example. They often arrived through recommendation from their first schools who could do little more for them, and occasionally Jack or his staff would find them almost by accident. Jack was once driving along the North side of Clapham Common in London, possibly coming from the Oval, when he saw some children playing cricket. It was not an official match and they were not wearing whites, and it didn't look as if they could afford them anyway. There was one lad who seemed to have some style. So much so that Jack stopped the car to watch, and what he saw interested him very much. He approached the boy, gave him a lift to his home and spoke to the parents, who must have gone from sheer disbelief to amazement in a matter of minutes. As usual Jack's hunch was completely justified. How many other headmasters could there be who would even contemplate putting ideas into action in a matter of minutes and generally making a success of it? If there was an element of gambling in it, that would be no barrier to Jack. It was fortunate for the likes of budding English cricketers with grubby knees on Clapham Common that Millfield could accommodate them. It mattered little to the school if a pupil spoke broad Somerset or broad Cockney when some could hardly speak English at all. However, there were others who were initially not so sure about Millfield's classless society, such as a noble duke whose son had failed for Eton and sought Jack's help. 'Meyer, do you mean to tell me that my son, heir to the line, might meet and get interested in someone like your butcher's daughter?'

'Well, you needn't worry, because the butcher isn't a snob and if his very intelligent daughter got interested in a rather fat, puddingy boy like your son I think you should be rather pleased about it.'

According to Jack the duke went purple, and Jack was about to phone for a doctor when his wife indicated that he was coming round. The boy came to Millfield.

Jack would find the money to back his worthwhile but penniless cases from better-off parents and supporters of the school. He could often be disarmingly frank in pleading his case.

Your son is not one of the brightest, and has little inclination to work. If he comes here he will be occupying much of the time of highly qualified, well-paid staff, and even then it is unlikely that he will distinguish himself. However, I have a dossier here of a girl from a dock yard family in Bristol. She's fifteen, probably going to leave school next year, thinks she wants to be a hairdresser and do you know, she must have an IQ of around 180. Now I am sure you will agree that the country needs people like her.

The fact that a proportion of the pupils who came on reduced fees would eventually support the school in terms of exams gained or athletic prowess did not escape the attentions of other public schools, who began to accuse Jack of 'poaching' bright pupils from other schools in order to bolster Millfield's achievements. This annoyed Jack intensely, and he would point out in so many words that since they had neither the charity nor the sense to contemplate doing likewise, what justification had they for criticizing him? Also they had sent him their rejects for repairs and were still happy to send them; having taken some three years' worth of fees they would pass the pupils on to Jack to achieve the 'O' levels in one year, which they had failed to achieve elsewhere. However, Jack was quite aware of the success of his unwritten policy of 'enlightened self-interest' which brought benefits to pupils, school, careers and country alike. In order to teach more groups with IQs of up to 170, staff of the highest calibre had to be employed, and they complemented the standards and versatility of Millfield for years to come.

In 1953, with Millfield being well organized and having obtained public school status, Jack decided once again to see if he could join the Headmasters' Conference. Membership would have given him great pleasure, since recognition would have made the school a member of a recognized body maintaining the exceptional standards and traditions of

Mark Cox (second left) with T.J. Reynolds, J. Baker and R.D. Jones, doubles finalists at the Junior Wimbledon Championships, 1959

the country's public schools. On the official front he was advised to come back later when academic standards were of a more even and higher order, but from a more reliable source he learnt that a member of the committee considering Jack's entry had apparently stated: 'Millfield? That place with women and tennis? God forbid!' It seemed that if recognition were needed for Millfield's achievements it would certainly not come from the HMC. Jack was somewhat alarmed to learn that co-education was to be a bar to his entry, because he held it to be one of Millfield's virtues. The derogatory reference to tennis was justified on the grounds that it was not a team game, and therefore would not breed the right attitude. The difficulty was that by this time the school was arousing considerable curiosity from the public and potential fee-paying parents through its remarkable achievements. Many established schools, and HMC members, viewed this with some suspicion because Millfield was in their terms highly unconventional, though obviously very successful. Also, it was only eighteen years old, and some good old-fashioned conservatism produced a strong and easily justifiable decision from the establishment to 'wait and see'. For his part Jack took the fact that he was not invited for membership rather personally. Among other things there were annoying quibbles like the way Millfield was listed in the *Public and Preparatory Schools Year Book*. Because it was not a member of the HMC, the information could not appear in the main part of the publication; it was listed instead under 'Tutors', where its full four-page long entry looked somewhat out of place. Jack had many close friends who did not altogether agree that membership was so 'all-important'. There was, after all, no doubt that Millfield was firmly on the map and offered a viable alternative to the other public schools, even though it could not boast a 400-year foundation.

Membership of the HMC was probably the last thing on the minds of Millfield's pupils in the early 1950s. There was far too much going on of more immediate interest and importance. With the structure of the school then in place, and its intake of pupils, who by natural selection – or perhaps Jack's selection – were of emerging ability and personality, there could be few dull moments. The sporting front carried news that not even those who hated sports could ignore. Fencing had been introduced in the 1940s and Millfield won the Somerset Junior Championships in 1948 and 1949. In 1950 the school took seventy-two places in the National Schools Athletic Championships, two boys winning the 440 and 220 yd races. This was also the decade when Millfield became the first school to have a polo team; new stables were constructed just beyond the Nissen huts, called 'the Camp' for obvious reasons, and a polo ground was laid out in Kingweston's spacious park. A sailing club was started, which met on Axbridge reservoir. It later transferred to Poole where it met on alternate weekends. An exploring society was founded by Dr John Paxton, who had been an assistant leader with the British Schools' Exploring Society's Arctic expedition in 1949, and organized parties to visit Spain, Morocco, Norway, Yugoslavia and Russia. There were also less vigorous activities like the budding school orchestra. Perhaps as another healthy antidote to Millfield's theme of excellence, the unofficial 'Rubber Dinghy Club' came into being. Its first craft was the 'Flying Banana' which took several trips around the fishpond and was soon joined by an enormous inflatable named 'The Sieve', which even ventured onto the nearby River Brue. Each year there was a major drama production which involved months of work by staff and pupils. On a more lowly but immensely entertaining level was the house play competition, in which the major houses competed over a couple of evenings to produce the best one-act play. Apart from one member of staff being invited to help each as a consultant, the direction and

Mary Bignal (Rand) with J.W. Archer receiving the thirty-sixth Bradford Cup from the Countess Mountbatten at the All England Schools' Athletics Championship, 1958

production of these plays was entirely the work of pupils, resulting in alternating fantastic, dramatic or hilarious episodes, as the quest for originality was fired with youthful imagination.

Mary Bignall's name will always be at the forefront of the many athletes the school produced in the 1950s. In typical fashion, Jack spotted her at her local school which he had been invited to visit on some other business. He spoke to her teachers and parents who were as delighted as she was at the promise of developing her sporting talents. She was an outstanding all-rounder, and in 1957, at the age of seventeen, having been at Millfield for two years, she was beating all-comers in the 80 m hurdles, clearing 18 ft at the long jump and attaining a high jump of 5 ft 3 in, better than any other woman in the country. Mary, who was also a member of the Bristol South Harriers, went on to take the Empire Games Silver Medal for high-jump while still at Millfield; in the 1964 Tokyo Olympics she took three medals, including a gold. Gordon Miller from Millfield was also a Tokyo finalist after taking the British high-jump record to 6 ft 10 in. On a more modest scale, in 1957 he was the school's best boy high jumper and achieved 5 ft 11 in at the Surrey County Championships. The school also had two excellent sprinters in Elizabeth Jennings and Derek Needham. Needham frequently clipped fractions off the county 100 yd dash record. Another was J.B. Melen, who perhaps could not have been classed as a boy at the age of nineteen, but took the 100 yd dash in 10.1 seconds at the Millfield School Athletic Championships, coming second to R.R.P. Grounds – once the country's fastest half-miler – in the 440 yd race. On this occasion the prizes were awarded by General Sir George Erskine who arrived in his helicopter, landing a few yards away from Jack's study window, to the consternation of the ducks.

Not for the first time Jack hit the headlines when the press released the following report:

> 'I have a boy of ten here, who will probably be the next squash champion of the world.' He said it with the calm assurance of a man who expects to recognise future world champions at any age. 'One of our girls is quite likely to become the first woman to high jump 6 ft. A lad here is almost certain to win Junior Wimbledon again this year and our cricket team is probably the best Schoolboy side in the country . . . and, by the way, I'm expecting another boy to break the javelin record at any time.'

This last reference was to Nicholas Head, and was quite modest in comparison to the treatment given him by the national press. The *News*

Chronicle headlined 'All the world is watching this boy', and Peter Wilson of the *Daily Mirror* put it as 'The kid with the giant throw'. Head's throw incorporated a rather different technique to the standard one; he could impart considerable acceleration by adopting an action similar to the discus thrower, but without spinning round. It was developed by one of the school's maths teachers, Mike Reilly, who also coached the boy, and was originally seen as a method of relieving 'javelin elbow'. Apparently the throw was approved as conforming to the regulations by the Somerset AAA but the international experts took a different view and rather killed the technique off before it could be used in anger. At about the same time, and possibly aggravated by this, Reilly, as excellent a maths coach as he was athletics coach, began to suffer disturbing mental trouble, and unhappily had to withdraw from teaching.

Perhaps it was the success of the girls' sporting events that helped to make Jack think again about accepting them at all ages, and not just as seniors. There was also healthy pressure from within the school. Conversion seems to have come from Edgarley when Jack gave the pupils their end-of-term speech, telling them what to expect when they went on to Eton, Haileybury or Millfield. In conclusion he asked if there was anything which any of them would like to ask him, and was rather surprised to see almost all of the girls raise their hands. 'Boss, why can't we come to Millfield?'

'Well, I think you have all seen the pamphlet and you know my views.'

Jack's published reason was that he felt the girls needed a headmistress who could lead and deal out fair justice in a way which he – a mere man – could not. He was quite unsure of himself regarding how to apply effective guidance or discipline to younger girls, hence his policy of only allowing entry to seniors. However, Edgarley's young ladies argued that this was unjust and unsound, and asked to make a bargain with him. Since there was little that Jack did not know about bargaining he felt fairly safe. The girls asked for the chance to come to Millfield, saying that if ever they betrayed his trust they would expect to be sacked, and if they ever felt that they were in acute need of a headmistress to do battle with they would tell him. Whatever the validity of the various arguments, the girls' conviction won the day, and in fairly small numbers they began to follow the boys into Millfield.

The increasing number of girls meant that Jack had to form some clearer policies on how to handle co-education in a boarding school. There was little in the way of precedent from what were known as 'progressive schools', and Jack knew that if the parents ever suspected that he was applying that kind of regime, most of the girls and quite a few of the boys would be whisked off overnight.

Millfield was co-educational, which made for a pleasant atmosphere from the start, free from innuendoes and sniggers heard all too often in single sex schools. Generally our pupils were given as much freedom as they could safely and sensibly use, and by treating them as responsible people, nine times out of ten they would be. I didn't want a school full of petty restrictions, just a few good common-sense rules based on good manners and consideration. Of course, it was inevitable and entirely natural that emotional relationships would develop, and clear guidelines were introduced to preserve the stability of school life. The first of these was to make it quite clear that fornication was not on the timetable. Boys and girls could go about as much as they liked together in public, but were not allowed 'private assignations' without the permission of their houseparents, who took all the details of where, when, with whom and what time back. We made it quite clear that any arrangement outside these parameters would almost certainly lead to premature departure from the school, and this rule worked very well. Few – even the most ardent – wished to be responsible for an expulsion. In the 1990s, this all looks rather old hat but it was, I think fairly enlightened for the time.

While the rules may have been enlightened, the establishment looked upon them with some distrust. 'Needless to say my ideas on co-education didn't go down too well with other established public schools where tradition and prejudice sometimes labelled us as "the school for slow boys and fast girls".'

However, during the 1960s one or two other schools started to look at co-education and occasionally their masters would get in touch with Jack to find out how he did it. By that time Millfield had accepted girls in growing numbers for around twenty-five years, and no appalling headlines, not even a 'tut-tut' had appeared in the press. As always, Jack would give the benefit of his experience, and therefore it was not without some justification that he was indignant to learn that the Master of Marlborough had announced to the world that he was about to 'pioneer' in the field of co-education. Jack first rather unkindly reminded him that it was one of his predecessors in the HMC who had dismissed Millfield as 'that place with tennis and women', and further reminded him of what Simon de Montfort had said about troops arrayed against him by his former pupil, the Prince of Wales, at the Battle of Evesham: 'By St James they come on in wise fashion, but it was from me they learned it.' Nonetheless the Master was correct on a technicality, because among the members of the Headmaster's Conference he certainly was pioneering.

If the co-educational side of Millfield did not make headlines, it often gave Jack cause for thought. Interviewing an American parent whose son was coming to add some academic qualifications to his love of tennis, Jack was surprised to hear that he was forbidden to beat the boy. 'Well in that case you either withdraw your application or agree to expulsion should a beating situation arise. You have the option.'

'Okay, I'll take it. I'll do that.'

So the boy came. Some time later, he, a couple of other boys and some girls were spotted enjoying a private smoking party in a field. In no time they were paraded into Jack's study. 'You know the rule, and you have been told time and time again. Right, the girls can start packing now, and I'll see the rest of you here at 9.15 Monday morning.'

'Sir, could we talk to you?' the American boy asked.

'Yes, you can talk to me. What do you want to talk about?'

'Well, the thing is, Sir, we don't think it's fair.'

'Fair? You can tell me on Monday morning whether you think it's fair or not. You've been warned often enough God knows, so get out and be here on Monday.'

They duly reported back to the study on time. 'Sir, there is something we would like to say.'

'Carry on. Carry on. I'm keeping as calm as I can. There's the cane ready.'

'Well, Sir, what we want to say is this. We don't think it's fair on the girls. We are only going to be beaten, Sir, and the girls are being thrown out.'

Jack said, 'Well, what else can I do? I can't beat the girls, so what else can I do?'

'Well, we just wondered Sir, if you could beat us twice and let the girls come back.'

This rather took the wind out of Jack's sails, after all a beating from the old Cambridge Blue was still formidable, and he knew it. 'Well now, although this is a very, very underhand trick, it is a chivalrous gesture and rather rare in this day and age, so I think I am going to accept it. Right, before I beat you three, you can go and phone the girls and tell them to get along to their classes immediately. Line up outside my study when you return, and because you are to blame for what happens, you will enter first,' he said to the American.

The boys returned quickly, and after knocking, the first victim entered. 'Well boy, you know what two sixes are, don't you? – Yes, twelve! Well, I can't believe it's safe to give you twelve, and in any case a dreadful thing has happened. The shock of finding out there's some chivalry left in the world has paralysed my right arm. I simply can't do my duty, but you can play your part.'

To the boys standing trembling outside the study door the strokes seemed to last an age, and they had never heard their friend yelp like that before. 'Right, get out through the dining-room door and remember, it will be twenty-four next time, so get the hell out! Next!'

By the time he finished he had to open a window to clear the haze of dust raised by thirty-six lashes to his ancient sofa.

Jack's observations uncovered another factor that he thought could enhance peaceful co-education; it involved the ratio of boys to girls. He knew that it was quite natural and healthy for several boys to seek the favour of any particular girl. Under normal circumstances their behaviour would not rise to the height of passion, and would remain within bounds even when the girl inevitably gave most or all of them a polite cold shoulder. Should girls outnumber or equal the number of boys he thought a different situation might arise where girls would compete for the same boy, and be tempted to show him favours in order to win him over. If this happened it could of course put behaviour at risk. In Jack's time there were just under three boys to each girl, and whether or not it was strictly valid, his argument seemed to work well in practice. It is possible that the proportion of girls could have been increased had there been a headmistress to share Jack's duties, but there never was, and he was always the main source of discipline and policy.

Jack would never have considered himself to be an expert on sexual matters, but he did discover that sex was occasionally at the root of unusual behaviour. It came to his attention that a girl in the school seemed to be an almost compulsive thief. It was quite out of character, because she was intelligent and working very hard for her exams. She hardly even knew that she was taking things. Jack took the simpler side of the question first, and asked her to clear a drawer into which she could place any item she found in her room that clearly did not belong to her. Her parents took her to a psychiatrist, whom Jack contacted, who suggested, 'Make sure you find the boy who has been interfering with her and throw him out of the school.'

'You mean it's sex?'

'Yes, it's a substitute for sex. She is obviously very sexually aware.'

Jack had in fact noticed that she became easily flushed in the company of boys. The important thing was that he did not throw her out of the school, and about ten years later she wrote, 'You know I will never forget how marvellously sympathetic you were, and how you helped me through that appalling stage.'

However, it was not only pupils who might have sex-related problems. An Old Haileyburian who had been at the college with Jack brought his son along for interview. The boy was quite bright, but Jack felt that there

'Boss' and his ducks, 1964

was something holding him back and wanted to question his father a little more, so out went the boy to feed the ducks. 'I've always led a very pure life,' said the father, 'but the sad thing is my wife is leaving me although I've always treated her with the greatest respect. May I tell you more?'

'Please do.'

'Well, as I say I have always treated her with the utmost respect and have never put upon her unless it was for procreating our children. I just cannot explain why there is this rift.'

Jack thought about it and said 'Well, I think I might have an idea. In fact I'm going to take your son but there is a condition. It is that you read that little book on the shelf there.'

'Which book? Oh, Marie Stopes's *Married Love*.' He flipped through a page or two, visibly tensed and said, 'Good gracious Meyer, this is utter filth. This is precisely the kind of thing we were told to avoid!'

'Yes I remember, though rather mistakenly I think you'll find. Anyhow my conditions are that you read it, and give it to your wife as well. Whatever happens after that I'll take your boy.'

Some two and a half years later the boy was obviously doing quite well and his father and mother came to see Jack. They seemed rather excited and perched close together on one end of the sofa not just, Jack noticed, because there was no room on it. After a few faltering starts they said, 'We've got something rather important to tell you.'

'You tell him.'

'No, you tell him.'

'Look,' said Jack, 'I'm not sure what the mystery is, but don't be afraid to speak. Your boy is doing very well you know.'

The father responded, 'Well, what's happened – well, you know when I first came here you made us read that book? We both realized that something had gone rather wrong with our marriage and we decided to try again and actually – well, actually we have a little daughter and we've called her after you – almost – her name is Jacqueline, I hope you don't mind.'

'I really am so proud,' said Jack. '

'And we want her to come to Millfield as soon as she is old enough.'

'And so she shall. Amothe will put her down now.'

The end of the decade saw Millfield's twenty-fifth anniversary, which was celebrated with a Parade Service, beer for the boys and champagne for the staff. A magazine entitled *Focus*, written and produced by the pupils, featured an anniversary supplement in the form of an interview with Jack. After many questions concerning the school's turbulent history his interviewer asked, 'Has it been worthwhile as far as you personally are concerned?'

'It has been abundantly worthwhile to me and I hope to those whom the school has helped; but whereas I thrive on it, it has almost killed my nearest and dearest supporters. I doubt whether it can have been fair on them though bless them they have never complained.'

CHAPTER TEN

The Years of Triumph

A *Times Educational Supplement* review of *Education Today*, a book written in 1964 by F.T. Willey, the now deceased Labour MP, suggested that Millfield was a school that gave its pupils a second chance and that it should therefore be allowed to carry on when a Labour Government had abolished the other public schools. Willey was the Labour Shadow Minister of Education who, among others, notably Shirley Williams, was pushing for the abolition of fee-paying schools. The review brought forth an indignant letter from a master at Winchester demanding to know why schools like Millfield, which had been going for only some thirty years, should remain open, while establishments such as Winchester might have to close after hundreds of years of service. As founder headmaster of Millfield, Jack wrote to express agreement, on the grounds that if Winchester and other famous old schools were not to have the opportunity of giving their pupils a first chance, Millfield surely wouldn't be able to give them a second. However, there was another, less frivolous side to the master's outburst which was especially relevant – its suggestion that Millfield could by no means justify its existence through having been around for hundreds of years. The school flourished only because parents wanted it, because from the start it was willing to take on pupils with whom other schools would not attempt to deal, or perhaps had tried and failed.

Labour did, however, make things difficult for parents regarding fees, by demanding a tax on childrens' trust funds and abolishing tax relief on overdrafts. Also, just as after the war, a great deal of capital had to be gathered to support Socialist ideals, so industry and the people had to pay. There were, of course, bright times ahead for any individual in developments on the construction industry front. Despite the unfavourable political climate, Millfield continued its whirlwind growth during the 1960s, and the press was rarely far behind to gather up news about the school's achievements. *The People*, a Sunday paper known at that time to be somewhat left-wing and occasionally a little scurrilous, devoted a page to Socialist views on private education, but one of its conclusions was:

If all public school headmasters were like the headmasters of Shrewsbury and Millfield there would be no demand for their closure. Meyer of Millfield states 'Show me a boy or girl with an IQ of 160 and I will guarantee to find the money for their school fees – and not necessarily at Millfield.'

The other side of the coin was the *Manchester Guardian*, which replied – referring to Jack – a few days later:

Somebody should tell this academic white-slaver, this gold medallist in the intellectual rat race that it is his duty to help every pupil equally and not treat intelligence as an entrance qualification!

Elegant copy this may have been, but the journalist was shooting from the hip, and a little more research would have easily uncovered cases like the sixteen year old whom Jack taught to read, and who went on to gain his two precious 'O' levels, giving him at least one leg up towards training for his farming career.

As always, Jack was the first to state that it was not he, but his staff who were performing miracles. They were all expected to take on duties beyond normal academic work, and these extra responsibilities were important to the school and had to be done well. Most subject tutors would normally take on three other duties, such as becoming a group tutor, helping with games and taking part in the Millfield Combined Training Scheme (MCTS). The latter scheme occupied around two hours each week during which non-Corps pupils would indulge in some largely outdoor pursuit. The scheme was comprehensively developed when Clive Thomas took over, and arts and crafts were also adopted into the scheme after a while. New tutors at Millfield were blessed if they were keen on any sporting activity, but should there be neither preference nor experience they would be steered to the nearest vacancy. With several hundred pupils involved in games at any one time there was no shortage of such opportunities. Selection on an MCTS activity would be on a similar basis. If extra duties were taken on with some reluctance, they certainly helped the new tutor to begin to feel part of the school, and to enjoy the humour – sometimes cynical – that accompanied these commitments. The real fly in the ointment for some was that all demanded 'yet more meetings' and could double the load of report writing towards the end of term. Senior tutors, heads of department, house masters and their assistants bore an even greater burden but were compensated by the 'Millfield Allowance' – a little extra salary, by no means automatically or evenly distributed. To confront Jack with the idea that they might be worth that little more was fairly daunting. Until tutors got to know his ways a none too uncommon experience would be to enter the study with a carefully memorized script which would surely justify one or two points on the Burnham salary scale. Twenty minutes later they would find themselves walking tall down the drive, glowing with compliments on how well this or that had gone, only to be brought up very sharply with the sudden realization that Jack hadn't actually awarded them a single extra penny!

Jack was not often seen around the school during term time and if he called the staff together it was either for something very successful or very wrong. There was, in any case, no room big enough to hold all of them comfortably until the late 1960s. Morning coffee was taken in one of the boy's common rooms in Millfield House and wheeled in on a trolley, and afternoon tea was served in a large hut, perhaps about 18 ft long by 14 ft wide which, for most of Jack's tenure at the school, was the official staff room. It was rather dingy inside, even with the lights on, but warm and clean and sported an assortment of very well worn armchairs and other furniture that could not be respectably displayed elsewhere in the school. This shed was the communication centre for every department of the school. Probably because of the goodwill of the staff, it worked extremely well, and the feature carrying this vital host of messages was nothing more than an end wall completely covered with pigeon-holes. Into these would be stuffed mail, memos and messages at the rate of hundreds every day. While sipping very hot tea the pigeonhole's owner could glance over the crowd in an attempt to judge the urgency of each message by the colour or quality of the

The daily 'bun fight' at morning break, 1967

paper. A ripped-off page of notebook was probably for squash with Frank on Thursday, while anything with the school crest required immediate investigation. On the other hand one or two tutors, fiercely independent types, appeared to be after the record to see how much could actually be stuffed into a pigeonhole. Some used the system for delivering messages more than others. John Davies, a man of singular energy who was Director of Physical Education, a House Master and MCTS committee member – and later went on from there – made so much use of it that he was more or less affectionately known as 'Davies the chit'. Almost the last word on pigeonholes might belong to Dougal Read. He possessed an acute eye for Millfield life on which he quietly commented with an understated, yet sharp wit. A big man with a military bearing, he was once caught in the act of putting dozens of chits into pigeonholes by means of folding them into paper darts, standing back and letting fly. But the last word really goes to the rather overzealous tutor who discovered a dead pigeon in his pigeonhole. Sean Walmsley, a brilliant young remedial teacher, had taken it upon himself to post witty Valentines to each member of staff, and earned the pigeon in response. For staff working under pressure, such bits of daftness were, on occasions, fairly essential, and certainly refreshing. Happily, spontaneity was a quality which hadn't left Jack, and he used it to remind staff that he was thinking of them. On one dismal, wet and cold January morning, coffee was supplemented by – some even abandoned the coffee – hot brandy punch which he wheeled in on the coffee trolley. The weather was also involved in his other and more frequent act of spontaneity. If it had been terribly wet and windy for days and suddenly brightened up, a prefect would visit each classroom stating 'Tutor's discretion, period 4.' A more popular name was 'sunshine periods' during which, if the tutor wished, he had the option of cancelling the lesson so that all pupils could get out into the sun and get rid of that jaded feeling. Knowing that Jack was thinking about the staff was also, perhaps, a pleasant way of keeping them slightly more on their toes.

A look around during break when the staff were together presented an extraordinary cross-section of people. From fit young sports coaches wearing, like John Davies, the latest in track suit fashion, through every age of Harris Tweed to venerable octogenarians to whom the chairs seemed to belong by right. These older members of staff had usually completed at least one career before coming to Millfield, and included headmasters, top servicemen, and a circuit judge. According to Jack they could teach for as long as they wished or until they went ga-ga. They did excellent work with gifted children who were progressing too

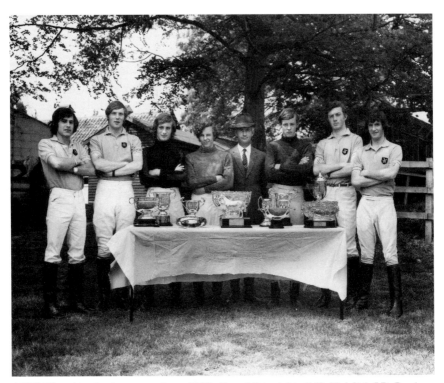

Millfield's prize-winning equestrians, 1971. From left to right: G.K. Makdisi, J.D. Davis, A.D. Griffiths, C.T. Jones, Major C.R. Burke, J.J.L. Harris, M.C.R. Emerson, R.J. Power

fast to stay in any one group, and for those who were just slow learners, but not dyslexics who needed specialist treatment. This freed other and perhaps more conventional staff whose qualifications ran from ordinary Cert.Eds to a fair crop of PhDs, to carry the bulk of teaching and administration. There were also many women on the staff and their presence was important to the general good atmosphere of the staffroom and school. Perhaps their only 'fault' was that they were more ready to be conscientious than some of their male colleagues. One characteristic shared by many of the tutors was that they had taught there almost since the school began. Jack's idea of 'never let a good man pass the door', had attracted a formidable array of talent, experience and personalities, and despite the demands of the standard six-day week practically all the staff would agree that one of the most attractive aspects of working at Millfield was that it was not like 'teaching in a school'.

In the early 1960s many of the staff who had come before or just after the war were still present, including the Reverend 'Daddy' Fisher, 'Jungle Jim' Bunbury, 'Gabby' Turner, Barry Tait, Emma Sawtell, Frank Slow and Alan Salisbury. GBA 'Gabby' Turner was also known to the pupils as 'Batman' from his initials and because he arrived at school each day on his trusty Velocette motorcycle wrapped up against the elements in an enormous trenchcoat. He was a devout, fatherly Catholic who spoke with authority on many subjects and lived in the nearby village of Butleigh where he had bought Robert Bolt's cottage. Although Bolt was considered by some a little leftish for Millfield, the success of his plays and filmscripts changed some of this opinion, and all agreed that he had been a brilliant head of the English Department while at the school. Millfield in fact had several literary giants on its staff at various times. John le Carré taught at Edgarley, and later Count Nikolai Tolstoy came and went twice. His history lessons were exciting and memorable, but perhaps he found the narrow confines of a syllabus too restricting for his deeper understanding of the subject. His true colours emerged later when he gallantly insisted on taking responsibility for a lampoon published by an acquaintance, which contained extracts from his book *Victims of Yalta*. To his cost, our legal system had no place for gallantry. The head of the English Department for most of the decade was George John, an irascible Welshman whose elegant command of the English language was proportionately spiced with vulgarity the more his thirst was quenched. Although he could be hurtful, most loved him. In this large and competent department no less an elegant voice belonged to a younger man, Frank MacCrea. Indicating superior literacy he actually wrote himself into the job while working in Canada, Jack replying, 'If you'll take a chance on me, I'll take a chance on you.' However, under Jack's eye virtues sometimes attracted some 'penalty', and Frank's was to coordinate *Windmill*, the school's annual. He also did pioneering work with the audio-visual (CCTV) studio to create a new 'O' level in Modern Communications. While conducting a summer holiday course, he was tutoring three young Americans in a small hut which was approaching ovenlike temperatures. Jack walked by, saw what was going on, and to the astonishment of all ordered Frank to continue the lesson in the swimming pool – which he duly did. Frank and his wife, Anna, also ran one of the larger girl's houses in nearby Somerton, following their experience as assistant house parents living in at Kingweston. The housemaster was then the Reverend Tom Wilkinson who was to become school Chaplain. Before the Wilkinsons' time Kingweston had one of the school's best known housemasters, Fred Stephenson and his wife, Sheila. He was a Northern Ireland hockey international and needed all

The first television studio, photographed in 1967

his strength to control some fairly unruly elements among the seventy-odd boys when he first went there. At the end of a term, when the coaches had arrived to ferry the boys to Castle Cary railway station, one of them reported £10 travel money to have been stolen. Notwithstanding all the drivers leaning on their horns and the inevitable wrath from Amothe, who had the whole operation organized with military precision, he insisted that all the boys stood by their beds until he cajoled an admission from someone who had the £10 stuffed down a sock. However, this tough Irishman had a ready smile and the patience to teach remedial maths. His wife, Sheila, was no less a faithful servant of the school and taught art as well as being Kingweston's housemother. Tony Robinson, another top hockey player, took part in around forty internationals and in the Olympics. He was a great man and conscientious to a fault and was at one time in overall charge of games. His burden was 'lessened' to running junior games when, as part of the maths department he had to oversee the introduction of modern maths. There is little doubt that his extra-curricular activities sent him to a premature retirement. It was extraordinary that even with so many staff at Millfield, such responsibilities could introduce a a workload doubling that for which the tutor had been employed.

Millfield had many husband-and-wife teams who taught in or otherwise supported the school. Although they would naturally tend to have similar problems, perhaps mutual sympathy helped a little. John and Jean Pike were typical. He was a bearded, sandal-wearing worshipper of wood, and Jean, who was rather more outgoing, taught English at Edgarley. One of John's achievements was to label all the trees around Millfield's campus. There was a remarkable variety planted by the Clarks, Jack's father, Rollo, and subsequent devoted gardeners like Fred Crossman. The arts and crafts facilities were perhaps rather later in development than other departments. 'Herbie' Davies taught metalwork, but perhaps his heart was more in the rugby he so enthusiastically helped to coach. His place was taken by Roger Cryer who, with a generous donation from the Desoutter family, elevated the metalwork shop to heights of precision and art with facilities for engineering more typically found in Colleges of Further Education. Although quite an 'angry young man' he had the kind of enlightened attitude that opened the doors of his department to other disciplines. He also quickly embraced the school's new audio-visual services, using both tape and slide sets as well as making instructional TV programmes to be called into the workshop on demand.

The television services were available to all, and were as useful for academic subjects as for crafts. Interesting technology was also evident in the language laboratories. Basically they were rooms full of individual booths where pupils could listen to pre-recorded material and also speak through a microphone directly to the tutor. Theoretically they reflected Millfield's ideas of individual teaching where the pupil could progress at his or her own rate, but they were initially a headache with endless niggling faults. Jacques Frati arrived at the same time as they did and masterminded their introduction. He also arrived at the same time as the demand for a new tutor to take over the school photographs, and there is rarely a time when a member of staff is more vulnerable than during his interview. Casual thought might conclude that this responsibility was not unreasonable, school photos only appearing once a year, but the reality was quite different. Each term there were different games, each have first, second and sometimes third teams, and several dozen different games were played every year. Then there were all the houses with their own boys or girls and their different house team photos. When he retired Jacques said it was like a black cloud lifted from his life to be free of this particular duty.

Rather more exotic languages were taught by Colonel Rex Barter and

Dick Snelling. Barter claimed that he taught twenty-two languages while at Millfield, while Dick Snelling tackled Serbo-Croat and Japanese, and other Far Eastern languages successfully. Like the craft departments, music was an activity which grew slowly, probably because of lack of facilities. When Peter Fox came to run this department it was rumoured that the only pianos that he could afford were from local pubs, because if a note stopped playing it was often because a few cigarette ends or bottle tops were obstructing the works. However, as Jack said, 'Peter Fox was the sort of man to get everyone playing, scraping or blowing something.' When Peter left Millfield his career took off in quite spectacular manner, and his place was taken by Geoff Keating who, with new buildings and more staff, developed the activity enormously. As a biology master, it is quite justifiable to describe Norman Parker's relationship with Millfield as symbiotic. He is an artist whose paintings are slightly surreal with a highly developed technique, a pianist for whom technical difficulties are overcome by happy insistence, an expert on and grower of orchids, and in the past was in charge of climbing for the Training Scheme while coaching trampoline for athletics. There are almost certain to be other sides to his approachable personality, and although it cannot be strictly true, his 'A' level students seemed to pass their exams after spending the greater part of their lessons exploring

Old Millfieldian Ian Balding winning at Sandown

some deep philosophical nicety, as opposed to the syllabus. All departments had their characters, but biology seemed generously endowed and it says much for the head of department, Mike Cole, that he made such a success of the job. Somewhat pragmatic, but always receptive, his intelligence and wit have ridden many storms and fathered many innovations. Another member of his department was to personify Millfield's rugby.

Well before the 1960s the position of director of studies was created to head the tutor, group tutor, senior tutor and head of department chain. The more the school grew the greater became the importance of the post, and in this decade the position was initially held by Frank Slow, one of Jack's most trusted and esteemed colleagues. He was also assistant headmaster for good measure. The first complete school timetable was created by R.L. Williams. The mental agility and tenacity required for the task could not be overestimated. He designed a matrix based around block subjects, yet which allowed many variations necessary to satisfy Jack's successful 'fitting the school to the boy' ideal.

Jack placed great importance on report writing and each subject and activity had its own page, bound into a small booklet before being sent to parents. Possibly of greater value to the pupils' education was the half-term report, because its strictly internal use meant that tutors could say what they liked about the pupil, the school and progress in general. The end of term reports had to be correct to the last detail, made in triplicate and passed to a pupil's group tutor. A whole afternoon was reserved for corrections while the lower part of the school was packed off to the cinema to watch a suitably uplifting epic. The group tutors moved into one of the new teaching blocks, three or four to a room. In the foyer of the building was a large board with a column of group tutor's names on the left, and the pencilled initials of those tutors whom they wished to see regarding reports which might not be up to scratch. Having written one, two or three hundred reports the sight of the tutor's initials scribbled all over the board was enough to send them over the edge. However, in response to the obvious tension the atmosphere was frequently hilarious. Colonel Tony Chadburn, a wonderful character who was CO of the school's Combined Cadet Force and took great parties of boys and girls on adventures throughout Europe, once provided a fairly startling welcome to anyone accusing him of a mistake by producing, with a grin, a service revolver from under his desk. Timothy Heneage's approach was quite different. 'Micheal, how nice of you to drop in. Now look, I think you're probably going to need a bit of a stiffener before we get down to business, so pull up a seat.' Upon which a bottle of sherry and a couple of glasses would appear. The whole appalling afternoon would often end in an unofficial binge at one of the local pubs where tutors could at last give vent about the pernickety old so-and-so who could have dotted the Is himself. Whatever the justification for such claims, little of it caused a cry of 'shame' from Jack, who had to write out a report on every pupil in the school – which meant 945 reports by 1970.

Since examinations were the passport to the next educational level they had to be high on the Millfield agenda. Jack always considered it unreasonably daft of the education authorities to hold exams in the summer when young people ought to be outside enjoying activities not possible during the winter. The hours of revision necessary could be achieved with fewer distractions during dark winter evenings, making concentration far more easy. However, the authorities were, and probably still are, too entrenched and reluctant to tolerate the upheaval necessary for change. As school numbers multiplied it became increasingly difficult to seat all exam candidates at the same time, and in the 1950s Jack had hit upon the idea of using a marquee into which he put hundreds of hired desks and folding chairs. It was the biggest one which he could find, possibly some 60 or 70 m long, and normally arrived having done duty at the Bath and West Show, which gave it a friendly, beery atmosphere until it had been up a week or two. Millfield's pupils did exceptionally well to give their best because the marquee could offer a variety of distractions. Moles surfaced for a walk, unfortunate butterflies endlessly sought the way out and thunderous wind and rain heralded the English summer. Birds happily flitted in and out, and after one had made a contribution to a boy's exam paper, the unfortunate candidate sensibly drew a ring around the deposit, which he annotated: 'Not my own work.' Since there were many exams, starting and stopping at odd times, the invigilator had quite a busy time of it, and it was especially difficult to communicate with pupils at the far end of the marquee. Therefore a loud-speaker system with a microphone on the invigilator's desk was rigged up to carry such doom-laden instructions as 'Turn your papers over now'. However, Millfield's technology was a little on the advanced side for them and they sometimes forgot to turn the microphone off once the exams commenced. The result was that pupils at the far end were distracted by the amplified, insistent ticking of the exam clock, and the click-clack of knitting needles. One boy stood up in an unsuccessful attempt to semaphore his message, then some ten minutes later he made another plea only for the marquee to be filled

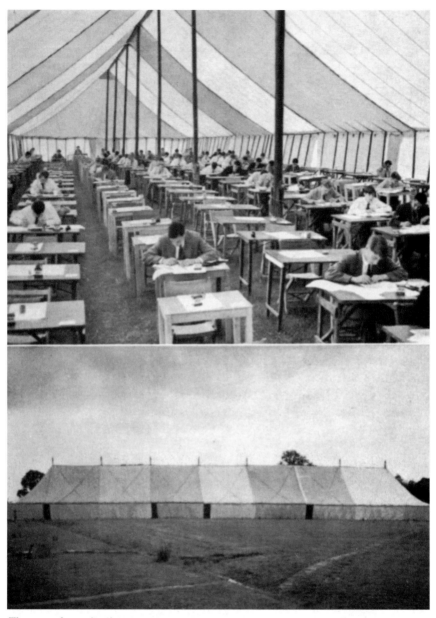

The annual examination marquee

with a booming 'Oh, there's that stupid boy again!' Invigilators' hands cupped invigilators' mouths!

Sports activity during the 1960s was no less spectacular than progress in any other part of the school. As usual it was the records that made the headlines, and Jack was sometimes irritated because the school's academic achievements were never greeted with the same enthusiastic publicity. In December 1958 the school suffered a great loss with the deaths of Walter Gluck and James Louden. They were returning from watching an inter-counties rugger match one evening when a poorly placed roadworks light caused their car to be steered into a deep ditch at the side of the road. Gluck, then a housemaster, had played an immense part in the school sports as Director of Games and master in charge of cricket, and his demise left a very big gap. His place was taken on the rugby front by Syd Hill, who was to take the game to such heights that only the best Welsh schools like Neath and Llanelli could give Millfield a good game. Syd, who had lived near Swansea, volubly shared his countrymen's passion for the game, and coached a XV containing Gareth Edwards, Vaughan Williams and Rod Speed who were a legend even at Millfield. In such a position he had Jack breathing flames of enthusiasm down his neck, and Syd was set two aims. First, to establish the rugby at the highest level and second to get the school re-accepted into the Public Schools Sevens competition at Rosslyn Park. He achieved both formidable tasks at a time when Millfield was being given a very cold shoulder by the public schools

Gareth Edwards in action at St Edwards School, Liverpool, 1969

establishment save for Kings College, Taunton, Marlborough College (thanks to Dennis Silk) and Llannelli Grammar School. He eventually surmounted both challenges, and won the Public Schools Sevens. He bore the brunt of much prejudice against Millfield, and was luckily built of the right stuff to brazen it out. Finding that a certain well-known school would only field a XV with eleven or twelve first-team players – the remainder being second team – Syd told their master in charge what he could do with his fixture. This school, although it was likely to be beaten something like 50–0, could still have used as an excuse for defeat the fact that it had not fielded its full first XV. Fearing what Jack would say when told he had lost a precious fixture, he was relieved to be backed up to the hilt in his decision. Syd's commitment to the game and Millfield was, and still is, phenomenal. He and Herbie Davies used to get boys back to school ten days before the beginning of term to start intensive training, and this would often commence after a 5 mile run from Millfield to Kingweston. It was also inevitable that so trustworthy and hardworking a couple as he and his wife should also be made houseparents. At Joan's kitchen they fed half the school every day and provided teas for visiting teams the whole year round. Notwithstanding this, Syd recently said:

> When the 'great call comes' if St Peter says 'You've been a good boy Syd (for most of the time anyway) so you have earned a rebate and can go back to earth for any ten years', then I would choose the years when I was in charge of rugby and in charge of Joan's kitchen.

The sad departure of Walter Gluck also meant that someone had to be found to take over the cricket, and Barry Hobson, an accomplished player, took on the responsibility. The first XI had many undefeated seasons and produced ten county players, including Peter Roebuck, who captained Somerset and has written so many eminently readable books on cricket.

Tennis, a sport not in favour with the old HMC, also flourished. Initially it was run by Colonel Malcolm Maclagan, who was joined by a professional coach, David Rundall, and David Kemp came in 1965, taking over the game in 1968. From 1958 to 1970 Millfield was never beaten in the schools' Glanville Cup. Every title in Junior Wimbledon was won, some of them several times. One of the first to bring Millfield's name to Wimbledon was Jim Tattersall, who twice won the men's junior singles. Two personalities always associated with Wimbledon are Mark Cox and Paul Hutchins, who spent many of their formative tennis years at the school. The Davis Cup teams were also well supported with ex-pupils like John Fever, Andrew Jarrett, J. Smith,

'Millfield, the cradle of British tennis.' Back row, left to right: David Rundle, Brian Gilkes, John Rudd, Stuart Greed, John Williams, David Kemp. Front row: Michael Mitchell, Colin Graham, Malcolm MacLagan, John De Mendoza

C. Dowdswell, P. Curtis and others. David Kemp now runs one of the most exciting coaching organizations in the south-west. At his interview Jack warned him that he might have to coach tennis seven days a week. His reply indicated that seven days a week was almost enough. Then one night Jack nearly shot him. A somewhat tedious side of being on the games staff was accompanying teams to away matches. With Millfield's fixture list this often meant travelling halfway across the country, or even staying away for a night or two. Having driven the tennis squad back from Torquay for one of the school's fixtures, and arriving after midnight, David was quietly making his way to the tennis hut when he was ambushed by Jack, Rigby at the ready. Having identified each other the first thing Jack wanted to know was the match score. Quite a few masters returning late had this kind of surprise, because one of Jack's recreations seemed to be to take a stroll round the grounds in the early hours to shoot the odd rabbit, or perhaps catch the not unknown intruder.

Millfield had the first full-time professional swimming coach in Britain,

Paddy Garratt coaches swimming, 1968

Paddy Garratt, who now coaches at national level. He produced
swimmers of Olympic standard, the last one under Jack's headmastership
being Duncan Goodhew. In his early days Millfield had a new pool which
was open and heated, much to the delight of the ducks who had to be
chased off their luxurious pond before training could begin at seven
each morning. Paddy took over from Patrick McArdle, possibly one of the
most caring and respected of Millfield's tutors. He would take it upon
himself to visit sick or retired elderly staff, winning everlasting respect
from Jack. He was originally made master in charge of swimming because
he was careless enough to let it be known that he had a life-saving
qualification, and from this small acorn grew another of Millfield's oaks.
To one side of the swimming pool, the meadow in front of Millfield
House had been turned into a nine-hole putting course. Its slope made it
quite a tricky round, but it helped to get three boys on their way to the
Open Championships, and produced such names as Brian Barnes,
Malcolm Gregson, Michael King and David Williams. Jack brought some
relief to such serious achievements by somehow acquiring a racehorse by
the name of Milkshake. With refreshing St Trinians flippancy, in order
that all could join the fun he once gave the school a half day off, with the
option to see her when she ran at nearby Wincanton Races.

Such sporting achievements and opportunities for all provided a welcome contrast to the examinations. But the development of the curriculum offered no less excitement. While noteworthy feats were achieved in dealing with dyslexia and remedial studies on the one hand, and the facility established to enable the very bright pupils to progress at their own furious pace on the other, new fields were still being pioneered. Dr John Paxton came in the early 1950s, and while he and his wife took pupils to some very wild and exotic corners of the world for the Explorers Club, back in his hut at Millfield he was creating one of the country's first Economics and Business Studies departments. Possibly because many parents ran businesses which their children would eventually join, the demand for Dr Paxton's teaching soon outstripped the flexibility of the timetable. His pupils found his teaching as memorable as others found his conversation, where a formidable though genial intellect would sear through pretension or less than sound argument.

The change to forty-minute periods was made in 1968, and although it allowed greater flexibility to the timetable those teaching at more advanced levels did not like it. Jack had started to publicize the attempt which he and others were making to have gifted children with very high IQs recognized as a group that required as much special treatment as the remedials. In 1966 he was closely involved with the establishment of the

Malcolm Tucker, swimmer and Commonwealth Games medallist, 1966

National Association for Gifted Children. For many years he had recognized behavioural disturbances in young pupils which he related to the frustration of not being allowed to progress at their own rate, mostly because that rate was simply not recognized by the ordinary teacher without the necessary training.

Another highlight of the early 1960s was the visit of a team of Her Majesty's Inspectors, who made a thorough examination of every aspect of the school lasting almost a week. Among other things the report concluded that 'the magnitude of the achievement of the headmaster in building so large a school (608 boys and girls in 1963), heterogeneous in constitution, yet as a community, marked by its tolerance and sense of responsibility, is fully recognised; he has impressed his personality and outlook upon it – this is an unusually interesting school to visit.' After the inspection, Dr Peter Davey, who had chaired Millfield's previous inspection, called a meeting with the school's governors to relate his findings.

> I have to tell you gentlemen . . . that we were very disappointed to find that Nissen huts, which we were assured by the headmaster would be removed – 3 June 1954 was his target – have not been removed but have greatly proliferated. Having said that, Mr Chairman, we want you to know that this has been the happiest week of our inspectorate. We have seen things here which we have only dreamt we might one day find in a school, and we have seen things here which we never even dreamt we would find in a school. In short, we want to tell you that we all consider you to be somewhere in the top six schools in England, in my opinion there can only be one place.

Suitably bucked by a generally very favourable report Jack once again sought some official recognition from a public schools body. He recognized that the HMC could and would still keep him out on the grounds that Millfield was co-educational, so he set his sights on the Governing Bodies Association (GBA), an equivalent organization. Almost by return of post his application was rejected on the grounds that the latest report showed that Millfield was still not up to standard and must not bother the authority again until it was. Quite naturally Jack was not going to accept that, so he contacted Dr Davey for support.

> Dr Davey wrote to them and I received a telephone invitation to go up and have a drink with the GBA secretary in his box at Lord's during the Australia v England Test Match, as there was a little matter he wished to discuss. I accepted the invitation, was greeted with a glass of champagne and a request for understanding.

Jack relates that the secretary informed him that:

I have put my foot in it. When your latest request was considered, I was simply told to get rid of you on any excuse I could think of (you know they are nearly all eaten up with jealousy of Millfield) and I took a chance on the report which I now see is excellent – as Dr Davey pointed out pretty sharply in a letter he wrote on behalf of your Governors. Now I shall get sacked by the committee for incompetence unless you forgive me and accept a promise that the next GBA meeting will vote you in by one vote.

Edgarley, Millfield's prep school, managed to gain recognition without the drama surrounding the GBA. From a Common Entrance tutorial establishment it developed into an institute no less adventurous than Millfield in producing innovations well ahead of its rivals. As a member of the Incorporated Association of Preparatory Schools it produced pupils who could confidently pass on to any British public school. However, like Millfield it accepted a very broad cross-section: from those requiring comprehensive remedial help to others with IQs of over 150. For pupils who were benefiting from remedial help, the Common Entrance exam necessary to enter public schools proved to be a disaster area, and a blow to the pupils' self esteem built up as part of Edgarley's remedial treatment; therefore the 'Millfield Transfer Exam' was introduced and designed to help the pupils show what they could do, rather on similar lines to the GCSE exams, which came some twenty-five years later. As Ben Rushton, the enlightened headmaster of Edgarley who had to oversee these innovations, said, 'The change over from "CE plugging" brought the balancing of the curriculum.'

Jack's interest in Edgarley and its pupils was, in Ben Rushton's words:

Unremittingly strenuous for those in charge. After a time I had to tell Boss that I went 'off-circuit' at 11.30 p.m. His response was to ring me at 11.25, and keep me talking until after midnight.

This was not idle chatter, and Ben was expected to have facts and figures at his bedside. Occasionally, and perhaps more so in the earlier days, Jack would pay a visit to Edgarley. 'Higgy' Higgins, Ben Rushton's predecessor, remembered one such occasion when he and Jack strolled around the gardens discussing all manner of important business. Then Jack spotted a boy with a golf ball. He went back to his car, brought out a niblick and borrowed the ball. Higgy reported that:

By this time a small gathering was watching (he was like a magnet to children wherever he went) and he pointed to a high dormitory window, part of which was open, and with the usual running commentary Boss dropped the ball, addressed it, and with graceful ease holed in one as it sailed through the small opening, finishing with his typical 'Well gentlemen, that concludes the entertainment for today,' normally heard after he had called down and fed the ducks. Less entertaining for Edgarley was the chaos caused by adventurous small boys subsequently attempting to emulate the shot.

A family that did great service for both Edgarley and Millfield was the Ludgates. Josephine taught at the prep school and Oliver at Millfield. Their two daughters also went through the system and Brenda came to teach at Millfield when she left college. Josephine's comment on Jack was that 'his instant assessment of character was disconcerting and fascinating, just as his impulsive generosity and trust were sincere and endearing.' She did much important work for the remedial pupils. The first real test of the brighter young pupils and Edgarley's teaching methods came in December 1960 when they were entered for a wide range of 'O' level GCE exams, all passing with a harvest of As and Bs. Dr Sandy Bridges joined Jack in establishing teaching methods for the very young (five to seven years) with high IQs. The results of his work were published in the early 1970s in a book entitled *The Millfield Experiment.*

At a public function held in a Bristol comprehensive school, Jack was asked the pointed question of how he would feel if he had to be headmaster of a state school, without all of Millfield's facilities. He replied without hesitation that to be such a headmaster where the buildings, staff, pupils and money were all found for him would be quite an attractive proposition.

With the bustling expansion of Millfield during the 1960s, money was as much of a problem as ever, and this was the decade of the great Appeals. They were crucial to Jack's plans because although his school commanded the highest fees in the country, extra money was vital for better buildings. Raising money had to be fun, and Jack went about the task with the same spontaneous delight apparent when he captained a cricket match. So effective and insistent was the process that one pupil writing in *Focus* was moved to plead for the formation of a 'National Society for the Prevention of Cruelty to Parents'. However, pupils were not safe either.

During a summer holiday I lent £1 to every pupil in the school with instructions to increase it by legal means on the lines laid down in the parable of the talents. One boy put the lot on a horse and lost it but three others excelled all expectations, another hatched chickens and sold them, and another bought the right to pick and sell apples. The best result of these goings on was achieved by two boys who used their father's Rolls to hawk Covent Garden vegetables and fruit all over London. They made more than £50, the Rolls was wrecked but the father was delighted to see his sons at last doing something sensible with their holiday time.

Jack's efforts on the appeal front meant fun and entertainment for all concerned.

Projects included a Gala Night at the London Palladium (Lord Grade and Lord Delfont), free shows at various theatres, one showing Irving Allen's *Cromwell* and Jack Gatti offering Julian Green's play *Salad Days* at his Vaudeville Theatre. Special gaming nights were organized by the Playboy (Victor Aubrey Lowndes the 3rd) and by the Cassanova (Miss Pauline Wallace). We also had generous patrons at Crockfords, the Olympic and the Ambassador. It was at these rather dangerous places that I met and made friends with distinguished visitors from at home

Results of the appeal. Two new classroom blocks, 1966

and abroad, many of whom were interested in acquiring places at
Millfield for their sons and grandsons – at any cost at all. This is largely
where the development money was to come from. One or two
'hazardous enterprises' were entered into (I had learned something
about hazardous enterprises during my few years in Bombay) and some
of them, especially those concerning horses, worked out better than
others. A monster raffle was organized with prizes offered which
included a fortnight's safari for two in Kenya with air fares and hotels
paid, an Aston Martin car at a very reasonable price, and a champagne
banquet for a hundred at the Waldof. Some splendid givers, mainly
those with Jewish backgrounds, simply took out their chequebooks and
earned a smile of approval from our Appeal Chairman, Joe Levy –
himself one of the most generous of men. Irving Allen, a man above all
others to put his money where his mouth was, gave us a marvellous
fencing Salle and his friend Dick Stewart a Judo Dojoh. The appeal
fund raised enough money to build two splendid modern classroom
blocks, and I borrowed £100,000 from Lloyds for a fine music school
on the site of the gardener's cottage, and benefactors (Mr Martin of
Martin and Baker – the ejector seat inventors – and Mr Sacker of Marks
& Spencer) gave us new chemistry labs and biology labs respectively.
The parents of Malcolm Tucker (our first Commonwealth games medal
winning swimmer) organised a fund which paid for the new indoor
swimming bath, which was to send out so many Olympic Games
swimmers.

The annual Parents' Day provided Jack with more opportunities to get
out the begging bowl. One of the most attractive features of the day,
when the whole school was on show, was the International Tent. As there
were about forty-two nationalities at Millfield there was never any lack of
orders for the limited number of pitches in the small marquee. Pupils
wrote home or contacted their embassies for goods to display and sell
which had a national flavour. The resulting displays, with pupils dressed
in national costumes, were fascinating, and often provided the only
chance any member of staff would have of tasting caviar, or riding on a
camel. The whole school buzzed with exhibitions and displays and the
Old Boys' cricket or tennis matches.

During one Parents' Day Jack set himself up as auctioneer on behalf of
the Building Fund. His repartee was brilliantly entertaining and
Sotheby's or Bonham's would have made a fortune with his services,
especially if they had the quality of buyers standing around his table on
that sunny afternoon. The goods for auction were practically anything he
could lay his hands on, mostly bricks to be used in building the new

The International Tent on Parents' Day, 1968

teaching block. With Jack's encouragement they went for hundreds of pounds each, except one which went to a little boy for two shillings. To complement the ducks a rather misguided parent had given some doves to the school, which bred like rabbits. They were also auctioned off, Jack providing even more entertainment with a tame one that sat on his shoulder. As he remarked afterwards, 'They did us proud, because they nearly always flew back to the school so we could auction them off again next year!'

In 1967 the Queen's Birthday Honours List announced the award of an OBE to R.J.O. Meyer, Esq., for Services to Education. For Jack, it was a greater compliment and recognition of the school's work than could ever have been achieved through the HMC. A week later the staff and school met at Saturday morning break to celebrate, and the senior prefect called for three hearty cheers of congratulation. After school the celebrations continued in a less formal style when Jack invited all staff to the Elms public house, and the ensuing party has gone down in Millfield's history. The award made Jack think about the succession to Millfield's throne, which had been on his mind for some time. Work was beginning to take its toll on Joyce, Amothe and himself. They had not had a single holiday since Millfield began, and the school was a far from easy ship to steer.

The study with 'Boss' and his school secretary, Amothe Sankey, in 1967

The fact that he had always pushed it and himself to gain that advantage meant that a high degree of vigilance was required to keep it on course. If he could have relaxed a little, perhaps consolidated what he had and ceased to expand the school for a few years life might have been far more easy. But such 'ifs' are fruitless to consider, because to sit back and admire his handiwork was not his way, one achievement was always a stepping stone to another.

> Round about 1965 I was faced with a dilemma when after about thirty on the whole very happy but exhausting years I found the strain beginning to tell, and realised that a successor would sooner or later have to be found. At sixty I could no longer obtain the much needed refreshment and relief which comes to the hard-pressed by engaging in some obliterating activity such as a golf championship or a County cricket match.

There seemed to be two alternatives. Jack rather fancied the kudos Millfield might acquire by attracting a well-known headmaster away from a great public school. On the other hand, the school functioned in such a unique fashion that it might be more sensible to groom someone within it to take over his routine duties, acquiring the title of Headmaster while Jack became Warden. In this position he envisaged being a kind of admissions tutor interviewing and finding prospective parents, sorting out fees and continuing his gentle 'Robin Hood' act on those who he knew could afford to be generous. Also Joyce and he had many pressing

Cricket coaching, c. 1963

invitations to visit friends and parents from all over the world, but such trips could never be accommodated with Millfield's busy routine as it was then.

Jack had brought Colin Atkinson to Somerset in 1961 to play for the County Cricket Club, joining Millfield's staff at the same time. The mid-1960s were turbulent years for the county side, and the players themselves voted Atkinson in as skipper from 1965 to 1967. He was a man who accepted responsibility easily, and Jack noticed that he seemed very businesslike in his attitude to cricket and Millfield. Of course responsibilities were one thing that Millfield quickly divulged to those with ability, and Jack made Atkinson a housemaster and master in charge of the PE department.

On the academic side he taught English and Latin and after his return to full-time teaching Jack gave him further responsibilities, finding him 'a discreet and effective trouble-shooter'. With his two favourites for the succession – Dennis Silk (Radley) and Ian Beer (Harrow) – unavailable, he decided to recommend Atkinson to the governing body as a candidate for the headmastership. Their reaction was confusing. There were factions who backed him strongly while others opposed him, and unfortunately the opposers were among Jack's strongest allies. In the face of no clear support Jack decided to proceed with preparing him for the job, making him deputy headmaster for a year and acting headmaster in 1969. The governors put their thinking hats on too, and produced a discussion paper outlining the pros and cons of three alternatives on similar lines to Jack's ideas. The only addition was to consider the possibility of advertising for a replacement. Atkinson had indicated that he had received two serious offers to go elsewhere, and was therefore keen to hear the governors' decision on the succession as soon as possible. However, they were still divided over his suitability for the post, and Jack was very sad to hear that his friend and loyal supporter Dean Ross Wallace was determined to resign his governorship should Atkinson be selected. This put Jack in a most difficult position, because he had already decided that Atkinson had to be Millfield's best bet. Jack thought that the year of acting headmaster was going well and he began to discuss plans for his wardenship with the governors. The agreement was that as life governor he would be consulted about all new policies, and would live in the bungalow to be built in the school grounds. Further, there was to be a generous pension in line with his 1953 agreement. The warden at Gordonstoun was receiving £10,000 per year, and they thought that Millfield could probably do better than that. As Governor Evan Stokes wrote: 'We will look after you well and do all we can to make things happy and easy for you.'

CHAPTER ELEVEN

Another Beginning and End

'R.J.O.M., the Man' had been the title of an interview in the 1965 edition of the pupils' magazine *Focus*. The questions varied between serious school and international topics to lighter stuff where Jack gave his opinions on Chelsea boots, the twist and thoughts on family planning for the Muscovy ducks, whose numbers were becoming an embarrassment. The editors considered Jack to be irreplaceable according to one question, and asked him what would happen to the school after he retired. He replied:

> It is very flattering to be thought irreplaceable, but it would be even more flattering to be thought to have enough sense to realise that plans have to be made which will prove as in all other organisations that no-one is irreplaceable – what I think may really happen is that in five or six years I may be 'kicked upstairs' – as they say when a Commoner goes to the Lords – and made Warden to make way for a young and efficient headmaster.

As he expected, in five or six years he was kicked upstairs – but he had not expected to be out of his school as well.

There is no easy way to tear a man's life's work from him, and the more the schism is examined, the louder becomes the question why? It is clear that Jack intended to continue a relationship with his school for the rest of his time. It was, after all, his life's work and the commitment and devotion that he, Joyce and Amothe had made over so many years was not something that could be switched off or simply waved goodbye. Certainly the staff and pupils were pleased that he was to be Warden, and Jack was looking forward to being able to spend more time with them. The administration required to run a school with numbers approaching twelve hundred was extremely demanding, and he sought to hand over the burden to a younger man while he, as Warden, would provide a liaison with Millfield for potential pupils, and continue raising money for the Building Fund or any other school activity that required support. He certainly had the contacts to do this, and he had made his plan clear to the governors, who were supportive during the lead up to his retirement. Some of Jack's methods of raising money were certainly unorthodox, but they were remarkably effective. The funds Jack brought back from his visits to the West End were not the actual results of gambling or winnings, they were genuine donations from very rich potential parents who wanted a place for their children in a few years' time. There were, and still are, people who say that Jack was a marvellous person, but for his gambling. While this sentiment is understandable, such an attitude excludes an important aspect of Jack's personality. If the odds looked possible, he would have a go, and luckily, with encouragement from his mother and Joyce who persuaded him that the odds were at least even, he started Millfield. There are, of course many different forms of gambling, and while some might be sympathetic to putting a few pounds on an up-and-coming golfer, the blind luck of the roulette wheel could be considered beyond the pale.

Jack was above all very big-hearted, and so was his school, and a very important side of that big-heartedness was the faith and trust he put in others. He had found throughout his life that if you let someone know that they were trusted, they would generally not let you down. This had also, of course, been his attitude to his pupils. Regarding the future of his school, he had put his trust in Colin Atkinson. There were reservations

Millfield, c. 1970

concerning his decision from some governors, staff and pupils, but as far as Jack could see there was no better man for the job. Jack had prepared him with increasing responsibilities over the years, and had no doubts about the efficiency with which he would carry out the role. Besides being a schoolmaster, Colin Atkinson was a very competent businessman, and Jack knew that the school would be in safe hands. However, he had set a formidable act to follow. Whoever was to succeed him as headmaster would find his fanaticism for education and the spontaneity with which he plucked solutions out of the air almost impossible to emulate. The educational side of the problem was alleviated by the great teaching machine being in place, with an excellent staff, highly qualified and motivated, who were supported with efficient administration. To have tried to follow the way in which Jack made money for the school might not have been something to be recommended. But at the time this was unimportant according to Jack, because he intended to continue in this role. However, as any businessman knows, control of the income is vital, and it has to be made reliable and, as far as possible, predictable.

There were two areas that should have given Jack cause for thought at this time. First, the resignation of Dean Ross-Wallace meant he had few strong supporters among the governors. Mrs Sankey and General Sir George Erskine had passed away and John Church was off the board. The support of the governors to Jack and Millfield in the early days had been vital, particularly because they recognized his qualities, and were willing to tolerate quips from him like 'I daren't tell them what I'm thinking – they wouldn't be able to sleep at night.' Once formed, the governors could select whomever they wished to join them, and the more recent recruits came more from a business rather than academic background. Certainly by 1970 they were, as a group, far more business-oriented. The second area Jack seems to have under-estimated, if not overlooked, was the way the world appeared from Colin Atkinson's viewpoint. He had been primed by Jack for the job, with a year as Deputy then a year as Acting Headmaster. By 1970 he had given the school nine years of excellent service during which he had accepted many important responsibilities, and a heavy burden of duties that he had carried efficiently in the last two posts. He was then expected to take up the position of full Headmaster with Jack still on his shoulder. The governors had already agreed that Colin should consult Jack on any changes he might want to make. If Jack had been some white-haired academic entering his dotage with little more on his mind than to potter around the golf course, and to finish his treatise on *Poèmes Antiques* by LeComte de Lisle the situation might have been workable. But of course Jack was not in the least like that. He had an immense amount of power and high expectations, and friends throughout the world who had an interest in Millfield. What was more, he was looking forward to a new lease of life by transferring most of the headmaster's responsibilities to Colin Atkinson.

During his two years as Deputy and Acting Headmaster Colin had had ample opportunity for looking at Millfield from the business angle. What he perceived was a conglomerate that included departments for boarding, transport, food and cooking, teaching, the sale of books, stationery and sport equipment and contingencies for riding and other special activities. Most of these items were expenses, apart from the book room and sports shop which just about held their own. The school had a turnover of around £1 million, with most parents paying the standard fees, but either side of them the rate varied from nothing to double fees and more. Rather more tantalizing were the massive sums – thousands of pounds – that arrived at somewhat irregular intervals through Jack. No-one but he knew the source of these amounts, and whether they would continue or cease when he became Warden. According to him, they were certain to continue and even multiply, as he had more time for his enterprises. Colin was a young man in his late thirties having vigour and energy and with the ambition not to merely have the title of Headmaster, but to be Headmaster on his own terms without having his wings clipped through being obliged to consult Jack at every twist and turn. He also saw a business which could, in business terms, be considerably streamlined, and potential for advancing the building programme without waiting for penny-pinching appeals. Happily for him, there were elements within the new governing body who saw things his way.

With hindsight it is clear that Jack's understandable wish to remain at the school he had built was creating a difficult position for Colin Atkinson. It was tragic that there seemed to be no-one of sufficient stature to discuss the situation with him. He would not, of course have been a sympathetic listener, but he might have considered advice from the likes of a General Sir George Erskine or Dean Ross-Wallace.

As it turned out, Jack presented the governors with another way round the problem, and the lever used to achieve their ends lay in his unorthodox methods of raising donations which were a by-product of his gambling. The majority of the governors, as Jack already knew, could not tolerate gambling, and when donations arrived, there was often £200 or £300 missing. Typical was the kind of incident where Jack would return from one of his London sessions and let it be known that £7,000 was on its way to the Building Fund. When it arrived it might be a few hundred pounds short, which was, according to Jack, the price of the chips used for the evening's entertainment. It was argued that this money was in fact part of the donation, and therefore the school's money, but Jack had lost out in that way before. He remembered rattling through Reading station,

'A connoisseur of rare sporting gifts', 1968

feeling very pleased with himself because he had a cheque for several thousand pounds glowing in his wallet when it dawned on him that if he had not given the donor £300 of his own money to keep him in the game, he might not have been invited for coffee the following morning to talk over the Appeal. So the glow of the donation was cooled somewhat through being a few hundred pounds out-of-pocket. There were other donors who required cash back-handers from their special reserve fund cheques – money which they could not personally lay hands on – and mixed up with the whole thing were deals concerning places for future sons and daughters. Luckily, Jack kept notes on them and later handed over paperwork to the value of some £60,000 to the governors. There was also information on longer-term deals that were thought to be worth potential millions. The back-handers, price of chips and arrangements for fees and places involved, as far as the school authorities were concerned, unacceptable irregularities. Despite the emerging crisis being kept quiet, somehow the rumour circulated that Jack was using the school's money for gambling. No-one asked how it was possible to get the school's money without the governors or bursar actually giving it to him. Before any binding agreements were made regarding the Wardenship, Jack was informed that the governors were not prepared to accept continued responsibility for the school unless he ceased to have any contact with present and future parents regarding finance, thus bringing such activities under the control of the school authorities.

The beginning of the end for Jack was now well under way as he felt his position within Millfield becoming remorselessly eroded. On 17 November 1970 he wrote to the chairman of the governors to confirm that he was resigning in the New Year. For him to have defended himself could have brought the whole school into disrepute, and it was a sad period for many, who, like the solicitor acting for him, had to look to his future when his loyalty was challenged, and naturally enough chose the path of security. In the end, Jack had lost the Headmastership, was no longer Governor, was Warden but not Life Warden, as he expected, had been moved out of his study – considered to be the seat of power – and had to settle for a quarter of the pension he had been led to expect.

Resignation was extracted from Amothe because the school authorities considered that in his new capacity, Jack would not require a full-time secretary. Amothe was, however, made of sterner stuff and continued to work for him in his new office in the chalet. Solicitor Kennard was now too old to be of much help, and Jack found that whatever protest or counter-claim he made, the ground had been cut from beneath him before he even put pen to paper. The whole operation was kept from the public and parents with hardly a squeak from the press. Staff and pupils only realized something was amiss when they were asked not to visit Jack in his chalet. However, in the early hours of the morning, boys followed the familiar route for breaking out of Millfield House. It was easier now that there was no light glowing from Jack's old study window, but a few tiptoed yards from the house brought its warm glow into view, with the promise still of understanding and advice. However, no matter who the visitor was or what the time of day or night, Jack continued to support the school.

If one were able to look at the coup in a cold-blooded manner, ignoring the hurtfulness and misery that were for some the inevitable outcome of its methods, one would have to admire it for its efficiency. The aims had been realized in only a few months and Colin Atkinson, having been released from the restrictions which he could see mounting before him, was then in a position to run operations as he had planned. Anyone viewing the fine buildings and layout of the school could not ignore his achievements, and he also maintained and improved the school's excellent financial status. Three years after his OBE for 'Services to Education' Millfield's founder retired without recognition or celebration from his school. Only the Old Boys later marked the occasion with a splendid party at London's Café Royal.

When the world heard that Jack was free of the Millfield headmastership, it formed an orderly queue to the chalet door. The three best offers came from Switzerland, Greece and America. The Greek idea seemed to be the one that attracted Jack most of all. Perhaps having established Millfield in 'England's green and pleasant land', he rather fancied the idea of starting another school at the very seat of learning. The first plan was suggested by Francis Noel-Baker, the former Labour MP for Swindon. His family owned Euboea, and this beautiful wooded island just to the North of Athens was to be the home of the new venture. At that time Greece was ruled by a military government known throughout the world as 'The Colonels'. Jack went out to Athens to see them in order to find out what reception a new school might get. Generally it was one of approval, because being an international school it would meet one of the Colonels' criteria – that the school should bring money into Greece, and not take it out. The story made the national and local papers at home, and caused a stir from within Millfield because it contravened one of the many stipulations of Jack's Wardenship: that he was not allowed to indulge in any consultancy or outside work. But as far as Jack was concerned he was acting in an unpaid consultancy, which did not contravene the conditions necessary for him to benefit from accommodation and receive his meagre pension. Possibly because of

Athens in the 1970s – back to the seat of learning

Francis Noel-Baker's recurring illness the venture never got off the ground. Instead Noel-Baker introduced him to an American school in Athens that was not going well. Campion School had been founded in 1970 by a vice-president of Citibank with a loan of $50,000. When Jack joined it in 1973 it had about a hundred pupils and no money because Citibank had refused to add to a $68,000 overdraft. It did not quite match dreams of Greek islands but it was a start. Those who knew and respected Jack in this country would have been shocked by his life style, and the way he was regarded in the early days in Athens. Colleagues knew little of his reputation, and so had little respect. What they saw was an old man who was supposed to get them out of the depressing mess that they were in. Jack had to roll his sleeves up and do the job from the beginning all over again. But the situation was a challenge, and challenges were important to Jack. Little by little success came to Campion and Jack thrived on it all, earning love and respect from staff and pupils. From his new study, where he slept on what he called his 'shelf', he built the school up in seven years to a roll of 1,450 pupils, and put $1 million into the school's bank. One astounding thing was that under Jack's direction it became the first foreign school to be accepted for membership of the Governing Bodies Association and Headmaster's Conference after a week-long inspection. Millfield, however, was still out in the cold as far as the HMC was concerned. Jack found that the Greeks were remarkably enlightened regarding the recognition and treatment of dyslexia, and was able to learn and contribute much to the work he found in Athens. Just when things seemed to be going smoothly the school's American founder decided to sack two Greeks – the bursar's secretary and lawyer who had played fundamental roles in building the school. Jack had made it a condition of his acceptance that no-one was hired or fired without his knowledge. However, the two were sacked and Jack walked out. So did many pupils and some of the staff.

Unbelievably, having built Campion School he proceeded to do the whole operation all over again, and founded St Lawrence College. Jack's energy, imagination and determination were again to the fore as he created this Greek school. A few years before, Brenda Ludgate, who had been both pupil and teacher at Millfield, had joined him in Greece and bears testimony to a side of Jack that none of his Millfield friends could have seen. Once again the school was a joyous success, and the 1983/4 Year Book, an album packed with informal photographs of pupils, staff, events and activities, bore the dedication:

> Some of us have known you for almost all of our school life. In most of our cases you were the one to set us on our way. Your door is always open and your time is always ours. When we need help or guidance, encouragement or sometimes admonishment you are there. To you we owe our belief in our own skills and talents and our hope that we, like you, can in turn make our contribution to a better world. With affection and with real gratitude for what you have so far made possible for us, we the pupils of St Lawrence College, dedicate this Year Book to you – Mr Meyer.

Notwithstanding the sentiments of pupils and staff the more successful the school became the more its Greek owners wanted it for themselves, and started to make life rather unpleasant for foreigners. It is a depressing thought that with his good, traditional upbringing Jack was never happy at taking the accolades or financial rewards that his efforts merited, with the result that during his life others with an eye on opportunity seemed to come along and take them for him.

The authorities at another school, Byron College, pleaded with Jack to come and work his miracles for them, and he accepted the invitation. During the two or three years at Byron Jack's health began to fail, and even the Greek sunshine was no match for the bronchitic condition which had increasingly afflicted him in his later years at Millfield. By 1987 it became clear that he had to return home for treatment. He was diagnosed as having emphysema and with intensive nursing from the National Health Service and Joyce made a recovery to the point where, although he was physically weak, and could never stray far from the oxygen bottle for long, he was mentally as sharp as ever. It was clear that he would be unable to return to his beloved Greece and he ended his contract with Byron College. Joyce had previously persuaded Millfield to let her have a house in Wells, and she prepared the first floor to become his new abode, with a large study, bedroom and bathroom. To anyone who had known his study at Millfield House, this new one was home-from-home. Joyce had arranged his enormous library on opposite walls, hanging the Cambridge UCC team photos on the others and had put in a desk, armchairs, television and his oxygen machine, which hummed away in the corner.

Seeing that he had at least reached a stable condition, Jack came to life again, taking a very active interest in all things sporting and educational, haranguing the press with letters and shouting at the television as another English wicket fell. It was not long before he was phoning around his many old friends in the racing fraternity for a little advice. Televised sport was an important recreation, and 'if you've got a couple of quid on Jack Niklaus you really get involved – you're on the edge of your seat'. However such pleasures were becoming increasingly interrupted as the news spread that he was back in Somerset. Letters, phone calls and visits multiplied from friends, relations, Millfield staff and pupils. Amothe came to help him keep up with correspondence, and, as she always had done, jogged his memory and filled in the details on this and that.

Last overs with the late Reg Sinfield, Gloucestershire and England cricketer, at Wells, Somerset, in 1988

In 1988 Wyndham Bailey wrote to Jack asking him to consider writing some memoirs for Millfield's Old Boys on the early days of the school. Wyndham had given something like twenty-five years of service to the Millfield Society and had been one of the first, in the early 1960s, to suggest a register of Old Boys. The request coincided with encouragement from other friends to write the history of the school or his own autobiography. Since one of his recreations in *Who's Who* was listed as conversation, the idea of sitting down and writing tens of thousands of words was not too attractive.

I was faced with a duty more than a pleasure of swapping peaceful oblivion for a demand to tell the strange story of how we planted Millfield in 'England's green and pleasant land'. Eventually a synopsis was cobbled together and with the advice and encouragement of a sincere friend, Dr John Paxton, then Macmillan's editor for *The Statesman's Year-Book*, a publisher was found.

This set Jack off on many delightful paths seeking information and memories from old staff, boys and sportsmen with whom he had shared so many adventures. Of great value to the venture would be Millfield's records, which the governors gave him permission to use, but at this point he was deeply shocked and horrified to learn that the school had destroyed all of its records up to the year 1958. The excuse, in the school which had put up so many fine buildings, was lack of storage space! A bonfire had taken three days to destroy all the documents. Trying to be philosophical, Jack could see that this particular incident of vandalism was complementary with the consistent attempt to remove his name from the school's history, and discount its achievements under his leadership, which had apparently been that of an eccentric headmaster who ran an expensive crammer.

Since his return Jack had been all too aware with rising indignation that press coverage and school publications carried this line. It was no figment of his imagination – the evidence is extant and apologies were offered by the press in one case. But any anger he may have had at the school for any of this was somewhat mollified when he learnt that Colin Atkinson was dangerously ill with an inoperable brain condition. Colin's health was deteriorating quickly and affecting his mobility. He wrote to Jack, asking if they could meet to talk things over. Regrettably the wound had gone too deep for Jack, who replied tersely that he regretted that Colin was enjoying his retirement as little as he was enjoying his. The school Chaplain and Joyce both tried to arrange meetings, but it was of no avail. As Jack said to a friend, 'There'll be no meeting this side of the pearly gates. That I can tell you.'

In the summer of 1990 Colin, who then called himself Principal of the school, and his Headmaster, Brian Gaskell, both retired and the governors selected Christopher Martin, the head of Bristol Cathedral School, to become Millfield's new headmaster. The choice has been an excellent one for the school, and he embraced the history of Millfield and the way it was when he came to it with a quality of natural leadership. In 1993, thirty years after Jack's last attempt, he and the school at last won the approval of the Headmasters' Conference. It is interesting to note that although the school was fifty-five years old in 1990 when he came, Christopher Martin was its first headmaster to have had any experience of that post elsewhere. A few months after taking up his position he came to have tea with Jack and Joyce; he apparently stayed for some three hours in deep conversation concerning Millfield and education in general. Jack and Joyce were then invited to go to Millfield for the Remembrance Day Ceremony, which happily they both managed to do although it was physically exhausting for Jack. However, he had the chance of seeing the wonderful buildings that graced the 100 acre campus and, some twenty years after he had left, there were still a

Millfield House, 1970

remarkable number of staff to whom he had given employment that came to meet him. In these two meetings Christopher Martin had reunited the founder with his school, achieving something that was beginning to look increasingly improbable. Christopher Martin's Millfield is very close to the spirit of Jack's, but thrives with the benefit of all the work that Colin Atkinson did to provide superb facilities.

Two months after their visit to Millfield, Jack collapsed in Joyce's arms; his heart had been working overtime for the past years trying to make up for the breathlessness of emphysema. Shortly afterwards, on 9 March 1991, he passed away, surrounded by his family.

Despite the sadness and heartfelt loss, his cremation and memorial service in Wells Cathedral were inevitably joyful occasions, as friends and relatives who had shared the diversity of his rich life recounted their memories of this extraordinary man. And so many of these stories produced smiles of admiration, incredulity or bouts of hilarity. Every few seconds could be heard, 'Did he really?' Naturally, Joyce was the centre of attention there, and as a member of the school's First XV who frequently saw her for repairs commented, 'She made you feel rather special, but then you found that everyone she saw felt like that, and you realized that it was Mrs M. who was rather special.'

Globe-trotting, as President of Millfield's Diamond Jubilee Appeal to

'– and a game of this or that'

visit Old Boys everywhere, she has helped to raise donations for the school's Meyer Theatre and a new maths complex.

Sadly, Colin Atkinson died a few months after Jack, and friends could only hope that at last they were inspecting the pitch together before playing on the same side in some Celestial XI. Jack's enthusiasm for cricket never ceased, despite spending many of his last years in a non-cricketing country, where of course he got them playing cricket. At the time of his death he had been working on 'A Crusade: The Art of Real Bowling', an article dealing in part with one of his heroes, Sydney Barnes, whom he first met in the late 1920s. It was published 'in tribute to the genius of Jack Meyer', by *The Cricketer* in August 1991.

Cricket was also in mind when Jack made known one of his last wishes – to have some of his ashes scattered on Millfield's pitch. The mended relationship with the school made this possible and on the appointed day a small group gathered at the ground. In keeping with the spirit of things, Gerry Wilson, the Chief Coach, had marked the scoreboard 'Last man in – 85', which would have been a pretty good score for Jack. Before walking onto the wicket to scatter his ashes, Joyce, in an almost matter of fact way, slipped off her shoes. Afterwards Tom Wilkinson asked her why. 'Oh, because when we were making this wicket before the war it was my job to weed it, which I did with Jacquie and Gill, who were still tiny, and Jack always made us take our shoes off first.' There could be no better place for his ashes than on Millfield's wicket, the school which he summed up as 'the very best teaching, ducks, the love of friends and a game of this or that'.

Index